PRAISE FOR
FROM #BLACKLIVESMATTER TO BLACK LIBERATION

"Keeanga-Yamahtta Taylor's searching examination of the social, political, and economic dimensions of the prevailing racial order offers important context for understanding the necessity of the emerging movement for black liberation."

—Michelle Alexander, author of *The New Jim Crow*

"Class matters! In this clear-eyed, historically informed account of the latest wave of resistance to state violence, Keeanga-Yamahtta Taylor not only exposes the canard of colorblindness but reveals how structural racism and class oppression are joined at the hip. If today's rebels ever expect to end inequality and racialized state violence, she warns, then capitalism must also end. And that requires forging new solidarities, envisioning a new social and economic order, and pushing a struggle to protect Black lives to its logical conclusion: a revolution capable of transforming the entire nation."

—Robin D. G. Kelley, author of *Freedom Dreams: The Black Radical Imagination*

"With political eloquence, intellectual rigor, and an unapologetically left analysis, the brilliant scholar-activist Keeanga-Yamahtta Taylor has provided a powerful contribution to our collective understanding of the current stage of the Black freedom struggle in the United States, how we arrived at this point, and what battles we need to fight in order to truly achieve liberation. *From #BlackLivesMatter to Black Liberation* is a must read for everyone who is serious about the ongoing praxis of freedom."

—Barbara Ransby, author of *Ella Baker and the Black Freedom Movement: A Radical Democratic Vision*

"Keeanga-Yamahtta Taylor has a strong voice, a sharp mind, and a clear, readable style that all come together in this penetrating, vital analysis of race and class at this critical moment in America's racial history."

—Gary Younge, editor at large, *Guardian*

"Keeanga-Yamahtta Taylor brings the long history of Black radical theorizing and scholarship into the neoliberal twenty-first century with *From #BlackLivesMatter to Black Liberation*. Her strong voice is deeply needed at a time when young activists are once again reforging a Black liberation movement that is under constant attack. Deeply rooted in Black radical, feminist, and socialist traditions, Taylor's book is an outstanding example of the type of analysis that is needed to build movements for freedom and self-determination in a far more complicated terrain than that confronted by the activists of the twentieth century. Her book is required reading for anyone interested in justice, equality, and freedom."

—Michael C. Dawson, author of *Blacks in and out of the Left*

"*From #BlackLivesMatter to Black Liberation* is a profoundly insightful book from one of the brightest new lights in African American Studies. Keeanga-Yamahtta Taylor invites us to rethink the postwar history of the United States and to place the actions of everyday people, including the hundreds of thousands of African Americans who participated in the urban rebellions and wildcat strikes of 1960s and 1970s, at the forefront of American politics. By doing so, she offers up a "usable past" for interpreting the current anti-state-sanctioned-violence movement sweeping the United States in the early twenty-first century. This timely volume provides much needed analysis not only of race and criminalization in modern American history but of the specific roles played by a bipartisan electoral elite, the corporate sector, and the new black political class in producing our current onslaught of police killings and mass incarceration in the years since the Voting Rights Act's passage. Taylor's fluent voice as historian and political theorist renders legible the accomplishments and, perhaps most importantly, the expansive possibilities of a new generation of black youth activism."

—Donna Murch, author of *Living for the City:*
Migration, Education, and the Rise of the Black
Panther Party in Oakland, California

"Keeanga-Yamahtta Taylor has given us an important book, one that might help us to understand the roots of the contemporary policing crisis and build popular opposition capable of transforming the current, dismal state of affairs. Equal parts historical analysis and forceful polemic, *From #BlackLivesMatter to Black Liberation* provides a much-needed antidote to the postracial patter that has defined the Obama years, but it also serves as a proper corrective for the "new civil rights movement" posturing of some activists. Against such nostalgic thinking, Taylor reminds us of the new historical conditions we face and the unique challenges created by decades of African American political integration. *From #BlackLivesMatter to Black Liberation* sketches a politics that rightly connects anti–police brutality protests and a broader anti-capitalist project. Everyone who has grown sick of too many undeserved deaths at the hands of police and vigilantes should read and debate this book."

—Cedric G. Johnson, author of *Revolutionaries to Race Leaders: Black Power and the Making of African American Politics*

FROM #BLACKLIVESMATTER TO
BLACK LIBERATION

Keeanga-Yamahtta Taylor

Foreword by Angela Y. Davis

Haymarket Books
Chicago, Illinois

© 2016 Keeanga-Yamahtta Taylor
Foreword © 2021 Angela Y. Davis
Chapter 8, "Where Is the Black Lives Matter Movement Headed," originally published as "Five Years Later, Do Black Lives Matter?" *Jacobin*, September 30, 2019.

Published by
Haymarket Books
P.O. Box 180165
Chicago, IL 60618
773-583-7884
info@haymarketbooks.org
www.haymarketbooks.org

ISBN: 978-1-64259-455-3

Trade distribution:
In the US through Consortium Book Sales and Distribution, www.cbsd.com
In the UK, Turnaround Publisher Services, www.turnaround-uk.com
In Canada, Publishers Group Canada, www.pgcbooks.ca
All other countries, Publishers Group Worldwide, www.pgw.com

This book was published with the generous support of the Wallace Action Fund
and Lannan Foundation.

Printed in Canada by union labor.

Cover image © 2021 Devin Allen.
Cover and text design by Eric Kerl.

Library of Congress CIP Data is available.

10 9 8 7 6 5 4 3 2 1

To the parents, brothers, sisters, partners, and friends of those who have been killed by police and other forms of state-sanctioned violence and yet remain committed to the struggle for a just world

Find out just what any people will quietly submit to and you have found out the exact measure of injustice and wrong which will be imposed upon them, and these will continue till they are resisted with either words or blows, or with both. The limits of tyrants are prescribed by the endurance of those whom they oppress.

—Frederick Douglass, 1857

Contents

Foreword

ANGELA Y. DAVIS

Given the entrenched tendency to assume that racism is a character flaw or a social problem emanating from individual attitudes, a tectonic shift occurred when the impact of the COVID-19 pandemic revealed incontrovertible evidence of the structural formation of racism. The entrance into public discourse of this *more* complex understanding of an issue, assumed by many to be resolvable simply by enlarging programs of diversity and inclusion, calls for the expansion of the kind of popular education campaigns usually associated with activist groups seeking revolutionary change. If we are to benefit from this historical conjuncture, Keeanga-Yamahtta Taylor is precisely the kind of theorist and educator we need in order to accomplish such a mass educational project. *From #BlackLivesMatter to Black Liberation* is the text that can guide us toward an intelligent engagement with structural racism and efficacious paths of resistance. The great value of this text is that unlike many of the mainstream efforts to define structural or systemic racism, capitalism is not relegated to the margins or ignored altogether.

In fact, this book pivots around Taylor's impressive facility to translate concepts drawn from the critique of the political economy of capitalism into popular terms that help us to comprehend the ways the culture of racism reflects its embeddedness in the country's foundational economic structures as well as within its housing, educational, health care, and, of course, its carceral and policing institutions. Those who were fortunate enough to read Taylor's incisive and edifying analysis of racism and Black resistance before the COVID-19 pandemic and the police murders of George Floyd and Breonna Taylor were well-prepared to explain how the paradigm of color-evasiveness not only fails to capture the way racism is produced but also can actually encourage its further reproduction.

While Taylor was writing the first edition of this book, we were attempting to comprehend what was taking shape as a new phase of the Black movement. Many of us wondered whether this moment of protracted protests in Ferguson, Missouri, in response to the police murder of Mike Brown would lead to the solidification of a new type of mass movement against racist state violence. What was new about this case was that the protests did not prove to be short-lived, as we had come to expect from past experiences of resistance to racist police killings. Rather they continued for days and weeks and months. What was also remarkable about the Ferguson protests is that they quickly garnered international support, thanks in part to the response of Palestinian resisters, who provided material assistance via social media by teaching the protesters in the US how to avoid injuries from the tear gas, which, as they pointed out, was produced by the same company as the tear gas the Israeli army used against them. Moreover, the demand to demilitarize the police not only emerged in response to the obvious evidence of military garments, weaponry, and vehicles but also because of the way Israel modeled police militarization, encouraging and training police departments throughout the world, including in Ferguson. Early on, therefore, there was a sense of connectedness with the Palestinian movement and with others around the world who were also challenging settler colonialism and its racist inheritances.

The emergent movement's feminist and abolitionist dimension was also new. This was a movement that did not seek to discover its public face in a charismatic male leader, who would stand in for the thousands of predominantly female and nonbinary activists whose labor created the very conditions of possibility for this new resistance. Not only were queer Black women central to new forms of collective leadership, but

Black trans women also began to play a crucial role. These new leadership paradigms demonstrated the extent to which strategies that were marginalized during earlier iterations of Black movements—Ella Baker's notion of collective leadership, for example—were given a new lease on life. As has been true of virtually all past Black movements, it was a movement for Black liberation, whose rank and file consisted of people of diverse racial and ethnic backgrounds. Among its abolitionist strategies was the explicit shifting of attention from the individual perpetrator to the racism inherent in the very structure of policing.

I know that I speak for many people when I offer my gratitude to Keeanga-Yamahtta Taylor for her decision to write this book, given that it proved to be a great gift as we struggled to understand the very meaning of the Ferguson protests and specifically how Black Lives Matter was introducing a new era of organizing, movement-building, and social justice–inflected research. However, no one could have predicted that under conditions of a global pandemic a much broader receptivity to structural analyses of racism would be generated in response to the police murders of George Floyd and Breonna Taylor. This new edition will certainly help us as we develop our capacity to curate deeper, more expansive conversations about the radical transformations that are necessary in our struggle for emancipatory futures.

Black Awakening in Obama's America

I am not sad that black Americans are rebelling; this was not only inevitable but eminently desirable. Without this magnificent ferment among Negroes, the old evasions and procrastinations would have continued indefinitely. Black men have slammed the door shut on a past of deadening passivity. Except for the Reconstruction years, they have never in their long history on American soil struggled with such creativity and courage for their freedom. These are our bright years of emergence; though they are painful ones, they cannot be avoided. . . . In these trying circumstances, the black revolution is much more than a struggle for the rights of Negroes. It is forcing America to face all its interrelated flaws—racism, poverty, militarism, and materialism. It is exposing the evils that are rooted deeply in the whole structure of our society. It reveals systemic rather than superficial flaws and suggests that radical reconstruction of society itself is the real issue to be faced. . . . Today's dissenters tell the complacent majority that the time has come when further evasion of social responsibility in a turbulent world will court disaster and death. America has not yet changed because so many think it need not change, but this is the illusion of the damned. America must change because twenty-three million black citizens will no longer live supinely in a wretched past. They have left the valley of despair; they have found strength in struggle. Joined by white allies, they will shake the prison walls until they fall. America must change.

—**Martin Luther King Jr.**, "A Testament of Hope," 1969

1

M artin Luther King Jr. wrote these words in the weeks before his assassination, while the "eminently desirable" Black rebellion rose in
the streets of the United States, exposing the triumphalist rhetoric
of the American dream as meaningless. While the United States may
have been considered an "affluent society," for the vast majority of African Americans, unemployment, underemployment, substandard housing, and police brutality constituted what Malcolm X once described as
an "American nightmare." Indeed, the relentless burden of those conditions would propel more than half a million African Americans—almost
the same number of troops sent to fight in Vietnam—to rise up in the
"land of the free" over the course of the 1960s.

It is almost never useful to compare eras; it is even less useful to
look at the past and say nothing has changed. But in King's words are
painful continuities between the present and the past that remind us
that, in some cases, the past is not yet past. Over the course of ten
months, spanning from the summer and fall of 2014 into the winter
and spring of 2015, the United States was rocked by mass protests, led
by African Americans in response to the police murder of a young
Black man, Michael Brown. In the summer heat of August, the people
of Ferguson, Missouri, rose up and brought the world's attention to the
crisis of racist policing practices in the United States. Eight months
later, some forty miles from the nation's capital, the city of Baltimore
exploded in fury at the police killing of young Freddie Gray.

King's words could easily describe the emergence of this protest
movement. What began as a local struggle of ordinary Black people
in Ferguson, who for more than one hundred days "slammed the door
shut on deadening passivity" in the pursuit of justice for Brown, has
grown into a national movement against police brutality and daily police killings of unarmed African Americans. It is no exaggeration to
say that the men and women in blue patrolling the streets of the United
States have been given a license to kill—and have demonstrated a consistent propensity to use it. More often than not, police violence, including murder and attempted murder, is directed at African Americans. Take Philadelphia: the birthplace of American democracy but
also home to one of the most brutal police departments in the country.
When the Department of Justice (DOJ) conducted an investigation of
the Philadelphia Police Department from 2007 to 2013, it found that

80 percent of the people Philadelphia police officers had shot were African American, even though less than half the city's population is African American.[1] Perhaps the most important finding, though, is that despite police shootings of unarmed people in violation of the force's own standards and rules, it is virtually impossible to punish—let alone indict, jail, or prosecute—police for this criminal behavior. For example, in Philadelphia, of 382 shootings by police, only 88 officers were found to have violated department policy. In 73 percent of those cases there was no suspension or termination.[2]

It should go without saying that police murder and brutality are only the tip of the iceberg when it comes to the US criminal justice system. Is it any wonder that a new movement has taken "Black Lives Matter" as its slogan when it is so clear that, for the police, Black lives do not matter at all? In fact, it is impossible to understand the intense policing of Black communities without putting it into the wider context of the decades-old War on Drugs and the effects of mass incarceration. Today, the United States accounts for 5 percent of the world's population but 25 percent of the world's prison population. There are more than a million African Americans in prison because Black people are incarcerated at a rate six times that of whites. The systematic overimprisonment of Black people, and Black men in particular, has conflated race, risk, and criminality to legitimize close scrutiny of Black communities as well as the consequences of such scrutiny. As Michelle Alexander has pointed out in her book *The New Jim Crow*, the imprisonment of Black men has led to social stigma and economic marginalization, leaving many with few options but to engage in criminal activity as a means of survival. When white men with criminal records are as likely to be hired as Black men with *no* criminal records, one can only imagine the slim prospects for legitimate work for Black men returning from jail and prison. The entire criminal justice system operates at the expense of African American communities and society as a whole.

This crisis goes beyond high incarceration rates; indeed, the perpetuation of deeply ingrained stereotypes of African Americans as particularly dangerous, impervious to pain and suffering, careless and carefree, and exempt from empathy, solidarity, or basic humanity is what allows the police to kill Black people with no threat of punishment. When Ferguson police officer Darren Wilson gave grand jury testimony about his engagement with Mike Brown, he sounded as if he were describing an altercation with a monster, not an eighteen-year-old. Even though Wilson and Brown were the same height, Wilson said he felt like he was being tossed around like a rag doll and that if Brown were to punch him in the face it would be fatal. Wilson went on to describe Brown as a "demon" who made "grunting" noises before inexplicably deciding to attack a police officer who had already shot him once and was poised to do so again.[3] Wilson attributed superhuman strength to Brown, whom he described as running through a hail of bullets, leaving Wilson with no alternative but to keep shooting.[4] It is an unbelievable story that hinges on the complete suspension of belief in Brown's humanity, his literal humanness.

The United States is often referred to these days as a "colorblind" or "postracial" society, where race may once have been an obstacle to a successful life. Today, we are told, race does not matter. Racial discrimination, sanctioned by law in the South and custom and public policy in the North over much of the twentieth century, caused disparities between Blacks and whites in employment, poverty, housing quality, and access to education. But in the aftermath of the Black freedom struggles of the 1960s, removing race from the law and shifting attitudes regarding race were supposed to usher in a new period of unfettered Black success and achievement. That an African American family inhabits the White House, an edifice built by slaves in 1795, is a powerful example of the transformation of racial attitudes and realities in the United States. Beyond the presidency of Barack Obama, thousands of Black elected officials, a layer of Black corporate executives, and many highly visible Black Hollywood socialites and multimillionaire professional athletes animate the "postracial" landscape in the United States. The success of a relative few African Americans is upheld as a vindication of the United States' colorblind ethos and a testament to the transcendence of its racist past. Where there is bad treatment on the basis of race, it is viewed as the product of lapsed personal behavior and morality, but it is "no longer endemic, or sanctioned by law and custom," as President Obama suggested in a speech commemorating the fiftieth anniversary of the Voting Rights Act.[5]

This is precisely why the spectacle of unchecked police brutality and murder has morphed into a political crisis. After all, the United

States does not passively contend that it is a colorblind society; it actively promotes its supposed colorblindness as an example of its democratic traditions and its authority to police the globe. The federal government and politicians in both parties have used this as an excuse to cut social programs and other aspects of the public sector, in denial of the central way that discrimination harms Black life in the United States. In other words, if a central demand of the civil rights movement in the 1960s was federal intervention to act against discrimination and act affirmatively to improve the quality of life for African Americans, promoting the United States as colorblind or postracial has done the opposite as it is used to justify dismantling the state's capacity to challenge discrimination.

The Supreme Court has done precisely this with voting rights, essentially ruling that racism no longer hinders access to voting, as it most clearly and demonstrably did in the era of Jim Crow. Chief Justice John Roberts said, when striking down the Voting Rights Act, "Our country has changed in the last fifty years." He added that Congress needed to "speak to current conditions."[6] Of course the country has changed, but the passage of time alone is not a guarantee that it has changed for the better. Justice is not a natural part of the lifecycle of the United States, nor is it a product of evolution; it is always the outcome of struggle.

Not only do these attacks have consequences for ordinary Black people, but they are also a "Trojan horse" shielding a much broader attack against all working-class people, including whites and Latino/as. African Americans, of course, suffer disproportionately from the dismantling of the social welfare state, but in a country with growing economic inequality between the richest and poorest Americans, austerity budgets and political attacks on social welfare come at the peril of all ordinary people. It is an example of how, counterintuitively, even ordinary white people have an interest in exposing the racist nature of US society, because doing so legitimizes the demand for an expansive and robust regime of social welfare intended to redistribute wealth and resources from the rich back to the working class—Black, Brown, and white. Conversely, it is also why the political and economic elites have such a vested interest in colorblindness and in the perpetuation of the myth that the United States is a meritocracy.

The spotlight now shining on pervasive police abuse, including the ongoing beatings, maimings, and murders of Black people, destabilizes the idea of the United States as colorblind and thus reestablishes the basis for strengthening regulatory oversight and antidiscrimination measures. In this process, larger questions inevitably arise as to the nature of such a society that would allow police to brazenly attack and kill so many African Americans. This is why the persisting issue of police violence is so explosive, especially in this particular historical moment of supposed colorblindness and the height of Black political power. Indeed, an African American president, attorney general, and Philadelphia police chief have led the national discussion on police reform. Yet, as near-daily reports on police brutality and murder fill the airwaves, this unprecedented display of Black political power appears to mean very little in the lives of ordinary Black people, who wield almost no power at all.

Two Black Societies, Separate and Unequal

How do we explain the rise of a Black president, along with the exponential growth of the Black political class and the emergence of a small but significant Black economic elite, at the same time as the emergence of a social movement whose most well-known slogan is both a reminder and an exhortation that "Black Lives Matter"? Examples of Black ascendance have been used to laud the greatness of the United States, as Obama echoed when he claimed that "for as long as I live, I will never forget that in no other country on Earth is my story even possible."[7] At the same time, Black poverty, imprisonment, and premature death are widely seen as the products of Black insolence and lapsed personal responsibility. In reality, these divergent experiences are driven by deep class differences among African Americans that have allowed for the rise of a few while the vast majority languishes in a despair driven by the economic inequality that pervades all of American society. Here, as in the rest of the world, the neoliberal era of free-market reform, the rollback of social spending, and cuts in taxes for corporations and the wealthy have produced social inequality on a scale unseen since at least the 1920s. As the Occupy movement of 2011 pointed out, the wealthiest 1 percent of the population controls 40 percent of the wealth. From 1978 to 2013, CEO compensation, adjusted for inflation, increased 937 percent compared to the anemic 10 percent growth in a typical worker's compensation over the same period.[8] As always, economic privation and social inequality have a disproportionate impact on Black America.

In fact, the gap between rich and poor is even more pronounced among Blacks than among whites. The richest whites have seventy-four times more wealth than the average white family. But among African Americans, the richest families have a staggering two hundred times more wealth than the average Black family. African Americans make up 1.4 percent—about 16,000 of the 14 million Black families in the United States—of the richest 1 percent of Americans. Each of those families' net worth averages $1.2 million, in comparison to $6,000 for the average Black family.[9] These class differences influence the ways in which they experience the world and the political conclusions they draw from those experiences. Class differences have always existed among African Americans, but the pall of legally instituted racism in an earlier era essentially tethered Blacks together into a Black community. Today, the absence of formal barriers to Black economic and political achievement has allowed for more differentiation among African Americans and has frayed notions of "community."

This does not mean that Black elites can transcend racism altogether. The Black elite is much smaller than the white elite; its members have greater debt and less overall net worth compared to rich whites. But it does mean that, in general, they experience racial inequality differently compared to poor and working-class African Americans and draw different conclusions about what these experiences mean. For example, a Pew Research Center poll conducted in 2007 showed that 40 percent of African Americans say that because of the "diversity within their community, blacks can no longer be thought of as a single race."[10] Additionally, 61 percent of Blacks believed that the "values held by middle-class Black people and the values held by poor Black people have become more different." Well-educated Blacks are more likely than Blacks with less formal education to say that the "values gap" within the Black community has widened over the last decade. Finally, low-income African Americans, according to the poll, suggest that the perception of differences over values and identity among Blacks "is felt most strongly by those Blacks at the lower end of the socio-economic spectrum."[11]

For Black elites, in particular, their success validates the political and economic underpinnings of US society while reaffirming the apparent personal defects of those who have not succeeded. Blaming Black inequality on Black people is not a new development, but the social movements of the 1960s made powerful structural critiques of Black poverty and deprivation as products of a society that, for much of its existence, thrived on the oppression and exploitation of African Americans. Black revolutionary Stokely Carmichael and social scientist Charles Hamilton coined the phrase "institutional racism" in their book *Black Power*.[12] The term was prescient, anticipating the coming turn toward colorblindness and the idea that racism was only present if the intention was undeniable. Institutional racism, or structural racism, can be defined as the policies, programs, and practices of public and private institutions that result in greater rates of poverty, dispossession, criminalization, illness, and ultimately mortality of African Americans. Most importantly, it is the *outcome* that matters, not the intentions of the individuals involved. Institutional racism remains the best way to understand how Black deprivation continues in a country as rich and resource-filled as the United States. This understanding is critical to countering the charges that African Americans are largely responsible for their own predicament.

The debate over the nature of Black inequality is not benign; it has deep political implications for the nature of American society more generally. The focus on Black culture as the source of Black inequality was never born out of hatred of Black people. Its function is to explain the Black experience as something that exists outside of the American narrative of unimpeded social mobility, the pursuit of happiness and equality for all: a way to exonerate the American system while simultaneously implicating African Americans in their own hardships. However, any serious interrogation of the history of Black life in the United States upends all notions of American exceptionalism.

After slavery, the popular explanations for Black poverty and marginalization drifted between biology and culture, but the ideas of free enterprise and American democracy "with contradictions" have never seriously been interrogated. The civil rights movement and the Black Power rebellion unfolding over the course of the 1960s pushed institutional racism, as opposed to Black cultural and familial practices, to the forefront as the central explanation for Black inequality. This was amplified by a commission's report based on the findings of a federal investigation into the causes of "civil disorder" throughout the 1960s. The Kerner Commission report plainly stated that "white racism" was responsible for Black poverty—"white society created it, white institutions maintain it, and white society condones it."[13] The complicity of the state itself in the subjugation of Black life legitimized the right of Blacks to demand that the state intervene and undo what it had played a clear role in creating. But this demand was only enforceable when the movement was on the streets. As the movement receded in the 1970s and as a bipartisan political attack on the welfare state gained traction, the mantras of the "culture of poverty" and "personal responsibility" reemerged as popular explanations for Black deprivation.

Today, the various problems that pervade Black communities are largely believed to be of Black people's own making. Indeed, President Obama, addressing an audience of Black graduating college students, exhorted, "We've got no time for excuses," as if the greater rates of unemployment and poverty experienced by African Americans were the products of "excuses." These are not just the admonishments by the Black elite: 53 percent of African Americans say that Blacks who do not get ahead are mainly responsible for their situation, while only 30 percent say that discrimination is to blame.[14] The premise that Black inequality is a product of the slackening of Black communities' work ethic and self-sufficiency has been bolstered by the visibility of the Black elite. In this context, the election of Barack Obama has been heralded as the pinnacle of Black achievement and, presumably, the end of racial grievances.

Black Awakening in Obama's America

There are, however, periodic ruptures in the US narrative of its triumph over racism as a defining feature of its society. The murder of Emmett Till in 1955 exploded the rhetoric of the moral and democratic superiority of American society when the United States was in the throes of the Cold War. The Black freedom struggle of the 1960s, while the United States was simultaneously waging a war in Vietnam (supposedly in the name of freedom), exposed the country as a whole as deeply racist and resistant to Black equality or liberation. More recently, the Los Angeles Rebellion in 1992 reignited a national discussion about the persistence of racial inequality. In 2005, the Bush administration's shameful response to Hurricane Katrina momentarily submerged the glowing self-appraisals of American society at a time when the country was, once again, locked in war and occupation, this time in Iraq and Afghanistan, respectively, in the name of freedom and democracy.

Today, the birth of a new movement against racism and policing is shattering the illusion of a colorblind, postracial United States. Cries of "Hands up, don't shoot," "I can't breathe," and "Black lives matter" have been heard around the country as tens of thousands of ordinary people mobilize to demand an end to rampant police brutality and murder against African Americans. It is almost always impossible to say when and where a movement will arise, but its eventual emergence is almost always predictable. On a weekly basis, social media brims with stories of police brutalizing ordinary citizens or killing the young, the Black, and—almost always—the unarmed. The advent of social media has almost erased the lag between when an incident happens and when the public becomes aware of it. Where the mainstream media have typically downplayed or even ignored public claims of police corruption and abuse, the proliferation of smartphones fitted with voice and video recorders has given the general public the ability to record these incidents and share them far and wide on a variety of social media platforms.

Historically, incidents of police brutality have typically sparked Black uprisings, but they are the tip of the iceberg, not the entirety of the problem. Today is no different. While it may be surprising that a Black protest movement has emerged during the Obama presidency, the reluctance of his administration to address any of the substantive issues facing Black communities has meant that suffering has worsened in those communities over the course of Obama's term of office. African Americans mobilized historic levels of support for Obama in the 2008 and 2012 presidential elections based on his promises of hope and change and his declaration that "yes, we can" end the war in Iraq. Perhaps most compelling to African Americans was their own hope of breaking free from the Bush administration's breathtaking indifference to Black suffering, as exemplified by the Hurricane Katrina catastrophe.

By any measure, however, African Americans under Obama are experiencing the same indifference and active discrimination; in some cases, these have become worse. Black unemployment has remained in the double digits throughout the Obama presidency. Even Black college graduates are more than twice as likely to be unemployed as white college graduates. Twelve percent of Black college graduates, compared to 4.9 percent of white college graduates, were out of work in 2014.[15] Even those African American college graduates who made "no excuses," went to college, and—as President Bill Clinton liked to say—"played by the rules" still fared significantly worse than their white peers.

Pundits and politicians alike have been celebrating what they describe as an economic recovery from the Great Recession of 2008, but for African Americans, the long winter of the downturn keeps churning on—demonstrated most sharply by the 27 percent of African Americans who live in poverty.[16] The national poverty rate for African Americans can obscure the even greater depths of Black economic deprivation concentrated in some parts of the country, especially across the southern United States. Across the Midwest, too, there is also intense Black poverty, including 46 percent in Minnesota, 39 percent in Wisconsin, and 34 percent in Michigan. Since Obama came into office, Black median income has fallen by 10.9 percent to $33,500, compared to a 3.6 percent drop for whites, leaving their median income at $58,000.[17] Poverty contributes to a host of other social ills: 26 percent of Black households are "food insecure," the government's euphemistic description of hunger; 30 percent of Black children are hungry; 25 percent of Black women are without health insurance; 65 percent of all new AIDS diagnoses are among Black women. In larger cities, Black women are as likely to be evicted as Black men are to be imprisoned: in Milwaukee, though Black women are 9 percent of the population, they account for 30 percent of all evictions.[18] The cascading effects of racism and poverty are unrelenting in the lives of working-class and poor African Americans.

Poverty is but a single factor in making sense of the ever-widening wealth gap between African Americans and whites. Over the last twenty-five years, the disparity in household wealth has tripled; today, white median wealth (as opposed to income) is $91,405, compared to $6,446 for African American households.[19]

If there were a single indicator to measure the status of Black women in the United States, it would be the difference in median wealth for single Black women compared to single white women. A 2010 study found that the median wealth of single white women was $41,500 compared to the paltry $100 for single Black women.[20] The historic crash of the American housing market in 2008 destroyed much of African Americans' wealth holdings. At the height of the mortgage lending boom in the mid-2000s, almost half of the loans given to African Americans were subprime. Today, according to the Center for Responsible Lending, almost 25 percent of Black families who purchased homes during this period are at risk of losing their homes as a result.[21] As has been widely reported, the crisis effectively destroyed tens of billions of dollars of Black wealth invested in real estate, as more than 240,000 African Americans lost their homes.[22] In Detroit, for example, a city that once boasted one of the highest Black homeownership rates in the country, more than one-third of Black families who borrowed between 2004 and 2008 have lost their homes to foreclosure.[23] The loans were "ticking time bombs" that eventually detonated, causing Black homeowners' already meager accumulated wealth to evaporate into thin air.[24]

Barack Obama became president right at a time when Black people needed help the most, yet he has done precious little. In fact, when he ran again in 2012, he reassured the nation (or at least white voters), "I'm not the president of Black America. I'm the president of the United States of America."[25] It's not only that Obama is reluctant to offer or support a Black agenda: he has also played a destructive role in legitimizing the "culture of poverty" discourse discussed above. At a time when the entire Western world was pointing to corrupt practices on Wall Street and illicit gambling in global financial markets as the causes of the global slump, there was Obama blaming Black fathers, "Cousin Pookie," families' eating habits, ESPN's *SportsCenter*, and Black parents not reading to their children at night for the absence of secure work and stable home lives in Black communities.[26]

"Hands Up, Don't Shoot"

The killing of Mike Brown, along with an ever-growing list of other unarmed Black people, drove holes in the logic that Black people simply doing the "right things," whatever those things might be, could overcome the perennial crises within Black America. After all, Mike Brown was only walking down the street. Eric Garner was standing on the corner. Rekia Boyd was in a park with friends. Trayvon Martin was walking with a bag of Skittles and a can of iced tea. Sean Bell was leaving a bachelor party, anticipating his marriage the following day. Amadou Diallo was getting off from work. Their deaths, and the killings of so many others like them, prove that sometimes simply being Black can make you a suspect—or get you killed. Especially when the police are involved, looking Black is more likely to get you killed than any other factor. In Ferguson, Missouri, in August 2014, people's exhaustion, sadness, frustration, and anger at the dehumanizing trauma inflicted by racism finally boiled over. But the outpouring of support and solidarity that followed was not only about Ferguson. The tens of thousands of people who poured into the streets over the summer, into the fall, and during the deep chill of winter were drawing from the deep wells of exhaustion among African Americans who have grown weary of the endless eulogizing of Black people—young and old, men and women, transgender, queer, and straight—killed by the police.

The explosion in Ferguson and the nationwide protests have deepened the political crisis, shattered the "postracial" proclamations, and inspired others to rise up against a worsening epidemic of police harassment, brutality, corruption, and murder that threatens to snatch the lives and personhood of untold numbers of African Americans in every city and suburb. But the sense of political crisis can be measured by the degree of attention it garners from elected officials scrambling to try and rescue the legitimacy of law-enforcement agencies and the rule of law itself. While many predicted the intervention of the Reverend Al Sharpton, Attorney General Eric Holder's appearance was unexpected. Holder traveled to Ferguson to announce that federal officials would ensure a fair investigation. Elected officials tweeted that they were attending Brown's funeral; President Obama was forced to make public statements acknowledging what he described as "mistrust" between "the community" and the police.[27]

The specter of crisis was also bolstered by cops' simple inability to stop killing Black people. Just prior to Brown's murder, forty-six-year-old Eric Garner of Staten Island, New York, unarmed and minding his own business, was approached by police and then choked to death as he gasped eleven times, "I can't breathe." Two days after Brown was killed, Los Angeles Police Department (LAPD) officers shot and killed another young Black man, Ezell Ford. Months later, autopsy reports would confirm that Ford was shot multiple times, including once in the back, while he lay on the ground.[28] In a suburb of Dayton, Ohio, police shot to death John Crawford III, twenty-two years old and African American, while he was talking on his cell phone and holding an air gun on sale in the aisle of a Walmart. And as the nation waited to hear whether a grand jury would indict officer Darren Wilson for Brown's death, Cleveland police killed thirty-seven-year-old, African American Tanisha Anderson when they slammed her to the ground, remaining on top of her until her body went limp.[29] The following week, police in Cleveland struck again, murdering a twelve-year-old boy, Tamir Rice, less than two seconds after arriving at the playground where Rice was playing alone. Making matters worse, the two Cleveland police stood by idly, refusing aid, while Tamir bled to death. When his fourteen-year-old sister attempted to help him, police wrestled her to the ground.[30] An earlier audit of the Cleveland Police Department (CPD) described the department as essentially lawless. It found that officers routinely "use unnecessary and unreasonable force in violation of the Constitution" and that "supervisors tolerate this behavior and, in some cases, endorse it." The report showed a "pattern or practice of using unreasonable force in violation of the Fourth Amendment," including the "unnecessary and excessive use of deadly force" and "excessive force against persons who are mentally ill or in crisis."[31]

We know the names of these people because of the nascent movement now insisting that Black lives matter. In the short span of a year, the impact of the movement is undeniable. It can be measured by some localities forcing police to wear body cameras or the firing of a handful of police for violence and brutality that was previously considered unremarkable. It can be measured by the arrest for murder of small numbers of police officers who would previously have gone unpunished. Perhaps most telling, it can be measured in the shifting discourse about crime, policing, and race.

After spending the better part of his presidency chastising African Americans for their own hardships, post-Ferguson, Obama has shifted gears to focus on what he termed the "criminal injustice system" in a speech on crime and punishment. In the summer of 2015, President Obama appeared at the national convention of the National Association for the Advancement of Colored People (NAACP) to deliver a sweeping speech on reforming the criminal justice system. The president highlighted the racial disparities that lead to vastly different punishments for Blacks, whites, and Latino/as, called for restoring voting rights to the formerly incarcerated, and argued that the $80 billion spent annually to maintain the nation's prisons could cover the cost of college tuition in every public college and university in the country. This transformation in Obama's rhetoric is welcome, but none of it would be possible without the rebellions in Ferguson and Baltimore or the dogged movement building that has happened in between. In other words, the radical movement of ordinary Black people has forced the federal government and its leader, the most powerful political figure in the world, to account for the war against Black life. The challenge, of course, will be going from recognizing Black humanity to changing the institutions responsible for its degradation.

The Future of Black Politics

The most significant transformation in all of Black life over the last fifty years has been the emergence of a Black elite, bolstered by the Black political class, that has been responsible for administering cuts and managing meager budgets on the backs of Black constituents. Today, a layer of Black "civil rights entrepreneurs" have become prominent boosters and overseers of the forces of privatization, claiming that the private sector is better suited to distribute public services than the public sector. This juncture between public and private is where Black incompetence fades to the background and government malfeasance comes to the fore as an excuse for privatization. Today there are many African American administrators who advocate for greater privatization of public resources in education, housing, and healthcare. Redevelopment programs often promise to include ordinary Blacks instead of pushing them out of urban communities—but when those promises fall through, Black officials are just as eager as white officials to invoke racist stereotypes to cover their own incompetence, from claims about cultural inferiority to broken families to Black criminality. There is growing polarization between the Black political and economic elite and those whom historian Martha Biondi and others have referred to as experiencing a social condition of "disposability." Biondi describes this condition as "encompass[ing] not only structural unemployment and the school-to-prison pipeline, but also high rates of shooting deaths as weaponry meets hopelessness in the day-to-day struggle for manhood and survival. Disposability also manifests in our larger society's apparent acceptance of high rates of premature death of young African Americans and Latinos."[32]

These relatively new tensions between the Black working class and the Black political elite raise new questions about the current movement to stop police abuse and, more fundamentally, about the future of the Black freedom struggle, which side various actors will be on, and what actual Black liberation would look like. More importantly, what is the relationship between the movement as it exists today and the ongoing and historic struggle?

Today's movement has similarities with the struggles of the 1960s but does not replicate them. The questions raised by the civil rights movement seemed to have been answered—but under closer inspection, those rights many thought had been won have come under withering attack. Audits of the nation's police departments reveal that police largely operate outside of the Constitution when dealing with African Americans. The right wing mobilizes stridently conservative candidates who seem to want to travel back to a time before the rights revolution of the 1960s, while the "colorblind" assault on voting rights—a very basic emblem of a supposedly free society—undermines Black voters' access to the voting booth. An estimated 5.8 million Americans are prevented from voting because of a prior felony conviction, including more than 2 million formerly incarcerated African Americans.[33] These and other violations of the basic rights of citizenship of Black people have not been resolved.

Black Lives Matter is not simply a replay of the civil rights movement. Typically, when more than six Black people assemble in one place to make a demand, the media instantly identifies a "new civil rights movement." But this elides the new and significantly different challenges facing the movement today—and obscures the unresolved questions of the last period. In many ways, the Black Lives Matter movement, now in its infancy, is already encountering some of the same questions that confronted the Black Power movement in the 1960s and 1970s. For example: Can the conditions created by institutional racism be transformed within the existing capitalist order? Housing, wages, and access to better jobs and education can certainly be improved, but can that be achieved on a mass level and not just for a few? Various sections of the movement believed these things could be achieved in different ways: some put their faith in electoral politics, others in Equal Employment Opportunity Commission (EEOC) litigation. Still others believed the movement should fight for those reforms within the context of a larger struggle against capitalism *and* fight for a socialist redistribution of wealth and resources. The intense debate over how to achieve Black liberation was interrupted by vicious government repression combined with cooptation and accommodation from within. The resulting decline muffled these questions but did not resolve them. Deepening inequality in Black communities—even as a Black man has ascended to the highest level of elected office in the country—is reviving these questions for a new generation of Black radicals who have come of age in a time of economic austerity and political bankruptcy.

This book explores why the movement marching under the banner of Black Lives Matter has emerged under the nation's first Black president. Police brutality is not a new phenomenon; it has existed, in some form or other, since the abolition of slavery. Why has abusive policing created a breaking point in the age of Obama? How does this fit into a larger historical pattern of explosive Black politics and the consistent denial of Black oppression in US society?

Chapter 1 looks at the ideas of "American exceptionalism" and the "culture of poverty," mutually reinforcing concepts used to explain the persistence of Black poverty while deflecting attention away from systemic factors rooted in the United States' history as a settler-colonial state that came to rely on slavery as its dominant mode of production.

Chapter 2 examines the origins of "colorblindness" as an ideological tool, initially wielded by conservatives in the Nixon era to resist the growing acceptance of "institutional racism" as the central explanation for Black inequality. An important contribution of the civil rights and Black Power explosions of the era was locating the roots of Black oppression in the institutional and material history of the United States. The high point of this recognition came with the publication of the Kerner Commission report, which blamed "white racism" for segregation and Black poverty. The threat of violence and rebellion curbed conservatives' efforts to roll back the welfare state—at least initially. Instead of mounting a frontal attack on the Black insurgency, they deployed the language and logic of colorblindness in such a way as to distinguish between intentional racism and the effects of racism wherever race was not specifically mentioned. This helped to narrow the scope of the meaning of "race" at the onset of the post–civil rights period. It also became a pretext for rolling back the gains of the 1960s: If the attainment of those rights was rooted in the acknowledgement that racism in both public and private sectors had harmed African Americans, then there was a claim for that harm to be cured. Instead, the absence of racial language in the law became a pretext for further diminishing the regulatory capacity of the state. Downplaying race meant, once again, emphasizing culture and morality as important to understanding Black progress.

Chapter 3 examines the rise of the Black political elite and the divergence of Black political interests in the post–civil rights era. I look at this development as a product of pressure from below and above—and thus one that is rife with contradictions. Black urbanites were demanding "home rule" and an end to political domination by corrupt white political machines; at the same time there was a general recognition that Black control of Black living spaces could help cool off the hot cities. Black politicians took over bankrupt cities with weak tax bases and were put in the position of having to manage urban economic crises on the backs of their Black constituents. The unmanageability of these conditions and the absence of real solutions meant that Black elected officials were also quick to blame Black residents as a way of absolving themselves. They became reliable mouthpieces for rhetoric that blamed Black people for the conditions in Black communities. The further the movement drifted into the background, the more conservative formal Black politics became—and the more disillusioned ordinary African Americans became with "Black faces in high places."

Chapter 4 examines the "double standard of justice" in the United States historically. Policing has always been racist and abusive, even after massive efforts to professionalize the police in the aftermath of the 1960s rebellions. These same racist practices inform policing today, but pressure to keep crime rates down in order to facilitate urban redevelopment has intensified them. Cities are increasingly two-tiered, with one tier for young, mostly white professionals and another for Black and Brown people who find their standards of living and quality of life in peril and are harassed by police along the racially segregated boundaries that outline the contours of gentrification. There are any number of conditions to protest in Black communities, but police violence has consistently sparked Black rage because it exemplifies the compromised citizenship of African Americans.

In chapter 5, I locate the roots of the current movement against police brutality in the raised expectations of the Obama campaigns, as well as Obama's ensuing silence on the critical issues facing African Americans even as he has parroted the worst stereotypes about Black culture and irresponsibility. The political action of young Blacks is not happening in a vacuum; it is a part of the same radicalization that gave rise to the Occupy movement and coalesced around the murder of Trayvon Martin.

Chapter 6 looks at the current movement, from the protests in Ferguson to the rise of Black Lives Matter, and its role in distilling class conflict among African Americans while providing a political alternative based in protest and rearticulating Black oppression as systemic phenomenon. It then looks at the issues involved in moving from the protests that have brought about more general awareness of the crisis of police terrorism in Black communities to a deeply rooted movement capable of transforming those conditions.

Finally, in chapter 7, I examine the relationship between the movement against police violence and the potential for a much broader anticapitalist movement that looks to transform not only the police but the entire United States.

CHAPTER ONE

A Culture of Racism

Negro poverty is not white poverty. Many of its causes and many of its cures are the same. But there are differences—deep, corrosive, obstinate differences—radiating painful roots into the community, and into the family, and the nature of the individual.

These differences are not racial differences. They are solely and simply the consequence of ancient brutality, past injustice, and present prejudice. . . . For the Negro they are a constant reminder of oppression. For the white they are a constant reminder of guilt.

Nor can we find a complete answer in the experience of other American minorities. They made a valiant and a largely successful effort to emerge from poverty and prejudice.

The Negro, like these others, will have to rely mostly upon his own efforts. But he just cannot do it alone. For they did not have the heritage of centuries to overcome, and they did not have a cultural tradition which had been twisted and battered by endless years of hatred and hopelessness, nor were they excluded—these others—because of race or color—a feeling whose dark intensity is matched by no other prejudice in our society.

Nor can these differences be understood as isolated infirmities. They are a seamless web. They cause each other. They result from each other. They reinforce each other.

—President **Lyndon Johnson,** Howard University
commencement speech, June 4, 1965

I understand there's a common fraternity creed here at Morehouse: "Excuses are tools of the incompetent used to build bridges to nowhere and monuments of nothingness." Well, we've got no time for excuses. Not because the bitter legacy of slavery and segregation have vanished entirely; they have not. Not because racism and discrimination no longer exist; we know those are still out there. It's just that in today's hyperconnected, hypercompetitive world, with millions of young people from China and India and Brazil—many of whom started with a whole lot less than all of you did—all of them entering the global workforce alongside you, nobody is going to give you anything that you have not earned. Nobody cares how tough your upbringing was. Nobody cares if you suffered some discrimination. And moreover, you have to remember that whatever you've gone through, it pales in comparison to the hardships previous generations endured—and they overcame them. And if they overcame them, you can overcome them, too.

—**President Barack Obama,** Morehouse University
commencement speech, May 20, 2013

On the same day that the Ferguson Police Department finally revealed the name of Darren Wilson to the public as the police officer who killed Mike Brown, police chief Thomas Jackson simultaneously released a grainy video that appeared to depict Brown in the act of stealing cigarillos from a local convenience store. Jackson later admitted that Wilson did not know that Brown was suspected of having stolen anything. But the real work of the tape had already been done. Brown had been transformed from a victim of law enforcement into a Black suspect whose death was probably justified.

Brown's depiction as a possible criminal did not derail the fight to win justice for him, but for the mainstream media and other political elites who had stuck their toes in the waters of social justice, Brown's possible involvement in a criminal act in the moments before his murder cast doubt on his innocence. The *New York Times* ran an unwieldy story about Brown's interest in rap music and reported that he had occasionally smoked marijuana—hardly alien activities for youth of any color, but the *Times* declared that Brown was "no angel." Months later,

Times columnist Nicholas Kristof tweeted that twelve-year-old Tamir Rice, killed by police in Cleveland, was a better face for the movement because his death was more "clearcut [*sic*] and likely to persuade people of a problem."[1] The attempt to differentiate between "good" and "bad" Black victims of state violence tapped into longstanding debates over the nature of Black inequality in the United States. Was Brown truly a victim of racist and overzealous police, or was he a victim of his own poor behavior, including defying police? Was Brown deserving or undeserving of empathy, humanity, and ultimately justice?

There are constant attempts to connect the badges of inequality, including poverty and rates of incarceration, to culture, family structure, and the internal lives of Black Americans. Even before emancipation, there were relentless debates over the causes of Black inequality. Assumptions of biological and cultural inferiority among African Americans are as old as the nation itself. How else could the political and economic elite of the United States (and its colonial predecessors) rationalize enslaving Africans at a time when they were simultaneously championing the rights of men and the end of monarchy and establishing freedom, democracy, and the pursuit of happiness as the core principles of this new democracy? Thomas Jefferson, the father of American democracy, spoke to this ironically when advocating that freed Blacks be colonized elsewhere. He said of the Black slave:

> His imagination is wild and extravagant, escapes incessantly from every restraint of reason and taste, and, in the course of its vagaries, leaves a tract of thought as incoherent and eccentric, as is the course of a meteor through the sky. . . . Upon the whole, though we admit him to the first place among those of his own color who have presented themselves to the public judgment, yet when we compare him with the writers of the race among whom he lived, and particularly with the epistolary class, in which he has taken his own stand, we are compelled to enroll him at the bottom of the column. . . .
>
> The improvement of the blacks in body and mind, in the first instance of their mixture with the whites, has been observed by every one, and proves that their inferiority is not the effect merely of their condition of life. . . . It is not their condition then, but nature, which has produced the distinction. Whether further observation will or will not verify the conjecture, that nature has been less bountiful to them in the endowments of the head.[2]

This naked racism flattened the contradiction between enslavement and freedom and, in doing so, justified slavery as a legitimate, if not natural, condition for African Americans. This, of course, was not driven by blind hatred but by the lucrative enterprise of forced labor. Historian Barbara Fields reminds us that "the chief business of slavery," after all, was "the production of cotton, sugar, rice and tobacco," not the "production of white supremacy."[3] The continuing pursuit of cheap and easily manipulated labor certainly did not end with slavery; thus, deep-seated ideas concerning the inferiority of Blacks were perpetuated with fervor. By the twentieth century, shifting concepts of race were applied not only to justify labor relations but more generally to explain the curious way in which the experiences of the vast majority of African Americans confound the central narrative of the United States as a place of unbounded opportunity, freedom, and democracy. This observation challenges the idea that race operates or acts on its own, with only a tangential relationship to other processes taking place within our society.

Ideologically, "race" is in a constant process of being made and remade repeatedly. Fields explains the centrality of ideology in making sense of the world we live in:

> Ideology is best understood as the descriptive vocabulary of day-to-day existence, through which people make rough sense of the social reality that they live and create from day to day. It is the language of consciousness that suits the particular way in which people deal with their fellows. It is the interpretation in thought of the social relations through which they constantly create and re-create their collective being, in all the varied forms their collective being may assume: family, clan, tribe, nation, class, party, business enterprise, church, army, club, and so on. As such, ideologies are not delusions but real, as real as the social relations for which they stand. . . . An ideology must be constantly created and verified in social life; if it is not, it dies, even though it may seem to be safely embodied in a form that can be handed down.[4]

The point is that explanations for Black inequality that blame Black people for their own oppression transform material causes into subjective causes. The problem is not racial discrimination in the workplace or residential segregation: it is Black irresponsibility, erroneous social mores, and general bad behavior. Ultimately this transformation is not about "race" or even "white supremacy" but about "making sense" of and rationalizing poverty and inequality in ways that absolve the state and capital of any culpability. Race gives meaning to the notion that Black people are inferior because of either culture or biology. It is almost strange to suggest that Black Americans, many of whose lineages as descendants of slaves stretch back to the first two centuries of the beginning of the American colonies, have a culture separate and distinct from other Americans. This framework of Black inferiority politically narrates the necessity of austere budgets while sustaining—ideologically at least—the premise of the "American dream." The Black experience unravels what we are supposed to know to be true about America itself—the land of milk and honey, the land where hard work makes dreams come true. This mythology is not benign: it serves as the United States' self-declared invitation to intervene militarily and economically around the globe. Consider President Obama's words in September 2014, when he declared a new war front against the Islamic State in the Middle East. He said, "America, our endless blessings bestow an enduring burden. But as Americans, we welcome our responsibility to lead. From Europe to Asia—from the far reaches of Africa to war-torn capitals of the Middle East—we stand for freedom, for justice, for dignity. These are values that have guided our nation since its founding."[5] What an utterly absurd statement—but that, perhaps, is why the US political and economic leadership clings so tightly to the framework of Black inferiority as the central explanation for Black inequality.

Finally, ideologies do not work when they are only imposed from above. The key is widespread acceptance, even by the oppressed themselves. There are multiple examples of African Americans accepting some aspects of racist ideology while also rejecting other aspects because of their own experiences. At various times, African Americans have also accepted that "culture" and "personal responsibility" are just as important in understanding Black oppression as racism and discrimination are. But the Black freedom struggle has also done much to confront explanations that blame Blacks for their own oppression— including throughout the 1960s and into the 1970s. The Black Lives Matter movement has the potential to shift this again, even as "culture of poverty" politics remain as entrenched as ever and Black inequality remains a fact of American life.

A Cultural Tailspin

Why are ideas about a defective Black culture so widespread when there is so much evidence for material causes of continued Black inequality? One reason is the way that the political system, elected officials, and the mainstream media operate—sometimes in tandem and sometimes independent of each other—to reinforce this "common sense" view of society. The hearty shouts of "culture," "responsibility," and "morality" come with reckless abandon when politicians of all stripes explain to the world the problems in Black America. Representative Paul Ryan used a commemoration of the fiftieth anniversary of Lyndon Johnson's War on Poverty programs as an opportunity to explicate what he considers its failures: "We have got this tailspin of culture, in our inner cities in particular, of men not working and just generations of men not even thinking about working or learning the value and the culture of work, and so there is a real culture problem here that has to be dealt with." Ryan did not need to invoke "race" explicitly. The code is well known, not only because white conservatives like Ryan readily invoke it but also because liberals both normalize and legitimize the same language.

For example, when Democratic Party leader and Chicago mayor Rahm Emanuel tried to garner support for his plan to curb gun violence, he focused on what he likes to describe as the "four Ps: policing, prevention, penalties, and parenting."[6] Here Emanuel parrots conventional wisdom about juvenile crime: that it requires better parenting and, perhaps, some preventative programming, but if those fail, there are always policing and penalties to fall back on. At other times Emanuel has been less charitable, simply saying, "It's not about crime, it's about values."[7] President Obama also linked youth gun violence in Chicago to values and behavior when he said, "We have to provide stronger role models than the gangbanger on the corner."[8] The problem, according to these examples, is that crime and poverty in cities are not products of inequality but of a lack of discipline. Black youth need better values and better role models to change the culture that produces their dysfunctional and violent behavior, which, of course, is the real obstacle to a successful and meaningful life. Mayor Emanuel made the distinction between his own kids' lives of privilege and luxury and those of Chicago's Black and Brown children clear when, after an extravagant South American vacation, he quipped to a local newspaper, "Every year, we try to take the kids to a different part of the world to see. When you . . . grow up . . . you want to be an Emanuel child. It's unbelievable."[9]

It is not just in the world of politics that elected officials blame poor Black children for their own hardships. The mainstream media provides a very public platform for these ideas—from the seemingly innocuous to the very serious. For example, the mainstream media made an enormous ruckus about the antics of professional football player Marshawn Lynch, who ignored the press during the Super Bowl in 2015. It was quite the topic of discussion during much of the week leading up to the game, but the media attention shifted when another African American football player, Larry Foote, chastised Lynch for sending the "wrong message" to kids from an "urban environment." He ranted,

> The biggest message [Lynch]'s giving these kids . . . is "The hell with authority. I don't care, fine me. I'm gonna grab my crotch. I'm gonna do it my way." . . . In the real world, it doesn't work that way. . . . How can you keep a job? I mean, you got these inner-city kids. They don't listen to teachers. They don't listen to police officers, principals. And these guys can't even keep a job because they say "F" authority.[10]

In other words, police violence against and higher rates of unemployment among Black youth exist because Black kids do not respect authority—and because Marshawn Lynch is a poor role model.

In a much more serious reflection on these issues, *New Yorker* columnist Jonathan Chait and *Atlantic* columnist Ta-Nehisi Coates debated in a series of articles whether a "culture of poverty" actually exists. According to Chait, some African Americans' lack of "economic success" is directly related to the absence of "middle-class cultural norms." The combination of the two can be reduced to the presence of a Black culture of poverty: "People are the products of their environment. Environments are amenable to public policy. Some of the most successful anti-poverty initiatives, like the Harlem Children's Zone or the KIPP schools, are designed around the premise that children raised in concentrated poverty need to be taught middle class norms."[11]

Chait blithely links Black success to programs promoting privatization—charter schools and "empowerment zones" that have hardly been proven to end poverty. This old argument disintegrates when we try to make sense of the Great Recession of 2008, when "half the collective wealth of African-American families was stripped away," an economic free fall from which they have yet to recover.[12] The "middle-class norms" of homeownership could not stop Black people's wealth from disappearing into thin air after banks fleeced them by steering them toward subprime loans. Nor do "middle-class norms" explain why Black college graduates' unemployment rate is well over twice that of white college graduates.[13] Coates responded with an argument that does not often elbow its way into mainstream accounts of Black oppression:

> There is no evidence that black people are less responsible, less moral, or less upstanding in their dealings with America nor with themselves. But there is overwhelming evidence that America is irresponsible, immoral, and unconscionable in its dealings with black people and with itself. Urging African-Americans to become superhuman is great advice if you are concerned with creating extraordinary individuals. It is terrible advice if you are concerned with creating an equitable society. The black freedom struggle is not about raising a race of hyper-moral super-humans. It is about all people garnering the right to live like the normal humans they are.[14]

American Exceptionalism

While the rest of the world wrestles with class and the perils of "class envy," the United States, according to the legend of its own making, is a place where anyone can make it. Much earlier, colonial leader John Winthrop famously described it as "a city upon a hill," adding that "the eyes of all people are upon us."[15] On the night he won the presidency in 2008 President Barack Obama said, "If there is anyone out there who still doubts that America is a place where all things are possible, who still wonders if the dream of our founders is alive in our time, who still questions the power of our democracy, tonight is your answer."[16] Former secretary of state Madeleine Albright has called the United States the "indispensable nation,"[17] while Ronald Reagan, years earlier, spelled out the specific metrics of the American dream:

> One-half of all the economic activity in the entire history of man has taken place in this republic. We have distributed our wealth more widely among our people than any society known to man. Americans

work less hours for a higher standard of living than any other people. Ninety-five percent of all our families have an adequate daily intake of nutrients—and a part of the 5 percent that don't are trying to lose weight! Ninety-nine percent have gas or electric refrigeration, 92 percent have televisions, and an equal number have telephones. There are 120 million cars on our streets and highways—and all of them are on the street at once when you are trying to get home at night. But isn't this just proof of our materialism—the very thing that we are charged with? Well, we also have more churches, more libraries, we support voluntarily more symphony orchestras and opera companies, non-profit theaters, and publish more books than all the other nations of the world put together. . . . We cannot escape our destiny, nor should we try to do so. The leadership of the free world was thrust upon us two centuries ago in that little hall of Philadelphia. . . . We are indeed, and we are today, the last best hope of man on earth.[18]

American exceptionalism operates as a mythology of convenience that does a tremendous amount of work to simplify the contradiction between the apparent creed of US society and its much more complicated reality. Where people have failed to succeed and cash in on the abundance that American ingenuity has apparently created, their personal failures or deficiencies serve as the explanation.

But there is something more pernicious at the heart of this contradiction than a simple morality tale about those who try hard and those who don't. The long list of attributes that Reagan proudly recites is wholly contingent on the erasure or rewriting of three central themes in American history—genocide, slavery, and the massive exploitation of waves of immigrant workers. This "cruel reality" made the "soaring ideals" of American exceptionalism and American democracy possible.[19] From the mutual foundation of slavery *and* freedom at the country's inception to the genocide of the Native population that made the "peculiar institution" possible to the racist promulgation of "manifest destiny" to the Chinese Exclusion Act to the codified subordinate status of Black people for a hundred years after slavery ended, they are all grim reminders of the millions of bodies upon which the audacious smugness of American hubris is built. Race and racism have not been exceptions; instead, they have been the glue that holds the United States together.

Historian James Adams first popularized the concept of the American dream in his 1931 book *Epic of America*. He wrote:

But there has been also the *American dream*, that dream of a land in which life should be better and richer and fuller for every man, with opportunity for each according to his ability or achievement. It is a difficult dream for the European upper classes to interpret adequately, and too many of us ourselves have grown weary and mistrustful of it. It is not a dream of motor cars and high wages merely, but a dream of social order in which each man and each woman shall be able to attain to the fullest stature of which they are innately capable, and be recognized by others for what they are, regardless of the fortuitous circumstances of birth or position.[20]

This powerful idea has lured immigrants to this country and compelled internal migrants to other parts of the country. But it is rife with contradictions, just as it was in the 1930s, when the failures of the American economy produced widespread insecurity and poverty, despite the personal intentions or work ethic of those most affected. At the same time, the Russian Revolution in 1917 cast a long shadow, and the threat of radical and revolutionary activity loomed over Europe. In this context, the mythology of the United States as different and unaffected by class tensions and dynamics took on new urgency. The New Deal legislation and the reorganization of capital was a reflection of this. As Hal Draper pointed about the 1930s, "The New Deal liberals proposed to save capitalism, at a time of deep going crisis and despair, by statification—that is, by increasing state intervention into the control of the economy from above."[21]

Indeed, Roosevelt referred to himself as the "savior" of the free-market system. In his bid for reelection, he said: "It was this Administration which saved the system of private profit and free enterprise after it had been dragged to the brink of ruin by these same leaders who now try to scare you. The struggle against private monopoly is a struggle for, and not against, American business. It is a struggle to preserve individual enterprise and economic freedom."[22] In an era when revolution was perceived not as idealistic but as a possibility, it was absolutely necessary to introduce new regulatory measures to create equilibrium in the system. But "preserving" the system was not only about change at an institutional level, it was also a political contest over collective ownership, for which socialists and communists organized, versus private enterprise, the lifeblood of capitalism. There were two significant shifts in the American political economy toward this aim. The turn to Keynesian economics and the bolstering of demand-based consumption helped to underpin perceptions of economic stability. In turn, the development of state-sponsored social welfare—Social Security, aid to mothers with children, public housing—created a bottom through which the vast majority of ordinary people could not fall. These, combined with the US entrance into World War II, revitalized the American economy and gave rise to the longest economic expansion in American history.

The robust postwar economy put flesh on the ideological scaffolding of the American dream. Massive government subsidies were deployed in ways that hid the state's role in the development of the American middle class, further perpetuating the mythology of hard work and perseverance as the key ingredients to social mobility.[23] This was especially true in housing. The private housing lobby and its backers in Congress denounced publicly subsidized housing as creeping socialism. The federal government therefore did not subsidize homeownership through direct payment but through interest-rate deductions and government-guaranteed mortgages that allowed banks to lend with abandon. Not only did it rebuild the economy through these measures—and on a sounder basis than the unregulated capitalism of the previous period—but it reinforced and gave new life to the idea of American exceptionalism and the good life. As David Harvey has explained,

> The suburbanization of the United States was not merely a matter of new infrastructures. . . . it entailed a radical transformation in life-styles, bringing new products from housing to refrigerators and air conditioners, as well as two cars in the driveway and an enormous increase in the consumption of oil. It also altered the political land-scape, as subsidized home-ownership for the middle classes changed the focus of community action towards the defense of property values and individualized identities, turning the suburban vote towards conservative republicanism. Debt-encumbered homeowners . . . were less likely to go on strike.[24]

But the fruits of these new arrangements did not fall to African Americans. Political scientist Ira Katznelson describes the uneven distribution of postwar riches in his well-known book *When Affirmative Action Was White*, including the initial exclusion of African Americans from Social Security collection and other New Deal benefits. When it came to homeownership, for example, federal mortgage guarantees were contingent on the recipients living in new, suburban housing, from which most African Americans were excluded. This meant that while the federal government subsidized suburban development, urban living spaces were an afterthought.[25] As businesses began to relocate their firms and entire industries to suburban areas because of lower land costs and taxes, the urban disinvestment dynamic was exacerbated, leaving cities bereft of the jobs that had initially lured millions of people to them in the first place.[26] Meanwhile, real-estate interests and their backers in government ensured that neither Black renters nor Black home buyers could participate in the developing suburban economy.[27]

Cold War Conflict

The aftermath of World War II introduced a new dynamic into American "race relations." The war itself created a new, bipolar world in which the United States and the Soviet Union were the "superpowers" that competed with each other for influence and control over the rest of the planet. The war also unleashed massive upheaval among the colonial possessions of the old world order. As the colonized world went into revolt against European powers, the superpowers made appeals to newly emerging independent countries. This made discrimination against American Blacks not only a domestic issue but also an international one.[28] How could the United States present itself as a "city upon a hill" or as the essential democratic nation when its Black citizens were treated so poorly?

Black migration out of the South picked up at an even greater speed than before the war. The postwar economic expansion offered Black laborers their chance at escaping the grip of Jim Crow. One hundred and twenty-five thousand Black soldiers had fought in World War II and were returning to cities across the North—to the most serious housing shortage in American history. Competition over jobs and housing in cities was an old story in the postwar period, but a renewed sense of sense of militancy among African Americans created a palpable tension. One army officer in the Morale Division reported that "the threats to the nation were 'first Negroes, second Japs, third Nazis'—in that order!"[29] A Black GI from Tennessee asked, "What I want to know is how in the hell white folks think we are going to fight for the fascism under which we live each moment of our lives? We are taught to kill and we are going to kill. But do you ask WHO?"[30] White violence directed at Blacks continued, especially when Blacks attempted to breach the boundaries of segregation. Southern whites' "massive resistance" in defense of Jim Crow is well integrated into American folklore, but this attempt at racist mob rule was not regional. In Chicago and Detroit, in particular, thousands of whites joined mobs to terrorize African Americans who attempted to move into white areas.[31] In both the North and South, white police either joined the attacks on African Americans or, as they had done so many times before, passively stood aside as whites stoned houses, set fires, destroyed cars, smashed windows, and threatened to kill any Blacks who got in their way.

The ideological battlefield on which the Cold War was fought compelled Northern political and economic elites to take progressively more formal stances against discrimination and to call for more law and order. This especially became necessary when African Americans began to mobilize against racial injustice and actively tried to bring international attention to it, greatly aware of American vulnerability in racial politics given its vocal demands for democracy and freedom. The Nazi genocide of Jews in the 1930s and 1940s had deeply discredited racism and eugenics; the United States had characterized World War II as a battle between democracy and tyranny. It was therefore increasingly concerned about international perceptions of its treatment of African Americans. Mob violence and physical threats against Black people collectively threatened its geopolitical positioning. The developing Black militancy, fueled by political dynamics within the United States as well as the global risings of Black and Brown people against colonialism, set the US state on a collision course with its Black population. African Americans had certainly campaigned against racial injustice long before the civil rights era, but the confluence of several overlapping events brought Black grievances into sharper focus. These factors combined to push the United States toward emphasizing its political commitment to formal equality for Blacks before the law; they also emboldened African Americans to fight not only for formal equality but for social and racial justice as well.

The United States' commitment to formal equality in the context of the Cold War was not only intended to rehabilitate its reputation on racial issues, it was also an effort to bolster its free-market economy and system of governance. The government and its proponents in the financial world were making a global claim that the United States was good to its Black population, and at the same time they were promoting capitalism and private enterprise as the highest expressions of freedom. American boosters sustained the fiction of the "culture of poverty" as the pretext for the persisting inequality between Blacks and the rest of the country. In some ways, this was even more important as the United States continued its quest to project itself as an economic and political empire. Cold War liberalism was a political framework that viewed American racial problems as existing outside of or unrelated to its political economy and, more importantly, as problems that could be fixed within the system itself by changing the laws and creating "equal opportunity." Themes of opportunity, hard work, resilience, and mobility could be contrasted to the perceptions of Soviet society as being impoverished because of its planned economies, prison labor, and infringement of freedom.

President Johnson, for example, described the contest between East and West as "a struggle" between two distinct "philosophies": "Don't you tell me for a moment that we can't outproduce and outwork and outright any communistic system in the world. Because if you try to tell me otherwise, you tell me that slaves can do better than free men, and I don't believe they can. I would rather have an executive vice president . . . than to have a commissar!"[32]

Upholding American capitalism in the context of a bitter Cold War had multiple effects. Elected officials in both parties continued to demonize social welfare as socialism or communism and an affront to free enterprise, as did private-sector actors who had a financial interest in seeing the American government shift its functions to private institutions. As scholar Alexander von Hoffman explains:

> From the 1930s onwards, private housing financiers, real estate brokers, and builders denounced the idea of the government directly helping Americans of modest means to obtain homes. It was, they cried, not only a socialistic plot, but also an unjustified give-away to a select undeserving group of people. It soon became evident, if it was not already, that self-interest, as much as ideology, fueled the hatred of the leaders of private industry for public housing.[33]

Historian Landon Storrs argues that anticommunism—the "Red Scare"—had an even more profound impact on public policies because it weeded out "employees deemed disloyal to the U.S. government." Between 1947 and 1956, "more than five million federal workers underwent loyalty screening," and at least 25,000 were subject to a stigmatizing "full field investigation" by the FBI.[34] An estimated 2,700 federal employees were dismissed and about 12,000 resigned.

Those most affected, according to Storr, "were a varied group of leftists who shared a commitment to building a comprehensive welfare state that blended central planning with grassroots democracy." The impact was indelible: "The power of these leftists was never uncontested, but their expertise, commitment, and connectedness gave them strength beyond their numbers. Before loyalty investigations pushed this cohort either out of government or toward the center of the political spectrum, the transformative potential of the New Deal was greater than is commonly understood."[35] Of course, McCarthyism's impact reached beyond liberal public policies; it was generally destructive for the entire left. The state specifically targeted leading activists and intellectuals involved in the fight against racism; antiracist campaigns were dismissed out of hand as subversive activity. As Manning Marable observes, "The purge of communists and radicals from organized labor from 1947 through 1950 was the principal reason for the decline in the AFL-CIO's commitment to the struggle against racial segregation."[36] More generally, anticommunism and the complicity of Black and white liberals in its witch hunts "retarded the Black movement for a decade or more."[37]

The volatile politics surrounding who should be eligible for public welfare also aided in creating the political categories of "deserving" and "undeserving." These concerns overlapped with the growing popularity of "culture" as a critical framework for understanding the failure to find the American dream. This political context, as well as the deepening influence of the social sciences as an "objective" arbiter in describing social patterns (sponsored by the Ford Foundation, among others), helped to map a simplistic view of Black poverty that was largely divorced from structural obstacles, including residential segregation, police brutality, housing and job discrimination, and the systematic underfunding of public schools in Black communities. The problem was described as one of "assimilation" for Blacks migrating from south to north. This fit in with a developing global perspective on US poverty that was shaped by the Cold War as well as the social sciences.[38]

In 1959, liberal anthropologist Oscar Lewis coined the term "culture of poverty" to describe psychological and behavioral traits in poor people in underdeveloped countries and "to understand what they had in common with the lower classes all over the world."[39] Lewis wrote, "It seems to me that the culture of poverty has some universal characteristics which transcend regional, rural-urban, and even national boundaries." He identified these cultures in locations as disparate as "Mexican villages" and "lower class Negroes in the United States."[40] The shared traits he identified included resignation, dependency, present-time orientation, lack of impulse control, weak ego structure, sexual confusion, inability to delay gratification, and sixty-three more.[41] These were overwhelmingly psychological descriptions, highly malleable and certainly not endemic to the condition of the people themselves outside of any larger economic context. Lewis was not a political conservative—he was a left-wing liberal who linked this "culture of poverty" to "class-stratified, highly individuated capitalistic societies." But, as Alice O'Connor notes, "the problem was that Lewis made very little attempt to provide direct evidence or analysis that actually linked behavioral and cultural patterns to the structure of political economy as experienced by the poor." The "culture of poverty" in its original incarnation was viewed as a positive pivot away from "biological racism," rooted in eugenics and adopted by the Nazi regime. Culture, unlike biology, was mutable and capable of being transformed. Finally, O'Connor argued, "by couching the analysis so exclusively in terms of behavior and psychology, the culture of poverty undercut its own radical potential and deflected away from any critique of capitalism implicit in the idea."[42]

Locating the Source

As insightful as Lewis's original iteration of the "culture of poverty" may have been, it did not account for the profound racial terrorism that confronted Black people in the North as well as the South. The movement against state-sponsored racism and violence across the South exposed to the world—and, more importantly, to the rest of the United States—the racially tyrannical regime under which African Americans were living. The 1963 March on Washington was the first national display of the breadth of the Southern civil rights movement. It focused on the many manifestations of racial discrimination and gave clear and definable contours to the constraints imposed on African Americans. In doing so, the march also communicated that the movement's understanding of freedom extended beyond simply repealing unjust laws in the South.

A portion of King's much-memorialized "I Have a Dream" speech speaks to the relationship between economic and racial injustice:

> There are those who are asking the devotees of civil rights, "When will you be satisfied?" We can never be satisfied as long as the Negro is the victim of the unspeakable horrors of police brutality. We can never be satisfied as long as our bodies, heavy with the fatigue of travel, cannot gain lodging in the motels of the highways and the hotels of the cities. We cannot be satisfied as long as the Negro's basic mobility is from a smaller ghetto to a larger one. We can never be satisfied as long as our children are stripped of their self-hood and robbed of their dignity by signs stating: "For Whites Only." We cannot be satisfied as long as a Negro in Mississippi cannot vote and a Negro in New York believes he has nothing for which to vote. No, no, we are not satisfied, and we will not be satisfied until "justice rolls down like waters, and righteousness like a mighty stream."[43]

Here King also links the codified racial discrimination of the Jim Crow South to the informal but equally pernicious de facto segregation of the urban North. In both cases, King clearly located the Black condition in public and private institutional practices throughout the United States. Of course, King was not the first to do this, but the scale, scope, and ultimate influence of the march elevated these arguments to a national level.

As early as the 1930s, and certainly throughout the postwar era, Blacks engaged in campaigns for "better jobs, an end to police brutality, access to new housing, representation in government, and college education for their children."[44] Malcolm X considered it "ridiculous" that civil rights activists were traveling to the South to fight Jim Crow when the North had "enough rats and roaches to kill to keep all of the freedom fighters busy."[45] In a speech given at the founding of his new Organization of Afro-American Unity, in the year before his death, Malcolm described the political economy of Black poverty in the North:

> The economic exploitation in the Afro-American community is the most vicious form practiced on any people in America. In fact, it is the most vicious practiced on any people on this earth. No one is exploited economically as thoroughly as you and I, because in most countries where people are exploited they know it. You and I are in this country being exploited and sometimes we don't know it. Twice as much rent is paid for rat-infested, roach-crawling, rotting tenements.
>
> This is true. It costs us more to live in Harlem than it costs them to live on Park Avenue. Do you know that the rent is higher on Park Avenue in Harlem than it is on Park Avenue downtown? And in Harlem you have everything else in that apartment with you: roaches, rats, cats, dogs, and some other outsiders disguised as landlords. The Afro-American pays more for food, pays more for clothing, pays more for insurance than anybody else. And we do. It costs you and me more for insurance than it does the white man in the Bronx or somewhere else. It costs you and me more for food than it does them. It costs you and me more to live in America than it does anybody else and yet we make the greatest contribution.
>
> You tell me what kind of country this is. Why should we do the dirtiest jobs for the lowest pay? Why should we do the hardest work for the lowest pay? Why should we pay the most money for the worst kind of food and the most money for the worst kind of place to live in?[46]

His influence and wide appeal across the Black North helped to articulate a different understanding of Black poverty and hardship as the products not of bad behavior but of white racism.

The passage of the 1964 Civil Rights Act and the 1965 Voting Rights Act removed the last vestiges of legal discrimination across the South. It was a surprising accomplishment that could not have been imagined even ten years before it happened. Its success was an amazing accomplishment by the ordinary men, women, and children of the civil rights movement, and it forced a monumental shift in the political and social order of the American South. But almost before the ink could dry on the legislation, its limits were displayed. Ending legal segregation and disenfranchisement in the South did not necessarily guarantee free and unfettered participation in the public and private spheres of employment, housing, and education. This was also true in the North. The civil rights movement had much clearer targets in the South; the means of discrimination in the North, such as housing and job discrimination, were legal and thus much harder to change. Black children went to overcrowded schools in shifts in Chicago and New York—all perfectly legal.

Five days after the Voting Rights Act was signed into law, the Watts Rebellion exploded in South Central Los Angeles. Cries of "Selma" could be heard above the chaos of rebellion.[47] The civil rights movement had hastened the radicalization of all African Americans. There had been smaller uprisings in New York City, Philadelphia, Rochester, and other cities the previous summer, in 1964, but the Watts Rebellion was on an entirely different scale. For six days, an estimated ten thousand African Americans battled with police in an unprecedented rebellion against the effects of racial discrimination, including police brutality and housing discrimination. Thirty-four people were killed, hundreds more injured. Four thousand people were arrested and tens of millions of dollars in property damage occurred.[48]

The fires in Los Angeles were evidence of a developing Black radicalization rooted in the incongruence between America trumpeting its rich abundance as proof of the superiority of free enterprise and Black people suffering the indignities of poverty. After the passage of civil rights legislation, Black suffering could no longer be blamed only on Southern racism.

The Black freedom movement of the 1960s fed the expansion of the American welfare state and its eventual inclusion of African Americans. Though the New Deal had mostly excluded African Americans, Johnson's War on Poverty and Great Society programs were largely responses to the different phases of the Black movement. In 1964, Johnson reminded his supporters in the Chamber of Commerce of the consequences of not backing social welfare:

> Please always remember that if we do nothing to wipe out these ancient enemies of ignorance and illiteracy and poverty and disease, and if we allow them to accumulate. . . . If a peaceful revolution to get rid of these things—illiteracy, and these ancient enemies of mankind that stalk the earth, where two-thirds of the masses are young and are clamoring and are parading and are protesting and are demonstrating

now for something to eat and wear and learn and health—[then] a violent change is inevitable.[49]

The War on Poverty and Great Society programs reflected Cold War antipathy toward total government control by emphasizing public-private partnerships and "equal opportunity," as opposed to economic redistribution. Nevertheless, Black protests polarized the political debates concerning the nation's welfare policies and the course of action needed to remedy the growing Black Power revolt—and debates over the nature of Black poverty reemerged.

Presidential consultant Daniel Patrick Moynihan penned a controversial report, titled *The Negro Family: The Case for National Action*, that blamed the problems endured by Black people on a "tangle of pathology." The Moynihan report, as it came to be known, claimed to ground the problems experienced in Black communities in theory and research. Instead, it was a more sophisticated recycling of stereotypes infused with an air of science that located social problems in the supposed behaviors of poor Black families. Moynihan claimed that the heart "of the deterioration of the fabric of Negro society is the deterioration of the Negro family."[50] This deterioration was rooted, he said, in the historic way that American slavery had broken up Black families. Moynihan blamed Black women for emasculating Black men, who then shirked their role as the head of the family. The result was antisocial behaviors experienced far beyond the borders of Black families. At one point, the report casually suggests that "it is probable that at present, a majority of the crimes against the person, such as rape, murder, aggravated assault are committed by Negroes"—then concedes in the next sentence that there is, of course, "no absolute evidence" for this claim. Moynihan identified these problems as the outcome of Black families led by single women.

It is important to note that Moynihan was a liberal serving with the Johnson administration. He viewed his ideas as progressive because he located the "root causes" of Black social pathology in family structure, which could be overcome by "equal opportunity" and other government action. This is where liberal and conservative thought converge, however: in seeing Black problems as rooted in Black communities as opposed to seeing them as systemic to American society. Moynihan offered little description of contemporary manifestations of racism. Instead, he emphasized the role of slavery in explaining the many problems that developed from the overwhelming poverty that most Black families were trying to survive. But the Black rebellion produced other explanations for entrenched Black poverty.

Over the next three years, violent and furious explosions of Black rage in American cities punctuated every summer. They shocked the nation. The triumphalism of the American dream withered with each convulsion. Black protests forged an alternative understanding of Black inequality. Black psychologist Kenneth Clark dislodged the Harlem rebellion from Moynihan's "tangle of pathology" in his book *Dark Ghetto*. Though Clark would later be accused of promoting his own theories about Black pathology, his descriptions of the Harlem rebellion could very easily describe the dynamic underlying all of the Black uprisings in the 1960s:

> The summer of 1964 brought violent protests to the ghettos of America's cities, not in mobilization of effective power, but as an outpouring of unplanned revolt. The *revolts* in Harlem were not led by a mob, for a mob is an uncontrolled social force bent on irrational destruction. The revolts in Harlem were, rather, a weird social defiance. Those involved in them, were in general, not the lowest class of Harlem residents—not primarily looters and semi-criminals—but marginal Negroes who were upwardly mobile, demanding a higher status than their families had. Even those Negroes who threw bottles and bricks from the roofs were not in the grip of wild abandon, but seemed deliberately to be prodding the police to behave openly as the barbarians that the Negroes felt they actually were.... [There was] a calm within the chaos, a deliberateness within the hysteria. The Negro seemed to feel nothing could happen to him that had not happened already—he behaved as if he had nothing to lose. His was an oddly controlled rage that seemed to say, during those days of social despair, "We have had enough. The only weapon you have is bullets. The only thing you can do is kill me." Paradoxically, his apparent lawlessness was a protest against the lawlessness directed against *him*. His acts were a desperate assertion of his desire to be treated as a man. He was affirmative up to the point of inviting death, he insisted upon being visible and understood. If this was the only way to relate to society at large, he would rather die than be misunderstood.[51]

Clark's description of how, at least, the Black male psyche was essentially repaired through the course of fighting against racism reflected the widespread growth of Black political organizations in response to every conceivable issue. But it was not just Black men who were being "repaired" through fighting racism; Black women were also at the forefront of many of the most important struggles in the 1960s. From tenant unions to welfare-rights organizations to Black public-sector workers demanding union recognition, ordinary African Americans organized to both define and combat racial injustice.[52]

Lyndon Johnson's administration churned out legislation in an effort to stay in front of the mounting protests and "civil disorder." The most obvious way to keep up was by expanding the American welfare state.[53] The limits of the American welfare state have been the subject of intense debate, but Johnson's Great Society programs included job training, housing, food stamps, and other forms of assistance that inadvertently helped to define Black inequality as primarily an economic question. The greater emphasis on structural inequality legitimized Black demands for greater inclusion in American affluence and access to the benefits of its expanding welfare state. Theresa Vasta spoke for many women on welfare when she said that she had "no time for games. My children are hungry and my oldest one is missing school because I have no money to send her. . . . I am American born. I think I deserve the right treatment. Fair treatment, that is."[54]

The expansion of the welfare state, the turn to affirmative action practices, and the establishment of the EEOC by the end of the 1960s reinforced the idea that Blacks were entitled to a share in American affluence. The development of Black struggle over the course of the decade, from the protest movement based in the South to the explosion of urban rebellions across the country, changed the discourse surrounding Black poverty. Johnson noted this in his well-known commencement address at Howard University:

> The American Negro, acting with impressive restraint, has peacefully protested and marched, entered the courtrooms and the seats of government, demanding a justice that has long been denied. The voice of the Negro was the call to action. But it is a tribute to America that, once aroused, the courts and the Congress, the President and most of the people, have been the allies of progress. . . . But freedom is not enough. You do not wipe away the scars of centuries by saying: Now you are free to go where you want, and do as you desire, and choose

A Culture of Racism

the leaders you please. You do not take a person who, for years, has been hobbled by chains and liberate him, bring him up to the starting line of a race and then say, "you are free to compete with all the others," and still justly believe that you have been completely fair. . . . Thus it is not enough just to open the gates of opportunity. All our citizens must have the ability to walk through those gates. . . . We seek not just freedom but opportunity. We seek not just legal equity but human ability, not just equality as a right and a theory but equality as a fact and equality as a result.[55]

The phrases "freedom is not enough" and "equality as a result" pointed to structural inequality and affirmed the demand for positive or affirmative action on the part of the state to cure impoverished conditions brought on by centuries of discrimination.

Hundreds of thousands of Black Americans drew even more radical conclusions about the nature of Black oppression in the United States as they were drawn directly into the radicalizing movement; hundreds of thousands more sympathized with the rebellions. The struggle broke through the isolation and confinement of life in segregated Black ghettos and upended the prevailing explanation that Blacks were responsible for the conditions in their neighborhoods. Mass struggle led to a political understanding of poverty in Black communities across the country. Black media captured stories of injustice as well as the various struggles to organize against it, feeding this process and knitting together a common Black view of Black oppression while simultaneously providing an alternative understanding for white people. A Harris poll taken in the summer of 1967, after major riots in Detroit and Newark, found 40 percent of whites believed that "the way Negroes have been treated in the slums and ghettos of big cities" and "the failure of white society to keep its promises to Negroes" were the leading causes of the rebellion.[56] Many, including Martin Luther King Jr., began to connect Black oppression to a broader critique of capitalism.

King began to make those connections in his politics, especially when his organizing brought him in direct confrontation with Northern ghettos and residential segregation. At a Southern Christian Leadership Conference convention in the summer of 1967, he gave a speech that raised broader questions about the economic system:

Now, in order to answer the question, "Where do we go from here?"

which is our theme, we must first honestly recognize where we are now. When the Constitution was written, a strange formula to determine taxes and representation declared that the Negro was sixty percent of a person. Today another curious formula seems to declare that he is fifty percent of a person. Of the good things in life, the Negro has approximately one-half those of whites. Of the bad things of life, he has twice those of whites. Thus, half of all Negroes live in substandard housing. And Negroes have half the income of whites. When we view the negative experiences of life, the Negro has a double share. There are twice as many unemployed. The rate of infant mortality among Negroes is double that of whites and there are twice as many Negroes dying in Vietnam as whites in proportion to their size in the population.[57]

The Black Panther Party for Self-Defense (BPP) went even further when it declared its intent to rid the United States of its capitalist economy and build socialism in its place. The Black Panthers were not a fringe organization—far from it. FBI director J. Edgar Hoover declared the party the "greatest internal threat" to the security of the United States. Formed in Oakland, California, directly in response to the crisis of police brutality, the Panthers linked police brutality to the web of oppression and exploitation that entangled Black people across the country. Not only did they link Black oppression to its material roots, they connected it to capitalism itself. Panther leader Huey P. Newton made this clear:

> The Black Panther Party is a revolutionary Nationalist group and we see a major contradiction between capitalism in this country and our interests. We realize that this country became very rich upon slavery and that slavery is capitalism in the extreme. We have two evils to fight, capitalism and racism. We must destroy both racism and capitalism.[58]

The Panthers were not a mass party, but they had appeal that stretched far beyond their actual numbers. At its high point, the BPP was selling an astonishing 139,000 copies of its newspaper, the *Black Panther*, a week.[59] In this paper, readers would have seen multiple stories about police brutality in cities across the country. They would have also read the Panthers' Ten-Point Program, a list of demands intended to explain the aims and goals of the party, which linked capitalist exploitation and the American political economy to Black poverty and oppression.

In doing so, the party audaciously made demands on the state to fulfill
its responsibility to employ, house, and educate Black people, whose
impoverished state had been caused by American capitalism.
The Panthers were a regular topic of discussion in Black mainstream media. For example, in 1969, *Ebony*, the most popular weekly
magazine in Black America, allowed Newton to pen an article from
jail to articulate the Panthers' program in his own words. The article
included a detailed discussion on the relationship between capitalist
exploitation and racism. It read, in part, "Only by eliminating capitalism and substituting it for socialism will all black, *all* black people, be able to practice self-determination and thus achieve freedom."
This was not just the observations of a marginal left: this was the most
well-known Black revolutionary organization making a case to a much
broader Black population about their oppression. The Panthers, who
were deeply inspired by Malcolm X, linked the crisis in Black America
to capitalism and imperialism. Racism could not be separated from
the perpetual economic problems in Black communities. In fact, the
economic problems of Black America could not be understood without
taking account of racism. Blacks were underemployed, unemployed,
poorly housed, and poorly schooled *because* they were Black.

Identifying structural inequality or institutional racism was not
just of scholastic interest; linking Black oppression to structural and
institutional practices legitimized demands for programs and funding
to undo the harm that had been done. This logic underlined calls for
what would become "affirmative action" but also much broader demands for federal funding and the enforcement of new civil rights rules
to open up the possibility for greater jobs, access to better housing, and
improvement in Black schools.

The entire dynamic of the Black struggle pushed mainstream politics to the left during this period, as evidenced by the growth of the
welfare state and the increasing number of mainstream voices that
identified racism as a problem. The Black struggle also heightened an
already intense political polarization. Of course, racists and conservatives had always existed and dominated politics, but the growing
movement now put them on the defensive. The political establishment was split over how to respond. Where some liberals gravitated
toward including more structural arguments about Black inequality,

conservatives clung to stereotypes about Black families. The more ghetto inhabitants rebelled, the more conservative politicians' ideas about the ghetto and the people who lived there hardened.

Generally speaking, however, the positive impact of the struggle could be measured by shifting opinions among the public regarding social programs. There was a nuanced public response to the riots in the late 1960s, not just a backlash. The emphasis on backlash by historians and political figures has simplified the multiple factors that contributed to conservative shift in formal politics by the end of the decade and into the 1970s. To be sure, there was resentment against the uprisings, the tone of which can be captured by a liberal *New York Times* editorial, written only a few weeks after the riots in Detroit, that read in part, "The riots, rather than developing a clamor for great social progress to wipe out poverty, to a large extent have had the reverse effect and have increased the crises for use of police force and criminal law."[60] Yet the totality of that perspective did not appear to correspond with a number of polls taken ten days later that showed wide-ranging support for expanding social programs aimed at mitigating the material deprivation that many connected to the spreading violence. In a *Washington Post* poll of African Americans published in 1967, Blacks linked deteriorating conditions in their communities with the uprisings. Fully 70 percent of Blacks "attributed rioting to housing conditions." Fifty-nine percent of Blacks said they knew someone living in rat-infested housing. In the same poll, 39 percent of whites said they believed the condition of Black housing was responsible for the ongoing riots. In another poll of African Americans and whites, strong majorities came out in support of antipoverty programs. A *Washington Post* headline read, "Races agree on ghetto abolition and the need for a WPA-style program." Sixty-nine percent of *all* Americans supported federal efforts to create a jobs program. Sixty-five percent believed in tearing down ghettos. Sixty percent supported a federal program to eliminate rats and 57 percent supported summer-camp programs for Black youth.[61]

In some ways, these findings prefigured the coming results of a federal investigation into the regularly occurring Black rebellions. In the spring of 1967, Johnson impaneled a federal commission to investigate them. The Kerner Commission, named after Illinois governor Otto Kerner, interviewed Black people in every city that had experienced urban uprisings over the previous three years. The findings were a damning embarrassment for the Johnson administration. The report's introduction was quite clear in assigning blame for the discord in American cities. It read, in part:

> We have visited the riot cities; we have heard many witnesses. . . . This is our basic conclusion: Our nation is moving toward two societies, one black, one white—separate and unequal. Segregation and poverty have created . . . a destructive environment totally unknown to most white Americans. What white Americans have never fully understood—but what the Negro can never forget—is that white society is deeply implicated in the ghetto. White institutions created it, white institutions maintain it, and white society condones it. Social and economic conditions in the riot cities constituted a clear pattern of severe disadvantage for Negroes compared with whites, whether the Negroes lived in the area where the riot took place or outside it.[62]

The top three grievances it found in Black communities were police brutality, unemployment and underemployment, and substandard housing.

Johnson was angered by the report because it indicated that, even after his administration had spent tens of millions of dollars, hundreds of millions more were still needed to respond adequately to the depth of the "urban crisis." Despite Johnson's disappointment and his refusal even to mention the report during the first week of its release, more than two million copies were sold to the public, making it one of the most widely distributed government reports in history. The Kerner Commission, like most liberal bodies by the late 1960s, espoused both structural critiques and cultural arguments about Black families. In the end, though, the report called for massive investment in existing welfare programs to undo segregation and poverty in the United States.

Conclusion

A concerted effort continues to link Black poverty to Black culture and the Black family. As always, both conservatives and liberals make these arguments. It is not hard to understand why. There can be significant political disagreements between them, but the shared limits of their political imagination follow the same parameters as the existing society. They cannot see beyond that which exists. To really address the systemic and utterly destructive institutional racism throughout the country would have two immediate consequences, both of which would be unacceptable to liberals and conservatives alike.

The first would be to fundamentally undermine America's continual efforts to project itself as the moral leader of the world. Addressing institutional racism is not the same as firing a racist cop or punishing some other individual for a racist transgression. It is also not the same as blaming slavery or history for the continuation of racial discrimination. It would require a full accounting of the myriad ways that racial discrimination factors in and shapes the daily lives of African Americans, in particular working-class and poor African Americans. The second consequence would be a massive redistribution of wealth and resources to undo the continuing damage.

Instead, the political establishment clings to cultural explanations for the frightening living conditions in places as varied as West Baltimore, Oakland, North Philadelphia, and Overtown in Miami, because such explanations require them to do very little. When social and economic crises are reduced to issues of culture and morality, programmatic or fiscal solutions are never enough; the solutions require personal transformation. This is why Black neighborhoods get police, not public policy—and prisons, not public schools. For example, in the raging debates over the future of public education, corporate education-reform advocates deny that poverty has any bearing on educational outcomes.[63] Instead, they describe Black children as being disinterested in education because to be smart is to pretend to be white. (The president of the United States once argued that this explains why Black students do poorly.[64]) All that remains is an overwhelming focus on charity and role modeling to demonstrate good behavior to bad Black youngsters as opposed to offering money and resources. Obama has organized a new initiative, My Brother's Keeper, specifically aimed at young Black and Brown boys and teenagers, whose problems, it says, exceed the capacity of government policy to address. It relies on corporate philanthropic donations, role models, and willpower. Obama, in introducing the measure, was quick to clarify that "My Brother's Keeper is not some big, new government program . . . [but] a more focused effort on boys and young men of color who are having a particularly tough time. And in this effort, government cannot play the only—or even the primary—role."[65]

The widespread and widely agreed-upon descriptions of Black people as lazy cheats rationalizes the social and economic disparities between African Americans and the rest of the population and absolves the economic and political systems from any real responsibility. This is not only a problem for African Americans. It also helps to disguise the greater, systemic inequities that pervade American capitalism. So, even while the ranks of the white poor continue to grow, their poverty is seen as somehow distinct from "generational" Black poverty. The growing ranks of the white incarcerated are distinguished from Black incarceration, which is supposed to be an outgrowth of Black irresponsibility. In the DOJ report on the Ferguson Police Department, released in March 2015, "several" officials told investigators that the reason Blacks received a disproportionately large number of citations and tickets was a "lack of personal responsibility."[66] Pathologizing "Black" crime while making "white" crime invisible creates a barrier between the two, when solidarity could unite both in confronting the excesses of the criminal justice system. This, in a sense, is the other product of the "culture of poverty" and of naturalizing Black inequality. This narrative works to deepen the cleavages between groups of people who would otherwise have every interest in combining forces. The intractability of Black conditions becomes seen as natural as opposed to standing as an indictment of the system itself, while the hard times befalling ordinary whites are rendered almost invisible. For example, the majority of poor people in the United States are white, but the public face of American poverty is Black. It is important to point out how Blacks are overrepresented among the poor, but ignoring white poverty helps to obscure the systemic roots of all poverty. Blaming Black culture not only deflects investigation into the systemic causes of Black inequality but has also been widely absorbed by African Americans as well. Their acceptance of the dominant narrative that blames Blacks for their own oppression is one explanation for the delay in the development of a new Black movement, even while police brutality persists.

There is, however, reason for hope. This chapter has tried to show the fluidity of political ideas and the conditions under which they can be challenged and ultimately changed. Public perceptions about poverty changed in the 1930s when it became clear that the actions of bankers had sent the economy into a tailspin—not the personal character of workers. The connections between capitalism, corruption, and the condition of the working class were made even clearer by communists and socialists, who linked the living conditions of the working class to an economic system rather than just bad luck. The political and economic elite responded by burying the left and its critiques of capitalism—while honing and deploying the "culture of poverty" theory to explain poverty in the "land of plenty." But this state of affairs was not etched in stone. The political uprisings of the 1960s, fueled by the Black insurgency, transformed American politics, including Americans' basic understanding of the relationship between Black poverty and institutional racism—and, for some, capitalism. Ideas are fluid, but it usually takes political action to set them in motion—and stasis for the retreat to set in.

CHAPTER TWO

From Civil Rights to Colorblind

If the problem of the twentieth century was, in W. E. B. Du Bois's famous words, "the problem of the color line," then the problem of the twenty-first century is the problem of colorblindness, the refusal to acknowledge the causes and consequences of enduring racial stratification.

—**Naomi Murakawa**, *The First Civil Right: How Liberals Built Prison America*

In his book *Black Reconstruction in America*, W. E. B. Du Bois described the promise of Reconstruction as a "brief moment in the sun" for Blacks, before its disastrous end moved African Americans "back again toward slavery."[1] The receding of the Black Power insurgency during the 1970s didn't return Blacks to a state of neo-slavery, but the hope and expectations raised by the movement of the 1960s proved elusive.

By the end of the 1970s, there was little talk about institutional racism or the systemic roots of Black oppression. There was even less talk about the kind of movement necessary to challenge it. Instead, when Ronald Reagan ran for the Republican presidential nomination in 1976, he made a play for the racist vote by complaining about a fictitious "strapping young buck" using food stamps to buy T-bone steak. He famously invented the stereotypical "welfare queen," who, he said, "used 80 names, 30 addresses, 15 telephone numbers to collect food stamps, Social Security, veterans' benefits for four nonexistent deceased veteran husbands, as well as welfare. Her tax-free cash income alone has been running $150,000 a year."[2] These were familiar racist baits for the white conservative electorate: lazy Black welfare cheats getting something for nothing. But in the aftermath of the "Black revolution" of the 1960s, politicians no longer felt comfortable displaying their racist credentials upon their sleeves. The "strapping buck" and the "welfare queen" were assumed to be Black—but, politically, Reagan and others could not risk saying so. Even with its coded language, Reagan's conservatism was at this point considered on the extreme right of mainstream politics—it would take the rest of the decade to become dominant. The Black movement of the 1960s had disgraced outward displays of racial animus, even as race continued to animate American politics by other means. Ultimately, Reagan lost the nomination to Gerald Ford by a narrow margin, but the trajectory of mainstream politics was clear. It was not just the right: the Democratic Party was also moving quickly to abandon its very recent association with the civil rights movement. On a campaign-trail stop in Indiana, Jimmy Carter, who was campaigning for the 1976 Democratic nomination, remarked:

> I have nothing against a community that's made up of people who are Polish, Czechoslovakian, French Canadians or blacks who are trying to maintain the ethnic purity of their neighborhoods. . . . But I don't think the government ought to deliberately break down an ethnically oriented community deliberately by injecting into it a member of another race. . . . I'm not trying to say that I want to maintain with any kind of government interference the ethnic purity of neighborhoods. What I say is the government ought not to take as a major purpose the intrusion of alien groups into a neighborhood, simply to establish that intrusion.[3]

The country was entering an era of post–civil rights "colorblindness." This was not the benign, long-sought absence of "race" from the legal strictures governing the United States. The 1968 Kerner Commission report's detailed descriptions of racial discrimination by public and private institutions had established a basis upon which African Americans could stake a claim to federal aid.

Instead, "colorblindness" aided politicians in rolling back the welfare state, allowing Congress and the courts to argue that the absence of racism in the law meant that African Americans could not claim racial harm. Not everyone believed this so soon after the Black movement had turned the country upside down demanding an end to racism. But the political framework of colorblindness allowed portions of the political establishment to separate Black hardship from the material conditions that activists had worked so hard to expose. It was as if the signing of civil rights legislation had wiped the slate clean and African Americans had been given a new start. Only ten years earlier, Lyndon Johnson had given his speech declaring that "freedom is not enough" to achieve racial equality, but now those vying for the presidency were contending that formal freedom was more than enough.

Nothing could have been further from the truth. Decades of disinvestment and under-resourcing had left African Americans surrounded by substandard and dilapidated housing, poor job options, underfunded schools, and a bevy of other problems that only massive financial investment could repair. The politics of colorblindness helped to shroud not only racism but also its companion: the economic crisis of the early 1970s. At the precise moment when the Black movement was demanding enormous infrastructural investment to revive urban enclaves, the booming American economy of the postwar era was grinding to a halt. With its end came a relentless ideological assault on the kinds of public expenditures needed to attend to deep economic deprivation. Colorblindness helped to explain this retreat from public expenditure as the consequence of moral decay and the rise of criminality in the "inner city." Nixon cabinet member George Romney would describe it as the "crisis problem people"—using the old "culture of poverty" framework the movement had pilloried in the 1960s. The point was to restore order while defanging continued Black demands on the state. These kinds of political attacks had persisted throughout the 1960s as the right hardened its political opposition to civil rights and welfare legislation. The difference then, however, was that the strength of the movement, in both its Southern and Northern expressions, exerted a tremendous amount of pressure on the federal government to make repeated concessions.

The end of the long postwar economic boom, along with a slowing Black political movement, created the first opportunity in a long while for the political right wing to recalibrate and take the offensive. American politics had been deeply polarized for much of the 1960s, but relentless protests had effectively thwarted the right's efforts to demobilize the movement. The racial common sense underwriting the "culture of poverty" had been severely compromised by the Black movement and its demands for full citizenship and an end to racial discrimination. It was hard to argue that people putting their lives in harm's way for the right to vote were "culturally defective." Not only was the Black movement a threat to the racial status quo but it also acted as a catalyst for many other mobilizations against oppression. From the antiwar movement to the struggle for women's liberation, the Black movement was a conduit for questioning American democracy and capitalism. Its generative power provided a focal point for the counteroffensive that was soon to come. This counteroffensive, launched by the business class, would affect not only Blacks but everyone who benefited from the expansion of social welfare.

This alone was enough to galvanize the right and all of mainstream politics. It was one thing to identify a political need to absorb some portion of African Americans into the mainstream of society—including through access to middle-class jobs, homeownership, higher education, and electoral politics. It was quite another to continue to acquiesce to Black demands in a way that threatened to compromise core ideological tenets of American capitalism, including the image of the United States as a land of equal opportunity, not "equal outcomes."[4] The battle in the sixties had legitimized Black demands; now that legitimacy had to be rolled back. In 1981, Republican Party strategist Lee Atwater explained how this was to be done and the role that colorblind politics could play:

> You start out in 1954 by saying, "Nigger, nigger, nigger." By 1968 you can't say "nigger"—that hurts you, backfires. So you say stuff like, uh, forced busing, states' rights, and all that stuff, and you're getting so abstract. Now, you're talking about cutting taxes, and all these things you're talking about are totally economic things and a byproduct of them is, blacks get hurt worse than whites.... "We want to cut this" is much more abstract than even the busing thing ... and a hell of a lot more abstract than "Nigger, nigger."[5]

It is important to consider that this political attack was intended not only to discipline rebelling African Americans but to reestablish order in a society where demonstrations, illegal strikes, riots, and rebellion had become legitimate means of registering complaints, including those of ordinary working-class white people, against the state and forcing reforms from hostile political forces. This chapter explores the ideological and political restoration of order in efforts to rehabilitate the system itself.

Understanding the "Conservative Backlash"

Richard Nixon's victory in 1968 signaled that not everyone was pleased with the radicalism sweeping across the United States. Nixon articulated the anxiety experienced by many white workers who chafed at the pace at which Blacks were demanding change. He especially embodied the anger of a ruling class that wanted to reestablish control over the direction of the country. This meant ending street protests as well as curtailing public-sector programs and work. The reassertion of Republican control began with binding the loose threads of the party. The GOP had been deeply divided for most of the sixties among the hardcore Goldwater right, the buttoned-up business elite of the Northeastern corridor, and the liberal civil-rights wing of the party. The tumult of social upheaval and the war in Vietnam had blown the existing Democratic Party apart, leaving its segregationist Dixiecrat wing without a home. This gave the GOP an opening to reestablish itself as the political home for conservatives, including the racist Southerners displaced from the Democratic Party.

Integrating the Dixiecrats into the GOP was central to a broader strategy the Republicans referred to as the "Southern strategy," which at its core was about winning white Democrats, particularly poor and working-class Democrats, to the Republican Party on the basis of racism. The Southern strategy was contingent on two assumptions: that the Democratic Party would implode across the South, and that Republicans could appeal to the racism and resentments of white workers, whom they presumed were chafing at what Blacks were gaining through protest. Nixon referred to all of these potential voters as the "silent majority"—insinuating that those protesting for civil rights and against the war in Vietnam were a vocal minority. In 1969, Nixon advisor Kevin Phillips wrote a book titled *The Emerging Republican Majority*, which essentially argued that elections are won by focusing on people's resentments.[6] Nixon, once in office, mapped out a strategy to do just that, transforming ordinary whites' anxieties, brought on by growing economic insecurity, into resentment against Blacks. Nixon's chief of staff, H. R. Haldeman, said as much in his diary of daily events in the White House. He wrote that Nixon had "emphasized that you have to face the fact that the whole problem is really the blacks. The key is to devise a system that recognizes this while not appearing to."[7]

There was a grain of truth to this: the Black movement was the nexus of social protest throughout the 1960s. King recognized as much in the months before he was killed: "In these trying circumstances, the Black revolution is much more than a struggle for the rights of Negroes. It is forcing America to face all its interrelated flaws—racism, poverty, militarism and materialism. It is exposing the evils that are rooted deeply in the whole structure of our society."[8] From the movement against the war in Vietnam to a revived movement for women's liberation, new struggles were unfolding. The gay liberation movement came into being with a riot in New York City in the summer of 1969; a strike wave in the late 1960s and early 1970s had even greater repercussions in American politics. Nixon's strategy for responding was an old one: divide and conquer.

That strategy, however, would take some time to develop. When Nixon was elected, the country was deeply divided. The last great gasp of urban rebellion came in the spring of 1968, in the aftermath of King's assassination—but the nation's elected officials did not know this in the early 1970s and assumed that more was around the corner. The threat of violence, which had propelled social policy for the better part of a decade, still hung thick in the air; nonwhite communities were having enough skirmishes with the police that Nixon had to temper his desire to cut social welfare. San Francisco mayor Joseph Alito reminded his colleagues in 1974 that "there are emotions in the cities that can be as disruptive as 1967, 1968, 1969 . . . [and] it would be a serious mistake to think the cities cannot erupt."[9] Nixon described the country as on the verge of unraveling—and tapped into the resentments and anxieties of white workers, stirring generational resentments between older white workers and the students, Blacks, young workers, and radicals who were taking over the cities and the campuses. Rising crime, rising taxes, and inflation capped the long economic expansion of the postwar period.

In the background, the war in Vietnam appeared endless and was on the verge of expanding. Nixon homed in on the uncertainty that ruled the moment and led a charge to link this national sense of insecurity to liberals and the pace at which Blacks were demanding even more. Part of the concern was that Black protests were not just affecting legislation: they were also having a direct influence on the economy. Workers' real wages were being eaten away by inflation (spawned by the war in Vietnam) while workplace conditions were getting worse. The demands of automation in many industries meant laying workers off and expecting those who remained to do more. Black autoworkers in Detroit referred to this process as "niggermation," describing how one Black worker was expected to be as productive as three white workers. The pace was grueling, the consequences were deadly, and the profits rolled in. According to one report, "In 1946, some 550,000 auto workers had produced a little more than 3 million vehicles, but in 1970 some 750,000 auto workers had produced a little more than 8 million vehicles."[10] "Niggermation," Dan Georgakas and Marvin Surkin explain in *Detroit: I Do Mind Dying*, was directly responsible for the deaths of more than 16,000 autoworkers. One 1973 report found "63,000 cases of disabling diseases and about 1,700,000 cases of lost or impaired hearing."[11]

The demand for higher wages to offset the corrosive effects of inflation and compensate for the dramatic rise in production helped to spur workplace militancy. This put Black and white workers on the same picket lines. Workplace action also spread to the public sector, even while public-sector strikes were illegal. After President John F. Kennedy signed an executive order in 1960 allowing federal workers to unionize, though not strike, public-employee union membership grew from 400,000 in the late 1950s to four million by the mid-1970s. This opened up enormous access to good, stable jobs because antidiscrimination legislation ensured more fairness in public-sector jobs than in private white-collar employment. However, the inability to strike often meant that federal workers, regardless of their ability to form unions, relied on welfare to supplement their take-home pay. By the mid-1960s, public-sector workers were beginning to engage in illegal strikes to raise their wages and bring dignity to their workplaces. Poverty wages in garbage collection, nursing, teaching, mail delivery, and other public jobs prompted unprecedented and illegal workplace action. The most famous example is the sanitation workers in Memphis, whose attempts at organizing a union brought King to their city; he addressed them the night before he was murdered. Hundreds of thousands of African Americans had participated in social-movement activism over the course of the 1960s, and they did not simply leave their politics at the door when they arrived at work. Instead, the struggle over social conditions in their neighborhoods catalyzed their struggles at work. In 1960, there had been thirty-six public-sector strikes. By 1970, that number had grown to 412. Black sanitation workers and nurses went on strike across the South for union recognition and collective bargaining rights.[12]

The most dramatic episode of workplace activism during this era was an illegal strike of more than 200,000 postal workers in March 1970. For two weeks, postal workers in more than thirty cities refused to sort or deliver the mail. Instead they walked the picket lines, demanding an increase in wages. The strike began in New York City, where the top salary postal workers could earn after twenty-one years of employment was still less than the average cost of living in the city. In 1968, President Johnson suggested to Congress a modest pay increase for postal workers. Congress took no action, but in 1970 it offered them a puny 4 percent raise—and a week later voted itself a 41 percent salary increase. The ensuing postal strike was the largest workplace action ever taken by federal workers. At one point Nixon mobilized the National Guard to sort and deliver the mail, but postal work was hard, skilled work and untrained soldiers could not easily perform it. The breakdown of discipline was palpable. Of the 26,000 soldiers called up to intervene in the strike, only 16,000 bothered to show.[13] Within a matter of two weeks, the disproportionately Black postal workforce won a 14 percent wage increase and the unprecedented right to collectively bargain their wages. Nixon's labor secretary glumly noted, "There's only one thing worse than an illegal strike: a wildcat that wins."[14] *TIME* magazine observed, "The government's authority was placed in question and the well-being of business, institutions, and individuals in jeopardy."[15]

The postal strike was the crest of a wave of workplace actions from 1967 through 1974. During that period there was an average of 5,200 strikes per year, compared with a high of 4,000 strikes in the previous decade. The number of workdays lost to strikes was also growing. From 1967 to 1971, strike days averaged 49.5 million, peaking during the year of the postal strike with 66.4 million days lost in 1970—the highest yearly loss due to labor unrest since 1946.[16] It was no coincidence that this strike wave coincided with the most militant phase of the Black insurgency—and it affected the entire workforce, not just Black workers. This was the real threat. As labor journalist Lee Sustar explains:

> Several Black caucuses, such as the Society of Afro-American Postal Employees, became centers of agitation for industrial struggle that necessarily involved white workers. Comprising over 20 percent of the 700,000 postal employees, Black workers were central to the weeklong, illegal wildcat postal strike in 1970. Black postal workers were concentrated in cities where the strike was strongest. Organized against the efforts of union leaders, the illegal walkout was broken only when President Richard Nixon sent in the National Guard. The strike, denounced as "labor anarchy" by the *Wall Street Journal*, almost certainly involved the largest number of Black workers ever in a U.S. labor dispute.[17]

Black labor played a prominent role in the strike wave, but its success would have been impossible if millions of white workers had also not taken action. This fact challenges the assumption that white workers were politically monolithic, dutiful adherents to "silent majority" politics. It challenges the simplistic narrative of racial backlash pitting ordinary whites against the Black struggle. None of this is to say that many white workers were not racist during this period; many were indeed resentful, perceiving that Blacks were getting too much at the expense of white families.

The political drift to the right, however, was not linear; it was complicated by changing racial and economic dynamics and by the real impact of the "Black Revolution" throughout the entire country, which provoked or even hardened some resentments and anxieties but also upended negative attitudes toward Blacks that were largely based in racist stereotypes. Black demands for inclusion, including access to the supposed benefits of American citizenship, subverted or, at least, confronted the idea that Blacks were lazy and parasitic.

According to Barbara Ehrenreich, polls taken between 1965 and 1968 showed sharp increases in the number of people who said they "often feel bad" about the way "Negroes [are] treated." The number of whites willing to vote for a Black president jumped from 38 percent in 1958 to 59 percent in 1965 to 70 percent in 1970.[18] Polls found majorities in favor of affirmative action, against the death penalty, and for integrated neighborhoods—the numbers, across the board, were higher in the early 1970s than they would be even a few years later. This speaks to the powerful sway of the social movements of the 1960s, not to an unbridgeable gap between white and Black. Ehrenreich goes on to point out:

> America's blue-collar workers were in revolt in the late sixties and seventies, but not along the right-wing traditionalist lines sketched by the media. The late sixties saw the most severe strike wave since shortly after World War II, and by the early seventies the new militancy had swept up autoworkers, rubber workers, steelworkers, teamsters, city workers, hospital workers, farm workers, tugboat crewmen, grave diggers and postal employees. For all the talk of racial backlash, Black and white workers were marching, picketing and organizing together in a spirit of class solidarity that had not been seen since the thirties. Nixon's "silent majority" was yelling as loud as it could—not racial epithets but the historic strikers' chant: "Don't cross the line!"[19]

The growth of left-wing consciousness over the course of the 1960s helps to explain why Nixon turned to colorblindness and racial code words as a way to conceal, or at least obscure, later efforts to undo aspects of the Johnson welfare state. If the white majority were as racist as the "conservative backlash" narrative makes them out to be, then why this strategy of codes and subterfuge? There was never any national directive declaring an end to the use of racial epithets in the public utterances of elected officials. Nor had public displays of racism simply become unfashionable. Instead, the Black movement had rendered such behavior completely unacceptable, not least because it had demonstrated, some fifty years before the slogan would appear, that Black lives mattered. It has been the relative strength or, lack thereof, of the movement that would ultimately determine whether or not the public nature of racism would persist. By the end of the sixties and into the early 1970s, the movement made racism unpopular; by the end of the decade this would begin to change.

In addition, Nixon could not unleash a frontal assault on the Johnson welfare state because poor and ordinary whites were also benefiting from the War on Poverty. This foreshadowed a strategy that Reagan and Clinton would employ as well—using racial codes and innuendo to build a case against programs that benefit poor and working-class whites, while undermining the potential for solidarity among those who have the most to gain by uniting and the most to lose by continuing to be divided. These were the politics of race in the new "postracial" era.

Restoring Order

In 1969, *Life* magazine published a series of articles on revolution. One front cover read:

> Revolution:
>> What are the causes?
>> How does it start?
>> Can it happen here?

It may read as a conspiracy theory today, but by the late 1960s these were serious questions confronting the elite, what today we regularly refer to as the 1 percent. This was not an anticommunist rant but evidence of genuine concern of the rising fortunes of the left. The *Wall Street Journal* raised similar questions in the wake of militant student activism overseas, openly wondering what impact the protests would have in this country:

> In a modern world reduced to the size of a village by high-speed communications it is possible to mobilize an international following with such an attractive idea [revolution]. Whether it is possible to foment a worldwide revolution with enough force to destroy the existing balances of power and order is a debatable topic. But this is no doubt the puzzling question that is in the back of the minds of many people when they see, on their TV screens, the forces of disorder at work.[20]

This continued worry about radicalization was coupled with a looming concern about the state of the economy. The core concern here was not about the economic health of the average American; rather, "capitalists in the early seventies felt threatened by changes in the world economy, by the decline of American hegemony, and by the consequences and implications of domestic political mobilizations."[21]

When a *New York Times* journalist and a graduate student were allowed to sit in on a series of retreats for business executives in 1974 and 1975, "they found a mood of vulnerability and a concern about the long range implications of recent social and economic policies." In their book *Ethics and Profits: The Crisis of Confidence in American Business,* Leonard Silk and David Vogel conducted a wide-ranging survey of 360 anonymous executives from some of the most powerful corporations in the nation about their attitudes concerning the health of business and free enterprise. They found a range of emotions, from anxiety to contempt, directed at the great mass of American society. One executive suggested, "The American capitalist system is confronting its darkest hour. . . . If we don't take action now, we will see our own demise. We will evolve into another social democracy."[22] Another bemoaned the role of Congress and stressed that business had to lead the country: "It is up to each of us, not some prostitute of a Congressman pandering to get reelected, to decide what should be done."[23] They debated whether or not American democracy had gone too far, asking, "Can we still afford one man, one vote? One man, one vote has undermined the power of business in all capitalist countries since World War Two."[24] Some discussed how to jolt the public out of its dependence on social welfare spending: "The recession will bring about the healthy respect for economic values that the Depression did. . . . It would be better if the recession were allowed to weaken more than it will, so that we would have a sense of sobriety . . . we need a sharp recession."[25]

These insights from the stewards of American business showcased concern, but also the lengths to which some capitalists were willing to go to reinvigorate their profits. These business leaders were not wholly confident in American politicians' ability to lead the economy. The challenge for Nixon was to restore confidence and profitability by quieting the decade-long social and political instability. Since the Black movement had been the nexus for social activism, would an attack on the Black movement have the same generalizing effect? This was a multipronged strategy that included physical repression of the movement through the use and expansion of the policing state; an ideological attack on poor and working-class African Americans as undeserving, lazy, and violent; and eventually the cultivation of a functioning Black middle class that could politically discipline poorer African Americans while also rehabilitating the idea that everyone could prosper in the United States.

Freedom and Choices

Nixon's first term functioned as a bridge between the civil rights era and a burgeoning period of postracial, colorblind political paradigms. The Nixon administration was reluctant to fully dismantle Johnson's programs, fearing that the cities would reignite, but it was also limited by the Democrats' control of Congress. Nixon worked to close the civil rights period not by being antagonistic but by changing the terms of the debate. Where the Black movement had, as a result of protests and theorization, succeeded in defining racism as systemic and institutional, Nixon officials worked to narrow the definition of racism to the intentions of individual actors while countering the idea of institutional racism by focusing on "freedom of choice" as a way to explain differential outcomes. Nixon made clear that his administration would fight against "intentional racism," but differentiated this from disparate outcomes produced by institutional discrimination that was harder to identify. For example, Nixon and others called the division between rich and poor "economic discrimination" but defended it, citing the right of property owners, in particular, to protect and maintain their property values by limiting the incursion of the poor into their communities (referencing the ongoing debate concerning the placement of low-income housing). But Nixon was addressing much larger issues as well. In a little-discussed 1971 statement on housing, he spelled out the logic of the post–civil rights "colorblind" paradigm:

> The goal of this administration is a free and open society. In saying this, I use the words "free" and "open" quite precisely. . . . Freedom has two essential elements: the right to choose and the ability to choose. . . . Similarly, an "open" society is one of open choices and one in which the individual has the mobility to take advantage of these choices. An open society does not need to be homogenous, or even fully integrated. There is room within it for many communities. In terms of an open society, what matters is mobility. The right and the ability of each person to decide for himself where and how he wants to live, whether as part of an ethnic enclave or as part of a larger society—or as many do, who share the life of both. We are richer for our cultural

diversity; mobility is what allows us to enjoy it. Instead of making man's decisions for him, we aim to give him both the right and the ability to choose for himself—and the mobility to move upward.[26]

He ended the statement by attempting to separate economic discrimination from racial discrimination: "What is essential is that all citizens be able to choose among reasonable locational alternatives within their economic means, and that racial nondiscrimination be scrupulously and rigorously enforced. We will not seek to impose economic integration upon an existing local jurisdiction; at the same time, we will not countenance any use of economic measures as a subterfuge for racial discrimination."[27]

This statement bears all of the hallmarks of colorblind logic: from the absence of racist language, we are expected to infer the absence of racist action. The statement in its entirety ignores the effects of the recent past when it comes to discrimination—particularly in the housing market. There is no accounting for the ways in which historic patterns of housing discrimination—which had only legally ended three years prior to this statement—shaped the contemporary metropolitan geography. There is no recognition of how historic and contemporary discrimination sharply limited African Americans' economic choices. The statement deliberately lacks context and history while at the same time suggesting that neighborhood configurations were shaped by "freedom," "choice," and cultural considerations, as opposed to redlining and racism. Nixon's emphasis on "mobility" and "the ability to choose" ignores the heated, ongoing debates over the 1968 Fair Housing Act (FHA). But this rhetorical and political shift would fit nicely with the demands of the business elite. Three years after the passage of the FHA, when Nixon made this speech, the National Association of Real Estate Boards, the nation's largest association of real estate brokers, continued to oppose fair housing, referring to it as "forced integration."[28] This was not accidental language; it was part of a larger effort to reframe the political debates that went far beyond housing. By disconnecting the contemporary crisis from a history of racial discrimination encouraged by public policy and acted upon throughout the US private sector, Nixon was commenting more broadly about disparities between Blacks and the rest of American society. In Nixon's world, a "free and open" society was more than enough; poor choices were the only real constraint on the "mobility to move upward." "Bad choices" could produce a lifetime of poverty or crime.

Law and Order under Nixon

Since the Truman administration the theme of "law and order" had served a function in presidential governance,[29] but the rise of the civil rights movement and then civil disorder gave new context and meaning for understanding crime, policing, and imprisonment. I explore these ideas more fully in chapter 4, but for the purposes of this chapter, it is important to understand Johnson and Nixon's turn to law and order as a means of confronting the Black insurgency and recasting Black demands for justice as a pretext for ramping up the policing and prison state.

To do this, Nixon picked up an earlier thread in conservative politics that conflated civil rights protests and Black demands with criminal activity. In a 1966 interview, for example, he said that the deterioration of respect for law and order "can be traced directly to the spread of the corrosive doctrine that every citizen possesses an inherent right to decide for himself which laws to obey and when to disobey them."[30] Nixon harnessed this logic, along with pointing to rising crime rates and the notion that the United States was spiraling out of control, as reasons to expand the powers and equipment of the criminal justice system dramatically.

Johnson's Omnibus Crime Control and Safe Streets Act of 1968 was passed in the weeks after the murder of Martin Luther King Jr., which prompted hundreds of riots across the United States. The legislation capped Johnson's years of efforts to professionalize law enforcement around the country where it had been wracked by lack of training, coordination, and organization. This was certainly not simply about "fighting crime," despite the attention to rising crime rates: Safe Streets greatly enhanced local officials' intelligence-gathering capacities, including wiretapping, "to protect the United States against the overthrow of the Government by force or other unlawful means, or against any other clear and present danger to the structure or existence of the Government."[31] The bill also called for greater integration of the FBI into state and local law enforcement and a 10 percent budget increase to "develop new or improved approaches, techniques, systems, equipment and devices to improve and strengthen law enforcement."[32] More generally, the Law Enforcement Assistance Administration, a subsection of the omnibus crime bill, was a conduit guiding federal resources toward states and cities to allow for more consistent approaches to police work. Indeed, within ten years, "the federal government was able to spend approximately $7.5 billion to beef up the nation's law-and-order apparatus in little more than a decade."[33]

Journalist Christian Parenti has pointed out the many specific ways the Nixon administration wielded the legal apparatus to harass and intimidate the left. For example, Nixon signed the Racketeer Influenced and Corrupt Organizations (RICO) Act into law in 1970 as part of a larger bill against organized crime, ostensibly to fight the influence of the Mafia. The RICO legislation, however, could be just as quickly used against the left. For instance, the legislation

> loosened the rules pertaining to the use of illegally obtained evidence by prosecutors; it created new categories of federal crime; it allowed the federal government to seize assets of any organization deemed to be a criminal conspiracy; it created new penalties and policing powers over the use of explosives and finally it created 25-year-long sentences for "dangerous adult offenders."[34]

Using the new powers of RICO, the Nixon administration subpoenaed more than a thousand antiwar activists, including leaders of Vietnam Veterans Against the War. Thousands of journalists, Black Panthers, and Puerto Rican nationalists were also forced to testify in grand jury hearings that were nothing but fishing expeditions to get information about the left.[35] Surveillance as a crucial aspect of social control was a major component of the widening Nixon policing state. Consider that in a matter of four years, the number of states with functioning "criminal justice information systems" mushroomed from ten to forty-seven. A $90 million investment allowed for greater integration of local systems with the FBI's master intelligence system, the National Crime Information Center (NCIC). When the NCIC was first formed, its database had 500,000 pieces of information, but by 1974, it had collected 4.9 million entries.[36]

The growing policing state was not just an attack on the organized left; it was also directed at policing the "unruly" Black population. Most experts chart the beginning of the phenomenon called "mass incarceration" in the 1970s. Anti-Black policing and law-and-order rhetoric had a much earlier start, but the exponential growth of imprisonment and the turn toward hyper-punitive prison terms began after the Black Power uprisings of the 1960s had ended. Between the 1980s and 1990s, the chances of receiving a prison sentence following arrest increased by 50 percent, and the average length of sentence increased by 40 percent.[37] As historian Heather Ann Thompson has pointed out, there were many markers highlighting the shifts in law enforcement over the 1960s and 1970s, but the vicious crackdown against a mostly Black uprising in the Attica prison in upstate New York, was, perhaps, most indicative. Inmates in Attica took forty-two prison staff members hostage to draw attention to their political demands to improve the quality of life in the prison, including improved sanitation, an end to guard brutality, better medical care, and better food, among many others. For five days inmates negotiated in good faith with state officials, but on the morning of September 13, 1971, the governor of New York

> gave the green light for helicopters to rise suddenly over Attica and blanket it with tear gas. As inmates and hostages fell to the ground blinded, choking and incapacitated, more than 500 state troopers burst in, riddling catwalks and exercise yards with thousands of bullets. Within 15 minutes the air was filled with screams, and the prison was littered with the bodies of 39 people—29 inmates and 10 hostages—who lay dead or dying. "I could see all this blood just running out of the mud and water," one inmate recalled. "That's all I could see."[38]

The brutal suppression of the Attica uprising was a way for law enforcement to act out violent revenge against the same kinds of people who had rebelled on the outside. It was a way for the state to impose its authority in ways that it had been unable to in the hundreds of rebellions that had rocked the country throughout the 1960s. Rockefeller used the state-led assault on Attica as an opportunity "to take a hard line and rethink how he had been handling New York City's 'fringe elements'—whether inmates, activists, or addicts. Determined to show conservatives in his party that he was tough on crime," Governor Rockefeller "not only chose to put down the Attica rebellion with deadly force but he publicly committed himself to certain "enduring principles" such as society's need for law and order."[39]

New York State's Rockefeller Drug Laws also indicated the punitive turn in sentencing in the 1970s.[40] After a 31 percent increase in drug-related arrests in the early 1970s, supposedly liberal-leaning Republican Nelson Rockefeller called for harsh sentences even for drug possession, including a mandatory minimum sentence of fifteen years to life for four ounces of narcotics—the same sentence as for involuntary manslaughter.[41] The effects were incontrovertible. Over the next twenty years, the proportion of drug offenders in New York's prison population grew from 11 percent in 1973 to a peak of 35 percent in 1994. In 1978, the state of Michigan tried to outdo New York by concocting the "650-lifer" law, which *required* judges to impose life sentences on anyone convicted of delivering 650 grams (less than one and a half pounds) or more of narcotics.[42] The effects of the growing policing and prison state were clear by the end of the decade: In 1970 the American prison population, including those in state and federal facilities, was 196,429—as small as it had been since 1958—but by 1980 it had grown to 315,974, the largest number of Americans ever imprisoned.[43] In addition, while white people—then as now—were always the predominant group of drug users, the ever-expanding powers of the police were directed at the "unruly" Black and Latino neighborhoods where authority had broken down and whose activism and discontent were a constant source of tension.

Nixon's turn to focusing on crime fit snugly with his broader use of colorblindness to champion his domestic policies. There was no need to invoke race in this campaign for law and order, but the consequences of the policies could not have been clearer. Crime was committed by bad people who made bad choices—it was not the product of an unequal social order that left Blacks and Puerto Ricans, in particular, isolated in urban enclaves with little access to good jobs, housing, or schools in a worsening economy. Instead, inequality left poor and working-class people of color to their own devices to advance in a society that had made next to no provisions for them to do so through legal or normative means. These kinds of constrained "choices" were made in white enclaves as well, but those were less surveilled and less likely to be criminalized by the police and the criminal justice system as a whole.

Elected officials' ability to manipulate and politicize crime was not wholly based on fiction. There was a surge in the numbers of crimes committed in the late 1960s and into the 1970s. Some of this had to do with a greater focus on counting crimes, including absorbing "criminal acts" committed in the midst of political rebellion into the overall numbers. The number of reported violent crimes grew from 161,000 in 1960 to 487,000 by 1978. There were also major fluctuations and variations in the numbers and locations of criminal activity over time and place. For example, homicides dropped by 4 percent from 1975 to 1978, as did property crimes.[44] But what did not change was the propensity for African Americans to lead in virtually all categories as *victims* of crime. Over the course of the 1970s, a Black man's chance of being murdered was six to eight times greater than that of a white man. Black families were more likely to be victims of burglary and car theft. Even Black middle-class families, because of their physical proximity to poverty, were much more likely to be victims of crime than their white peers. Politicians were quick to manipulate crime numbers that showed the disproportionate burden of Black communities as an excuse to expand the powers and reach of the policing state; they did so using public funds that were needed to develop the kinds of public institutions and civil infrastructure that could mitigate poverty and criminal activity. To be sure, this often meant that Black people were the ones to call on the state for greater protection from law enforcement—but this happened in a context where almost all the alternatives had been taken off the table.

The Crisis Problem People

In 1973, Richard Nixon declared an end to the "urban crisis." The significance of this was that the "crisis in the cities," as Johnson had described it, had been the catalyst for federal aid to American cities for much of the 1960s. But in the spring of 1973, several weeks before he was to offer a draconian budget that included suspending all federal housing subsidies, the president declared the urban crisis to be over. In a radio address, Nixon declared, "A few years ago we constantly heard that urban America was on the brink of collapse. It was one minute to midnight, we were told, and the bells of doom were beginning to toll. One history of America in the 1960s was even given the title *Coming Apart*. Today, America is no longer coming apart."[45]

Crisis magazine was much more skeptical than the president. An editorial replied, "The rosy portrait of the state of the Union with its implications of a cool summer followed the unveiling of the President's alarming budget . . . [and] came three months before the summer vacation period during which hundreds of thousands of poor and unemployed ghetto youth will be released from school to roam the teeming streets of their quarters practically 24 hours a day."[46] Nixon never mentioned any repair to or improvement in the conditions of urban dwellers, including African Americans. He also made no effort to quantify how the end of the urban crisis could be measured: An end to police brutality? An end to housing discrimination? What were the markers? Instead, he focused on the decline in the number of people living in substandard housing. That was an important marker, but it hardly spelled an end to the litany of problems outlined in the Kerner Commission report. Nixon was mostly interested in turning the page. He was not naïvely thinking that urban problems were now a thing of the past; he was extracting the federal government from its responsibility to resolve them. It had now been five long years since the last massive upheaval in a Black community, and Nixon seized the opportunity.

The new attack on social spending was buttressed with descriptions of urban populations as either not truly in need or beyond the help of federal antipoverty programs. The Nixon administration began to describe urban problems as being intractable because of the people who lived in the cities. In other words, where impoverished conditions still existed, it was time to look at what was wrong with those people. Nixon's new emphasis on the "free society" and "choice" was intended to reduce social inequality to individual behaviors. People, of course, could make right or wrong choices, but it was the individual, free of social constraints, doing the choosing. It was much easier to promote the idea of making do with less in the aftermath of the nation's longest economic expansion if the people being asked to make do with less were blamed for their own hardship.

George Romney, Nixon's first secretary of the Department of Housing and Urban Development (HUD), led the way in this shift by focusing on what he described as the "crisis problem people." In 1973, in a speech to the Detroit Economic Club to explain the scandalous collapse of a federal housing program, Romney explained why government malfeasance and private institutional fraud were not the culprits.

He said, "with deep regret, the things that have gone wrong with the housing subsidy and insurance programs . . . are my responsibility." He continued: "Even if we had been able to avoid all of the mistakes and errors that have occurred in the housing programs, we would still be up against the larger tragedy—the crisis of people with problems in our central cities." He would later elaborate on who these "people with problems" were: "Housing by itself cannot solve the problems of people . . . who may be suffering from bad habits, lawlessness, laziness, unemployment, inadequate education, low working skills, ill health, poor motivation and a negative self-image."[47]

These phrases were codes for the Black poor living in the cities. This also showed how colorblindness worked against the interests of African Americans not just in obvious ways but as a pivot for attacking living standards and programs for all working-class people. Nixon's declaration of the end of the urban crisis was not only a way to isolate poor, urban Blacks; it also began ideologically undoing the postwar welfare state. Carl Albert, Democratic Speaker of the House, recognized Nixon's draconian 1973 budget as, "nothing less than the systematic dismantling and destruction of great social programs and the great precedents of humanitarian government inaugurated by Franklin D. Roosevelt and advanced and enlarged by every Democratic president since then."[48] Albert may have been engaging in some partisan hyperbole. It would take the swinging axe of Ronald Reagan to completely destroy the Johnson welfare state, but Nixon helped to establish the ideological groundwork for Reagan's project by systematically discrediting the people who relied upon the programs.

Historian Alice O'Connor has described the emergence of the neoconservative right in the 1970s as most interested in "*redefining* the problem [of urban crisis] altogether along the lines earlier sketched out in Moynihan's sensationalized 1965 report on the *Negro Family: The Case for National Action*."[49] Conservative intellectuals gathered in think tanks and journals to articulate this process of redefining. They went farther than resuscitating the "culture of poverty" narrative, reaching back to earlier theories of biological racism. For example, one conservative described urban slums as "human cesspools . . . into which our worst human problems have flowed and in which, through some kind of bacterial action, a self-sustaining reaction has been created that is making matters worse despite the general improvement going on everywhere else."[50] Another conservative author described urban rebellions as little more than "outbreaks of animal spirits and of stealing by slum dwellers."[51]

Conclusion

It is important to understand "colorblindness" as much more than the denial of racism. Colorblindness has become the default setting for how Americans understand how race and racism work. It is repeatedly argued that the absence of racial insult means that racial discrimination is not at play. Indeed, the mere mention of race as a possible explanation, or as a means of providing greater context, risks accusations of "playing the race card"—a way of invoking race to silence disagreement. This is deployed to hide or obscure inequality and disparities between African Americans and whites. It has helped to elevate and amplify politics that blame Blacks for their own oppression.

Colorblindness is a critical weapon in the arsenal of the politically powerful and economic elite to divide those who have an interest in uniting to make demands on the state and capital to provide the means for a decent quality of life. Colorblindness and "postracial" politics are vested in false ideas that the United States is a meritocratic society where hard work makes the difference between those who are successful and those who are not. The history described in this chapter concerning the rise in class struggle, the anxiety of the business elite, the onset of economic crisis within global capitalism, and how the convergence of those different factors created an opportunity to undo the welfare state of the previous period is the context within which we should understand the emergence of the concept of colorblindness. The looming threat of explosive cities, still palpable in the spring of 1974 with Nixon's draconian budget cuts, stopped a frontal attack on the social welfare programs of the 1960s. Instead, barely coded language focused on the poorest of Blacks to explain the retreat from the cities, as did Nixon's abrupt announcement declaring the end of the "urban crisis." Most importantly, removing race and, ultimately, culpability for the conditions of the cities, meant there was no explanation for those conditions beyond the people living there. If culture was the issue, what was needed was personal transformation, not a robust public sector. All this prepared the ideological ground for the massive assault on social welfare that would come in the 1980s amid the so-called Reagan Revolution.

CHAPTER THREE

Black Faces in High Places

*Black American history's central axis is the tension between accommo-
dation and struggle.*

—**Manning Marable**, *How Capitalism
Underdeveloped Black America*, 1983

*And what we got here in this town? Niggers in high places, black faces
in high places, but the same rats and roaches, the same slums and garbage, the same police whippin' your heads, the same unemployment and
junkies in the hallways mugging your old lady.*

—**Amiri Baraka**, *Tales of the Out and the Gone*, 1972

E ight months after Black people in Ferguson, Missouri, took to the
streets to demand justice for Michael Brown, Baltimore exploded
in rage at the brutal beating and then death of twenty-five-year-old
Freddie Gray. Gray, from the poorest area of Baltimore, was Black and
unarmed—and when the police attempted to stop him for no reason,
he ran. He did not run inexplicably; he ran because Baltimore police
are notorious for the physical abuse they enact against people, particularly Black people, in their custody, as the *Atlantic* documents:

> Victims include a 15-year-old boy riding a dirt bike, a 26-year-old preg-
> nant accountant who had witnessed a beating, a 50-year-old woman

selling church raffle tickets, a 65-year-old church deacon rolling a cig-
arette and an 87-year-old grandmother aiding her wounded grandson.
Those cases detail a frightful human toll. Officers have battered dozens of residents who suffered broken bones—jaws, noses, arms, legs,
ankles—head trauma, organ failure, and even death, coming during
questionable arrests. Some residents were beaten while handcuffed;
others were thrown to the pavement.[1]

Though it fit into a frightening pattern, Gray's death almost went
unnoticed until cell-phone video emerged to show him being "disappeared" into the back of a police van, only to emerge much later with
his spinal cord cut almost in half. Freddie Gray was killed almost two
weeks after video footage from North Charleston, South Carolina,
showed a Black man named Walter Scott shot eight times in the back
as he ran helplessly from a white police officer. The reluctance of Baltimore officials to act stood in contrast to the quick action of officials
in South Carolina, who fired the cop, Michael Slager, almost instantly
and charged him with murder. In Baltimore, the six officers were
placed on "paid administrative leave" as questions mounted during a
slow-moving investigation. From the time of Gray's death there were
daily protests demanding the arrest of the six police involved; investigators preached patience. In the hours after Gray's funeral on Monday,
April 27, patience ran out when police attacked high school students
and the students fought back, touching off the Baltimore rebellion. A
federal survey estimated that the riots in Baltimore caused $9 million
worth of damage including the destruction of 144 cars and the incin-
eration of fifteen buildings.[2] More than two hundred people were arrested, including forty-nine children, half of whom were never charged
with a crime. One five-year-old boy was "brought to court in chains—
hands and feet shackled—before finally being released to his parents."[3]

The police violence that killed Freddie Gray was now on display for the world to see. But this was no Ferguson. Nor was it North
Charleston. What distinguishes Baltimore from Ferguson and North
Charleston is that the Black political establishment runs the city: African Americans control virtually the entire political apparatus. Mayor
Stephanie Rawlings-Blake and police commissioner Anthony Batts
were the most prominent faces of political power in Baltimore during
the rebellion, but Black power runs deep in the city: Baltimore's city

council has fifteen members, eight of whom are African American, including its president. The superintendent of the public schools and the entire board of the city's housing commission are African American. In Ferguson, where Blacks are 67 percent of the population, the city is run almost exclusively by whites. North Charleston has similar dynamics: African Americans compose 47 percent of the population but are governed by a white mayor and police chief and a white-majority city council (eight of eleven members). In Ferguson, the lack of Black political power and representation became a narrative thread in popular explanations for what went wrong. Electing African Americans into political office in Ferguson thus became a focal point for many local and national activists. Conversely, in North Charleston, the quickness with which the white political apparatus acted only drew attention to the sclerotic response of Baltimore's Black leadership.

If the murder of Mike Brown and the rebellion in Ferguson were reminiscent of the old Jim Crow, then the murder of Freddie Gray and the Baltimore uprising symbolize the new Black political elite. The dynamics of a Black rebellion in a Black-governed city highlight one of the most dramatic transformations in Black politics—and Black life in general. In fact, Baltimore is a scant forty miles from the White House, where the nation's first African American president resides. There are forty-six Black members of the House of Representatives and two Black senators—giving the 114th Congress the highest number of Black members in American history. Just as the West Side of Baltimore was erupting against the police killing of Freddie Gray, Loretta Lynch became the first Black woman appointed as attorney general—replacing the first Black man to have held the position. Across the United States, thousands of Black elected officials are governing many of the nation's cities and suburbs. Yet, despite this unprecedented access to political power, little has changed for the vast majority of African Americans. For example, three of the six police officers involved in the alleged death of Gray are African American. Judge Barry G. Williams, who is also African American, presided over the trial of Black police officer William G. Porter, which ended in a mistrial eight months after the death of Gray. Even though Porter confirmed that he did not buckle Gray into his seat or call an ambulance when Gray's injuries were apparent, the jury did not find that Porter had played a significant role

Gray's death. Even with the involvement of a Black cop, a Black prosecutor, and a Black judge, justice remained elusive for Freddie Gray.[4] The main difference is that today, when poor or working-class Black people experience hardship, that hardship is likely being overseen by an African American in some position of authority. The development of the Black political establishment has not been a benign process. Many of these officials use their perches to articulate the worst stereotypes of Blacks in order to shift blame away from their own incompetence.

Despite the lawlessness of the Baltimore Police Department, Mayor Rawlings-Blake reserved her harshest comments for those involved in the uprising, describing them as "criminals" and "thugs." A few days later, President Obama took the mayor's lead when he referred to "criminals and thugs who tore up the place." When Obama's spokesperson, Josh Earnest, was asked if the president wanted to clarify what he meant by "thugs," he doubled down: "When you're looting up a convenience store or you're throwing a cinder block at a police officer, you're engaging in thuggish behavior and that's why the president used that word."[5] Rawlings-Blake's outburst was hardly surprising: a month before the unrest in Baltimore, she had ranted that Black men were responsible for violence in the city. She claimed, "Too many of us in the black community have become complacent about black-on-black crime. . . . While many of us are willing to march and protest and become active in the face of police misconduct, many of us turn a blind eye when it's us killing us."[6] But Baltimore's Black mayor had "turned a blind eye" to the intense poverty in Freddie Gray's West Baltimore neighborhood, Sandtown, where residents experience 24 percent unemployment and have a median income of $25,000—less than half the median income in the rest of Baltimore. Surely there could be some connection made between the desperate levels of poverty in Baltimore and the crime that exists in those communities. In a context, however, where no programs and no money were on offer to transform those conditions, a mayoral press conference singling out Black men for crime in the city of Baltimore was deemed sufficient.

From the president to the mayor of Baltimore and beyond, Black elected officials use their "insider" positions as African Americans to project to the Black and white public that they have unique capabilities in the event of Black unrest. The utility of Black elected officials lies in their ability, as members of the community, to scold ordinary Black people in ways that white politicians could never get away with. Black elected officials' role as interlocutors between the broader Black population and the general American public makes them indispensible in American politics. Moreover, it gives them authority as people with particular insight into the "Black community," which they often use to do more harm than good while deftly escaping the label of "racist." For example, in Chicago in the spring of 2014, the African American commissioner of Cook County, Richard Boykin, called a press conference to lobby for legislation that would classify gang members as "domestic terrorists." Such a change in designation would increase the punishment for various crimes to twenty-year-to-life sentences. Boykin said of his proposal, "These dedicated groups of individuals—some black, some Hispanic—are destabilizing our community, and we must put an end to it, or else this violence will put an end to us."[7]

Black elected officials obscure their actions under a cloak of imagined racial solidarity, while ignoring their role as arbiters of political power who willingly operate in a political terrain designed to exploit and oppress African Americans and other working-class people. Consider the case of Marilyn Mosby, the state's attorney for Baltimore, and her decision to charge the six officers implicated in Gray's death with murder. Mosby endured barbs from the Baltimore police union as well as the media for "rushing to judgment" in charging the police, but the combined pressures of three days of rioting in Baltimore, escalating Black anger, and the growing Black Lives Matter movement shining a spotlight on police practices emboldened Mosby to act. She exemplifies the complicated role Black elected officials play. On the one hand, she was, perhaps, more susceptible to pressure from the Black electorate, but on the other hand, Mosby also bore responsibility for helping to create the conditions that led to Gray's death. Three weeks before police captured and killed Gray, Mosby had personally directed the police department to target the intersection where they first encountered Gray with "enhanced drug enforcement efforts."[8] Mosby told police assigned to that area that their supervisors would monitor their progress with "daily measurables." Baltimore police officer Kenneth Butler explained, "They want increased productivity, whether it be car stops, field interviews, arrests—that's what they mean by measurables."[9]

Mosby did not direct the police to nearly sever Gray's spinal cord, but the pressure to crack down on crime through the use of the police, prisons, and jails has predictable outcomes.

The dynamic propelling African Americans into political confrontations with each other has been in the making since African Americans became legitimate political contenders in urban contests toward the end of the 1960s. The pursuit of Black electoral power became one of the principal strategies that emerged from the Black Power era. Clearly it has been successful for some. But the continuing crises for Black people, from under-resourced schools to police murder, expose the extreme limitations of that strategy. The ascendance of Black electoral politics also dramatizes how class differences can lead to different political strategies in the fight for Black liberation. There have always been class differences among African Americans, but this is the first time those class differences have been expressed in the form of a minority of Blacks wielding significant political power and authority over the majority of Black lives. This raises critical questions about the role of the Black elite in the continuing freedom struggle—and about what side are they on. This is not an overstatement. When a Black mayor, governing a largely Black city, aids in the mobilization of a military unit led by a Black woman to suppress a Black rebellion, we are in a new period of the Black freedom struggle. This chapter explores the rise of Black political power and its consequences for the Black poor and working class.

A Class for Itself

The integration of Black politics into the political mainstream coincided with an aggressive effort to cultivate a small but stable Black middle class. One route to this was government employment. Although Johnson's War on Poverty and Great Society programs never included a strong jobs component, between 1965 and 1972 federal spending on social welfare increased from $75 billion to $185 billion.[10] This massive expansion of the federal government, combined with antidiscrimination mandates in federal hiring practices, created vast job opportunities for Black workers. By 1970, half of Black male college graduates and more than 60 percent of college-educated Black women were public employees, compared with 35 percent of white men and 55 percent of white women. And although only 18 percent of the labor force in 1970 consisted of government employees, 26 percent of African American adults worked for the government.[11] According to historian Thomas Sugrue, "No institution played a greater role than government in breaking the grip of poverty and creating a Black middle class."[12]

In 1974, 64 percent of all new federal employees came from minority groups.[13] These changes in Black employment overlapped with a more general rise in income and a more firm class differentiation under way. Between 1969 and 1974 the earnings of the top 5 percent of nonwhite families increased from $17,000 to $24,000. By 1977, 21 percent of all Black families had incomes between $15,000 and $24,000; another 9 percent earned above $25,000.[14] For Blacks in management and other professional positions, the rate of unemployment remained in the single digits over the course of the 1970s, while Black and white workers in manufacturing experienced double-digit unemployment.[15]

Although this relatively small section of Blacks continued to have racially discriminatory encounters with whites, there were also important new aspects of their experience that differed from that of the majority of African Americans. The overall unemployment rate for professional and technical Black workers was about half that of the wider Black civilian workforce. The unemployment rate for Black salaried employees was even lower. The number of Black-owned banks also doubled during this time, to twenty-four.[16] Only a small number of African Americans were employed in the fields of banking, commerce, law, education, and medicine, but "they were set apart from the vast majority of working class and impoverished blacks by their relative income parity with whites, their educational training and professional advancement; their political moderation and social conformity; their advocacy of the economics of capitalism and corporate owned mobility."[17] In four decades, Black households earning more than $75,000 grew from 3.4 percent to 15.7 percent. Between 1970 and 2006 the number of Black households making more than $100,000 annually increased from 1 percent to 9 percent.[18] In real numbers, six million African Americans had become wealthy enough to "live in spacious homes, buy luxury goods, travel abroad on vacation, spoil their children—to live, in other words, just like well-to-do white folks."[19]

The size of this group was less important than the fact that their existence would vindicate American capitalism. Politically, they gave the emerging Black political class a group to orient toward as well as collaborate with on the basis of shared values and goals. The experiences of this relatively small group of African Americans was in no way representative of the majority or even common Black experience, but they were heralded as examples of how hard work could enable Blacks to overcome institutional challenges. The moderate success of some African Americans also allowed for other, less "successful" Blacks to be chastised for not taking advantage of the bounty of "opportunities" in the United States. The more time passed, the more the radical Black movement's momentum ebbed. Personal stories of achievement and accomplishment began to replace the narrative of collective struggle.

From the ranks of the newly developing Black middle class came hundreds, then thousands, of Black elected officials, who began to officiate for and politically represent the communities from which they rose. The Black elite and political class have now grown beyond simple aspirations of inclusion into American capitalism; they hold real political power and authority, which distinguishes them from most ordinary Blacks. From the presidency to the halls of Congress to city halls across the country, they have the capacity to shape public policies and to amplify public debates that disproportionately affect Black life. They wield more political, social, and (potentially) economic authority than average people. Their position remains tenuous and potentially compromised as compared to white political power, but they can hardly be described as toothless or powerless.

The Black Man's City

By the late 1960s, calls for "community control" over the cities in which Black people lived became louder. It made sense. The Black migration of the previous generation had brought millions of African Americans into the cities and helped to elevate Black concerns at least into the realm of being discussed politically, even if rarely acted upon. It was also transforming the metropolitan demographics, as the migration of Blacks prompted an outmigration of whites. White political control of increasingly Black-populated cities exacerbated existing tensions over Black unemployment and poverty, underfunded schools, and substandard housing, among many other hardships, and gave rise to urban rebellions. In cities like Chicago, where Blacks were a third of the population, the wheels of patronage drew in some Black participation but without real Black political or economic control of the city's infrastructure. The destruction and instability rebellions had caused over the course of the decade softened the political elite to the idea that more Black control and ownership within the cities might help to calm the rebellious Black population. Given the conservative starting point of many Black elected officials today, it is hard to see how this turn to electoral politics could be considered radical or even relevant. But by the late 1960s, the potential for Black political and economic development was a welcome alternative to decades of neglect and disinvestment. The possibility of Black mayors running cities with large Black populations was called the "most amazing political revolution since the end of slavery."[20]

With no clear sense of where the Black movement was headed, the turn to electoral politics and "community control" appeared as a logical and pragmatic alternative. The unrelenting pressure that the federal government's counterinsurgency program, COINTELPRO, exerted on the left made that political direction seem risky. The assassinations of Malcolm X and Martin Luther King Jr., amid an atmosphere of intense surveillance and harassment, were intended to chill political opposition. One woman, speaking in the documentary film *The Black Power Mixtape: 1967–1975*, said, "I don't think there is much of a future at this point. Not much at all. They're just killing people."[21] Bobby Seale, former chairman of the Black Panther Party, said as much in an interview with *Ebony* about his run for mayor of Oakland in 1973. In an article titled "Shift to the Middle," Seale describes how, in the Panthers' relatively short existence, 50 members had been killed, 200 injured, and another 300 arrested; as a result, the Panthers had to shift strategies.[22] Included in that shift was a more collaborative approach with the Black middle class, utilizing their skills to fill the void created by the lack of public and private investment. Seale said, "We had to build a framework in which the Black middle class could work." The relentless assault on the Panthers and the Black left in general was isolating and exhausting. An alliance with the Black middle class meant tempering the Panthers' message to gain new allies. Seale rationalized the shift as allowing the

Panthers to expand their forces and carry through a program to provide services the state could not or would not provide.

This "pragmatic turn" away from revolution by sections of the Black revolutionary left created the conditions for civil rights organizations and Black militants to find some common ground. Carmichael and Hamilton described what Black urban governance could look like: "The power must be in the community, and emanate from there. . . . Black politicians must stop being representatives of 'downtown' machines, whatever the cost might be in terms of lost patronage and holiday handouts."[23] Black moderates may not have cared for the emphasis on Black control or power, but contrasted to the unpredictability of urban rebellion, Black political power seemed like a favorable alternative. As civil rights organizer Bayard Rustin counseled in an essay titled "From Protest to Politics,"

> If there is anything positive in the spread of the ghetto, it is the potential political power base thus created, and to realize this potential is one of the most challenging and urgent tasks before the civil rights movement. If the movement can wrest leadership of the ghetto vote from the machines, it will have acquired an organized constituency such as other major groups in our society now have.[24]

The revolutionaries Grace Lee Boggs and James Boggs wrote in the influential essay "The City Is the Black Man's Land" that the struggle for Black control of American cities was a "civil war between black power and white power, the first major battle of which was fought last August in Southern California between 18,000 soldiers and the black people of Watts."[25] The Boggses continued, "Negroes are the major source of the pay that goes to the police, judges, mayors, common councilmen, and all city government employees taxed through traffic tickets, assessments, etc. Yet in every major city Negroes have little or no representation in city government. WE PAY FOR THESE OFFICIALS. WE SHOULD RUN THEM."[26] Even King suggested that Black political power in the cities could stem the tide of rebellion by "more aggressive political involvement on the part of . . . Negroes." He anticipated the electoral turn of Black politics in the cities when he wrote: "The election of Negro mayors . . . has shown [Blacks] that [they have] the potential to participate in the determination of [their] own destiny—and that of society. We will see more Negro mayors in major cities in the next ten years."[27]

Promoting more Black political participation on a local level was a project of the Black movement, but the broader political establishment approved. The government and politicians widely promoted greater Black control of urban space as a preventive measure against urban uprisings, from including Black businesses in the Small Business Administration to Richard Nixon's fomenting Black capitalism to bipartisan support for greater homeownership in the inner city. Black people needed to have what Nixon liked to describe as a "piece of the action." Nixon said in a 1968 speech that "what most of the militants are asking is not separation, but to be included in—not as supplicants, but as owners, as entrepreneurs—to have a share of the wealth and a piece of the action."[28] Federal government programs, he said, should "be oriented toward more Black ownership, for from this can flow the rest—Black pride, Black jobs, Black opportunity and, yes, Black Power."[29]

"Keep It Cool for Carl"

In 1967, Carl Stokes of Cleveland, Ohio, became the first Black man to be elected mayor of a major American city. His election foreshadowed many of the dynamics that would come to characterize the Black mayoralties of the 1970 and 1980s. Stokes was a career politician who had served in the Ohio state assembly for two terms. He first ran for mayor in 1965 as an independent, and lost the race when the Cleveland Democratic Party machine helped to shut down his campaign. Shortly after Stokes's failed bid, the Hough area of Cleveland exploded in rebellion in response to the usual mix of police violence, poverty, and substandard housing. Stokes used this opportunity to launch a new campaign for mayor the following year, and suddenly became the popular candidate of various political interests. Stokes entertained the idea of running as an independent because of the deep animosity between him and the Cleveland Democratic machine, but Lyndon Johnson and the Democratic National Convention directly intervened and told him that if he ran as a Democrat, the national party would provide the necessary resources. The Stokes campaign became a focal point of the civil rights establishment, whose leaders were worried about the political drift of their organizations after the end of legal discrimination in the South and the urban uprisings in the North. Even King was drawn to the potential of Stokes's rejuvenated campaign. In 1966 he and the Southern Christian Leadership Conference (SCLC) were wrapping up a bruising and ultimately unsuccessful campaign against housing discrimination in Chicago. For the stewards of the Democratic Party, the mayoral race in Cleveland offered an opportunity to create a viable alternative to the rebellion in the streets. Civil rights organizations and their supporters concentrated their efforts there. However, the campaign was also seen as insurgent because of the opposition of the local Democratic Party, including many ranking Black Democrats, who denounced Stokes as "destroying Negro unity."[30] The Cleveland Democratic Party warned of a pending "Black government" and suggested that if Stokes won, King would soon be running city hall. Stokes was also concerned that King's presence in Cleveland might alienate white voters. He asked King to leave. King refused but promised not to engage in any direct action that might antagonize white voters.

To the concern of Stokes, the National Association for the Advancement of Colored People (NAACP), Congress of Racial Equality (CORE), Student Non-Violent Coordinating Committee, and SCLC, the Urban League, and the National Council of Negro Women arrived in Cleveland to register thousands of new Black voters in anticipation of the coming election. The Ford Foundation gave the Cleveland chapter of CORE an astonishing $175,000 grant ($1.2 million in 2015 dollars) to assist with the voter registration drive.[31] Civil rights organizations in Cleveland promoted the slogan "Keep It Cool for Carl" to hem in the campaign politically and ensure there were no confrontations between activists and the public. To this end, Stokes's growing list of admirers included local industrialists and capitalists, who contributed $40,000 to local Black nationalist organizations to help keep the city quiet through the election period, worried that the sitting mayor, Ralph Lochner, was no longer capable of running the city. As a result, by 1967 Stokes had raised an eye-popping $250,000.

Stokes proclaimed that, while he loved his "Negro heritage," he was running for mayor of *all* of Cleveland, regardless of race. In one typical campaign speech, he pledged to be mayor to "all people without favor or unfair special consideration . . . rich and poor, whites and Negroes, bankers and busboys are all equally entitled to the best possible . . . services."[32] Stokes was promising everything to everyone. He promised to deliver services and improve social conditions in Black neighborhoods. He promised whites that, as a Black man, he could be expected to keep the peace in Black neighborhoods and would not "tolerate violence in the streets."[33] He promised business a climate conducive to investment. Stokes beat Lochner in the Democratic primary, then went on to handily defeat the Republican challenger in the general election by more than 18,000 votes, including 15 percent of the white vote.[34]

In 1967 Stokes became mayor of the eighth-largest city in the United States. His success, heralded as a victory for all of Black America, came just months after Richard Hatcher took office as mayor in Gary, Indiana. Together these victories seemed to indicate a new direction for Black politics. But in Cleveland, Stokes's initial moves as mayor raised more questions than his victory settled. Among his first acts was the appointment of Michael Blackwell as chief of police. Police brutality had been a catalyst for the 1966 Cleveland uprising; appointing a white veteran with a forty-three-year tenure in the same force was a bizarre choice. Stokes also gave business a disproportionate role in the plans to redevelop the local economy. He appointed several business leaders who had supported his candidacy to his Urban Renewal Task Force. He said, "Business and industry built these cities. If they are going to be rebuilt it will take that same investment and ingenuity that was originally employed."[35] This was the backdrop to Stokes's decision to back a $4 million public-private venture called Cleveland Now. Like many of the public-private redevelopment projects of the period, Cleveland Now was championed by business and presented to the public as a project that would redevelop the local economy. But Stokes's real value to business interests came in 1968, when a riot almost broke out after an episode of police violence. A gun battle with local Black nationalists from an organization called New Libya led to a five-day rebellion in which three cops were killed. Stokes promised to crack down on the violence and rallied white support with the appointment of another white veteran police chief, who promised to restore order. He also spent tens of thousands of dollars on upgrading the weaponry of the police force. As the next election came closer, he played on fear of crime in Black neighborhoods to rally support, writing in internal campaign materials, "Fear is the one weapon that will effectively increase the turnout of Black voters in this election."[36]

The turn from "protest to politics" has been regarded as a sign of the Black movement's maturity. As historian Peniel Joseph has written, "Embracing protest *and* politics, Gary illustrated the new political understanding that revolution, far from being the hundred-yard dash that many predicted during the late 1960s, was in fact a marathon that required a community of long-distance runners."[37] Joseph was referring to a Black political gathering in Gary, Indiana, in 1972 that brought together Black revolutionaries and Black elected officials, with all of the inherent problems one might expect to arise in such a gathering. I discuss the Gary convention below, but Joseph's point was that the conference signaled an important transition in the Black political movement. The move into formal politics would raise many questions, but it also signaled the rise of a stultifying "pragmatism" and "realism" in place of aspirations to change the world. As this turn was happening, however, there were still critiques of the growing popularity of Black capitalism and its electoral outgrowth. For example, Huey P. Newton wrote in protest,

> Black capitalism is a hoax. Black capitalism is represented as a great step toward Black liberation. It isn't. It is a giant stride away from liberation. No Black capitalist can function unless he plays the white man's game. Worse still, while the Black capitalist wants to think he functions on his own terms, he doesn't. He is always subject to the whims of the white capitalist. The rules of Black capitalism and the limits of Black capitalism are set by the white power structure.[38]

Taking control of city hall or the local city council could not resolve the looming questions of how to fully attend to housing, jobs, public education, and healthcare needs amid shrinking tax revenue, cuts to federal spending, and growing hostility to welfare as an entitlement to the poor. The daily tinkering with the fiscal constraints and municipal minutiae was certainly time-consuming and distracted from the bigger picture of total social transformation. King, in a 1967 essay, also recognized that elections alone were not "the ultimate answer." He explained, "Mayors are relatively impotent figures in the scheme of national politics. Even a white mayor . . . simply does not have the money and resources to deal with the problems of his city."[39] The struggle for everyday reforms to better people's lives did not contradict revolutionary optimism about creating a different world, but entering the Democratic Party dramatically reduced the potential and possibility of both.

The Conscience of the Congress

By the early 1970s, the electoral turn was no longer a debate. It was already under way in all wings of the movement. From traditional Democratic Party liberals to the Black Panther Party, running for political office was part of the arsenal of available political weapons. There were earnest attempts to build independent political organizations outside of the Democratic Party. Local Democratic Party machines used their political weight to crush opposition outside of their control, as in Cleveland. But the national Democratic Party recognized reality: as whites continued to leave and Blacks emerged as the predominant group in cities, Blacks could no longer be disregarded. Moreover, as cities continued to go up in flames, the belief that a Black political machine could calm urban tensions and also more capably manage urban fiscal crises made Black political power look more attractive. Its ascendance was not confined to local machines and "community control"; more Blacks also began to contend in national political races.

The clearest evidence of the new Black political power nationally was the debut of the Congressional Black Caucus (CBC) in 1970. It formed with thirteen members and declared its mission to unite and address the legislative concerns of Black and minority citizens. The CBC's members intended to amplify Black interests by "speaking with a single voice that would provide political influence and visibility far beyond their numbers."[40] Riding the wave of new Black political power in their districts, they claimed to arrive in Congress with a clear sense of their constituency and their objectives as Black elected officials. John Conyers, a Democratic representative from Detroit, made this clear in an essay titled "Politics and the Black Revolution," contrasting electoral work and revolution. He claimed that "the one thing that characterizes almost all these new Black officials is that their allegiance is to Black people who elected them and not, as in the past, to white political manipulators, Northern and Southern variety, who have always been behind the scenes."[41] Conyers elaborated on the continuity between the Black revolution and the electoral turn:

> I am talking about politics from our point of view—from the Black point of view. Our own intelligence about the oppressiveness of the kind of society which would like to forget us along with other historical "mistakes" should give Black people a unique force in effecting

change in America. An infusion of Blacks into the political arena might provide the moral force of "soul" which America either lost or never had. No longer will we be content to stand on the sidelines and rail against the powerful forces that shape our lives. Instead, we propose to enter the political arena and wrest for ourselves a share of the decision making power. . . . Some see the Black American's choice as between withdrawing from this "hopeless" government or overthrowing the entire system. I see our choices as between political involvement or political apathy. America is the Black man's battleground. It is here where it will be decided whether or not we will make America what it says it is. For me, at least, the choice is clear.[42]

One writer described the opportunities that would be opened up by Black representatives claiming Congressional power: "With their $42,000 annual salaries, $170,000-plus for staffers and office equipment, unlimited access to House hearings, a Congressional Library for research, and a widely read *Congressional Record* to publish their views, Congress members are in command of resources heretofore unavailable to Blacks."[43] The cohesion with which the caucus functioned in its early days made it appear almost as if it were a political organization acting on behalf of all of Black America. CBC members were, by far, the farthest to the left in all of Congress in their opposition to the war in Vietnam and to Nixon's plan to dismantle Johnson's Great Society programs. They reinforced this perception when Nixon refused to meet with them and they, in turn, threatened to boycott his 1971 State of the Union address. Nixon aides reached out to the caucus to avoid an embarrassing snub, but they boycotted anyway. When Nixon did finally meet with them several months later, he insisted that his administration was doing all that it could and would continue to keep the lines of communication open.

The growing threat to the welfare state kept the CBC in an oppositional stance, heightening perceptions that it was an important or even radical political force. Often, however, Black members of Congress saw the inside maneuvering of the caucus as more critical, pragmatic, and purposeful than the old protests of the 1960s. At a fundraiser for the CBC in 1971, actor and activist Ossie Davis gave a speech complimenting the CBC for taking action as opposed to rhetoric. He said, "It's not the man, it's the plan. It's not the rap, it's the map."[44] Such statements recast the activism of the 1960s as "angry rhetoric" that produced little actual change in the cities. The ability to "get things done" was the new measure of political acumen. Yet when it came to getting things done, the CBC had a weak record. Most of its activity seemed to involve endless hearings and studies quantifying Black oppression. By the early 1970s, the plight of Black neighborhoods was old news; many other organizations had performed similar studies for years. The limitations of the CBC kept options for the Black left very much alive.

In 1972, Black political players converged on the city of Gary, Indiana, home of Richard Hatcher, one of the first Black mayors of the era. The National Black Political Convention was unprecedented in bringing together the entire spectrum of Black politics—from radicals and revolutionaries to more than 2,000 elected officials. More than 8,000 delegates attended. Charles Diggs, a congressman from Detroit and a member of the CBC, was one of the organizers of the event, signaling the existing ties between the Black left and Black elected officials. The debates at the gathering were representative of the political tensions between various wings of the Black liberation movement and the resulting difficulties of forging a direction forward for the movement.

The convention's preamble reflected the radical politics of one section of the movement, as well as the deep connection between the insurgent past and current debates over the direction of the movement. It read, in part,

> A Black political convention, indeed all truly Black politics, must begin from this truth: The American system does not work for the masses of people, and it cannot be made to work without radical fundamental change. . . . The profound crises of Black people and the disaster of America are not simply caused by men, nor will they be solved by men alone. These crises are the crises of basically flawed economics and politics, and of cultural degradation. None of the Democratic candidates and none of the Republican candidates—regardless of their vague promises to us or to their white constituencies—can solve our problems or the problems of this country without radically changing the system by which it operates.[45]

The tone of the statement did not quite reflect the developing fissures evident in the gathering itself. While the radicals and the nationalists may have been insisting that it was "nation time," the growing implantation of Black politicians in mainstream electoral politics presented a dilemma. In fact, though a CBC member was one of the conveners of the convention, the CBC as an organization refused to endorse the event or any of the statements it produced. Those who attended were there as individuals, not as representatives of the CBC. The Gary convention eventually came undone under the weight of its own contradictions, which could not be papered over in the name of racial solidarity. Denouncing capitalism and calling to overthrow the system while simultaneously supporting candidates within the Democratic Party was unwieldy at best. Meanwhile, the more that CBC members were drawn into the norms of congressional life, including committee work, fundraising, and simply navigating the world of compromise and negotiation that defines the legislative process, the less enamored they were with "community politics" and a narrowly defined, race-based agenda.

As the vibrancy of the Black insurgency faded, less pressure was exerted on Black elected officials. The retreat of the movement also signaled to Black workers and the poor that Black elected officials and whatever assistance they could offer would have to be enough, because help was not coming from anywhere else. Both realizations, over time, had a conservatizing effect, as Black politics moved to the right in accord with the general conservative pall overtaking mainstream American politics. The Democratic Party had opened itself up to Blacks, women, and youth for fear that these constituencies would pull voters away from mainstream politics and, in doing so, leach support from the party. In search of resources, support, and perhaps legitimacy in the face of a cloudy future for the Black movement, activists entered the party believing they could use it for their own purposes. But instead of the left turning the party, many activists found themselves having to conform to Democratic Party objectives.[46] In some cases, radicals and revolutionaries not only stayed in step with the narrow and conservative agenda of the Democratic Party but jumped ship on liberalism altogether and defected to the right wing.

From Protest to Peril

Over the course of twenty years, American cities had changed from being dominated by white political machines to being the site of actual Black political power. It was, of course, an unfortunate time to take over American cities. Tax dollars were drying up as millions of individuals and businesses left the cities. Although the process of "deindustrialization" had begun in the 1950s, the term became popular in the 1970s "when a wave of plant closings changed the employment landscape."[47] According to one analyst, from 1966 to 1973, corporations moved more than a million American jobs to other countries:

> Even more jobs moved from the Northeast and Midwest to the South, where unions were scarce and wages lower. New York City alone lost 600,000 manufacturing jobs in the 1960s. . . . The workers laid off in the 1960s and '70s were disproportionately Black. The U.S. Commission on Civil Rights found that during the recession of 1973 to 1974, 60 percent to 70 percent of laid-off workers were African American in areas where they were only 10 percent to 12 percent of the workforce. In five cities in the Great Lakes region, the majority of Black men employed in manufacturing lost their jobs between 1979 and 1984. A major reason was seniority; white workers had been in their jobs longer, and so were more likely to keep them during cutbacks.[48]

In the 1980s, Ronald Reagan put his ideological zealotry against the social welfare state into practice and led Republican efforts to curtail social spending dramatically. His budget cuts, which shredded the already frayed American welfare state, included:

- a 17 percent cut in unemployment insurance (during a recession);
- a 13 percent reduction in food stamps, making a million people ineligible;
- a 14 percent reduction in cash benefits through Aid to Dependent Families with Children, resulting in 410,000 being dropped from the rolls and 259,000 families' benefits being reduced;
- increasing Medicare deductibles while cutting Medicaid by 3 percent and tightening eligibility standards;
- simply eliminating 300,000 jobs financed through a federal jobs program—overwhelmingly affecting Black workers; and
- raising rent by 5 percent in federally subsidized housing units,

Perhaps the most draconian cuts were aimed at children. In 1982, $560 million was cut from the federal school lunch program, which subsidized meals for public schoolchildren. As a result, 590,000 children were dropped from the program. When Reagan could not get away with eliminating food for children altogether, he eliminated as much as he could from their plates by authorizing reduced portions, allowing the use of meat substitutes, and—infamously—classifying ketchup as a vegetable—all while raising the price of lunch by 20 cents.[49]

The impact on African Americans was swift and severe. In Reagan's first year in office, Black family income declined by 5 percent. The proportion of Black families living in poverty increased from 32 percent to 34 percent, while the overall number of poor families increased by more than two million. By 1983, Black unemployment across the country had soared to 21 percent.[50] The relentless attacks on the poor and working class of all races and ethnicities continued throughout the decade, but its apex was when Reagan summarily fired 11,000 air traffic controllers who had been on strike over salary and working conditions. He also imposed a million-dollar fine on the union and a lifetime airline-industry ban on rehiring the striking workers. It was barely a decade removed from the postal workers' strike, but the dramatic difference in outcomes underlined that a new era was upon the nation.

This was the backdrop against which the drama of Black urban political power was to unfold in the 1980s. African Americans were handed the keys to some of the largest and most important cities in the country: Los Angeles, Detroit, Atlanta, Chicago, Philadelphia, and New York, just to name a few, but they had few resources to financially manage these cities, which had a growing number of Black poor and unemployed.

It was also a time of deep political polarization, not only in the country as a whole but also within the Black establishment. A month after Ronald Reagan's election in 1980, 125 Black academics and businesspeople met in San Francisco for a conference to discuss the meaning of Black conservatism. Economist Thomas Sowell organized the conference, which was sponsored by the Institute for Contemporary Studies, and invited conservative luminaries such as Edwin Meese and Milton Friedman to participate. Historian Manning Marable described the meeting's significance as "dramatiz[ing] . . . the severe contradictions on major political, economic and educational issues which divided the members of the Black elite."[51] Reagan's victory created space for Black conservatives to operate openly and freely. Charles Hamilton, who had coauthored *Black Power* with Stokely Carmichael in 1968, now called for Black politicians to "deracialize" their political message to avoid alienating potential white voters.[52] For some, the political degeneration of Black liberals was stunning. Martin Luther

King's former lieutenants, Ralph David Abernathy and Hosea Williams, endorsed Reagan's candidacy in 1980 and even made the incredible suggestion that segregationist stalwart Strom Thurmond serve as a "liaison officer between Republicans and on behalf of minorities."[53] Black Democrats also sensed the changing tide and looked to realign their political message. At a CBC gathering in 1981, an NAACP official described the new challenge for Black leadership: developing "cadres of Black professionals." Another official agreed, "We've got to develop technical militants out of these middle class affluent Blacks who have received training, acquired good educations and have worked themselves into the mainstream of economic life."[54] Even Jesse Jackson Sr. urged Black businessmen to "move from civil rights to Silver Rights and from aid to trade," meaning that business development and the economy were the new terrain of struggle.[55]

It is impossible to understand the defection of Black liberals into the conservative camp without understanding the degeneration of the Democratic Party's relationship to Black America. Jimmy Carter became president in 1976 by a narrow margin only made possible by the Black vote. Yet, once in office, Carter was hostile to Black demands to commit to the welfare state after six years of the Ford and Nixon administrations. Instead, his officials "declared that no new social welfare, health care, or educational programs would be initiated."[56] Meanwhile, Black unemployment continued to rise. Black liberal organizations denounced Carter's inattention to Black poverty as "callous neglect" and complained that their cause had been "betrayed."[57] Carter did, however, increase the military budget, at that point, to its highest level in American history—$111 billion—and his capital-gains tax cut led to growth in corporate profits. While lining the pockets of the rich, he pushed "to increase the prices of dairy products, grain, meat, and other products, and to 'deregulate' transportation industries, fostering monopolization and unrestricted price increases."[58]

It was not surprising, then, that when Reagan challenged Carter in the 1980 election, only 33 percent of Democrats said they wanted Carter as their nominee.[59] The state of Black progress under Carter was evident from the trial in Miami, Florida, of four white cops implicated in the murder of an unarmed Black military veteran. Even though two police who were at the scene testified against them, an all-white, all-male jury acquitted the defendants. For three days, Miami's Black Overtown neighborhood coursed with anger. In the end, the tally of the riots included $100 million in property damage, eighteen people killed, and a thousand injured. The National Guard finally put the rebellion down. Carter traveled to Miami and told locals that federal aid would be on the way—once tensions were quelled.[60] This was not a revival of the 1960s, however; this time, the Black establishment mobilized to calm Black Miami. The era of protest was over. Electoral politics and the promotion of Black elected officials were presented as the only alternative.

By the late 1980s the Democrats, reeling under the weight of the Reagan Revolution, had adapted to the rightward shifting political agenda—from supporting various aspects of the War on Drugs to promoting an agenda that prioritized private investment over rebuilding the public infrastructure. The political choices of Black elected officials were not aligned with the politics of mainstream Black America, especially as ordinary African Americans continued to suffer through unemployment and the vicious slashing of social welfare programs.

After the passage of the 1965 Voting Rights Act, the number of Black elected officials had grown to 1,400 in 1970 and to nearly 5,000 by 1980, but changing metropolitan demographics pressured those who had previously run as "Black" candidates to transform into "electable" candidates. Such transformations, however, did not prevent Black politicians from bumping up against what political scientist Fred Harris described as a "glass ceiling" in politics.[61] In 1983, a Washington-based Black think tank brought together a range of Black political operatives to determine how to break this "glass ceiling"—meaning how to overcome the racism within the electorate. The key questions at the gathering were: "How does one transcend race? How do you raise issues to a level of rare and profound sophistication? How do you downplay race? How do you modify or how do you lessen the impact of race?"[62]

Not all Black politicians wanted to transcend race. In fact, they more often invoked their Blackness and racial solidarity to garner support for their electoral programs. In 1982, the recently formed National Black Leadership Round Table (NBLRT) produced a booklet titled *The Black Leadership Family Plan for the Unity, Survival, and Progress of Black People*, which it claimed was a new blueprint "to secure for ourselves and our posterity full freedom and an equitable share of the blessings of this nation."[63] The NBLRT was composed of more than 150 Black civic, business, and fraternal organizations intended to represent the broad leadership of Black America. Unlike the National Black Political Convention in Gary a decade before, no left or revolutionary organizations were included in the NBLRT. The group was initially funded and directed by the CBC and reflected its political objectives of harnessing Black voting potential to develop and consolidate electoral power.

Walter Fauntroy, a leading figure in the NBLRT, had been a stalwart figure of the civil rights movement, a personal friend of Dr. King, and the District of Columbia's first nonvoting Congressional representative. By 1982, Fauntroy was also chairman of the CBC.[64]

The focus of the pamphlet demonstrated the tremendous transformation in Black politics even in the small span of ten years. The 1972 public preamble introducing the Gary convention had been outwardly focused, identifying the flaws of American capitalism as the source of crisis in Black communities and declaring that only by changing the system could Black liberation be won. While these observations were true, the framework of electoral politics the preamble also advanced was incapable of delivering such change. The focus of the 1982 *Black Leadership Family Plan* was decidedly internal. Instead of calling for systemic change, this was a plan of

> daily living commitment to ourselves and families, to our people, and ultimately to a better America. For we must make a historical covenant with ourselves that the freedom and dignity of our people, while recognizing the responsibilities of other institutions, rest essentially upon what we do ourselves, and how seriously we take the mantle of leadership and self-determination.[65]

The NBLRT was attempting to consolidate resources in Black communities to "be an investment pool contributed by Blacks and other minorities for minority businesses; tap the public capital; and multiply . . . resources."[66] The actual architect of the pamphlet was a Black businessman named Theodore Adams; the pamphlet's objectives reflected the concerns of business, from economic development to general calls for a crackdown on crime in Black communities. The plan went so far as to suggest that youth organizations should "stop Black crime and support fair law enforcement . . . condemn the illegal use and sale of drugs . . . [and] inform on drug dealers to law enforcement officials and Black defense organizations."[67] Even as the organizers of the NBLRT embraced Black citizens in their organizing efforts, as opposed to the "deracialization" perspective, they envisioned Black politics much more narrowly than just a few years earlier during the Gary convention.

Moreover, the call for law and order in Black communities indicated a more conservative political current, even among Black liberal politicians. In some ways it reflected the difference between being in power and being outside power in a given locality. Historically high Black unemployment, the developing drug trade, and the cumulative effects of urban disinvestment made Black cities seem ungovernable and chaotic. Black elected officials governed conservatively in a political climate that did not allow for many alternatives for those acting within the parameters of electoral politics.

The conditions of urban governance in the 1980s were harsh, but many Black elected officials also embraced policies that, while promoted as economic development, in reality transferred public resources over to private control. As Adolph Reed has observed, they pursued "programs centered around making local governments the handmaiden to private development interests . . . with little regard to the disadvantageous impact of their constituencies."[68] By the mid-1980s, Black-led and -dominated administrations backed by solid council majorities governed thirteen US cities with populations over 100,000.[69] Not only were Black municipal officials without resources, but they accepted the premise of "pro-growth" government. Almost universally, they embraced tax cuts for private business, in combination with costly public-private partnerships that purported to redevelop commercial districts but often turned into expensive boondoggles. Mayor Coleman Young in Detroit granted tax relief to a $500 million private development project to renovate the city's waterfront area even while he was "reducing the workforce, department budgets and debt."[70]

The first African American mayor of Camden, New Jersey, Randy Primas, fought for six years against women-led community opposition to place an incinerator in the town. Of course, the suburban residents whose trash would be incinerated did not have to endure the resulting rising rates of asthma and other predictable health problems.[71] Primas sealed his legacy by allowing the New Jersey Department of Corrections to build a $55 million prison, capable of holding between five hundred and eight hundred inmates, in North Camden, saying, "I wouldn't fight it. I view the prison as an economic development project. In addition, I think the surveillance from the two prison towers might stop some of the overt drug dealing in North Camden." When community members protested, Primas lectured, "I need revenue to run a city. I don't think a prison is as negative as people make it out to be. It would create jobs, create revenue, and have a positive impact on the drug problem here. It's not the solution to Camden's problems, but it's realistic."[72]

Black Philadelphia mobilized to elect African American Wilson Goode to the mayor's office in 1983, but "from the outset, Goode was the obedient representative of corporate and financial interests."[73] In 1985 Goode orchestrated an assault on the Black countercultural organization MOVE. Police pumped more than seven thousand rounds of ammunition into MOVE's row house. The attack culminated with police dropping a bomb on the house, killing eleven people, including five children, and destroying sixty-one homes in the fires that consumed the block, leaving 240 people homeless.[74] The attack prompted little outcry from Black civil rights organizations or Black elected officials in the CBC.

Sharon Pratt, a former corporate lawyer and treasurer for the Democratic National Committee, was elected mayor of Washington, DC, in the early 1990s. She lobbied for the National Guard to occupy the streets of Black neighborhoods in the nation's capital as a crime-fighting measure.

In Chicago in 1983, a citywide movement of ordinary Black people organized to topple the white, racist Democratic Party machine that had been led by Richard J. Daley. To everyone's shock, Black Chicago delivered Harold Washington to City Hall, but he was unable to undo the decades of segregation and discriminatory practices that had resulted in a two-tiered Chicago. Of course, no one would expect the election of a Black mayor to reverse the economic and social damage done by years of discriminatory treatment, but the emphasis on local campaigns and elections did show how much the goals of the Black movement had shifted. Its horizons had narrowed from Black liberation to winning electoral majorities in American cities where African Americans lived, as a defensive stance against the conservative trajectory in national politics and ultimately as a more "realistic" and "pragmatic" path.

Perhaps nothing embodied the conservative direction of formal Black politics more than the CBC's cosponsorship of Ronald Reagan's Anti-Drug Abuse Act in 1986. Liberal congressman Ron Dellums from California, along with seventeen of the CBC's twenty-one members, supported the legislation. The act was considered an important tool in the mounting War on Drugs and would be instrumental in the explosion of Black incarceration. It codified more severe sentencing for possession and use of crack cocaine than for powder cocaine. It also allocated $1.7 billion toward the drug war, even as the nation's already fragile welfare state suffered relentless budget cuts. The 1986 act made "crack cocaine" the *only* drug that carried a mandatory minimum five-year sentence for a first-time offense.[75]

The CBC's robust support for law and order in Black communities reflected the deepening crisis of crime in urban centers, the foreclosure of other viable alternatives in an increasingly politically conservative environment, and the political maturation of Black elected officials. By the mid- to late 1980s, Black elected officials were no longer political neophytes: they were experienced executives and operatives in the American political system of constant compromise and negotiation. By 1985, in the midst of the 99th Congress, Blacks had gone from being passed over for coveted chairmanships to chairing five standing committees, two select committees, and fourteen subcommittees in the House of Representatives. Though Blacks composed only 4.6 percent of Congress, they held 22 percent of chairmanships in standing committees and 40 percent in select committees. The CBC cosponsored conservative law-and-order politics out of not political weakness but entrenchment in Beltway politics.

Post-Black Politics

By the 1990s, the retreat from the heady days when John Conyers described the difference between white politicians and Black politicians as the latter's "allegiance . . . to Black people" was complete. During the Clinton administration, Black elected officials lined up to sign off on legislation that was literally intended to kill Black people. In 1993, President Bill Clinton unveiled a new "crime-fighting" bill, the Violent Crime Control and Law Enforcement Act of 1994, that included expanded use of the death penalty, life sentences for nonviolent criminal offenses, 100,000 more police on the streets, and a gratuitously punitive elimination of federal funding for inmate education. Logically, it stood to reason that if legislation increased the number of people to be punished, there must be somewhere to place them—so the bill also included $10 billion in allocations to build more prisons. Clinton lobbied for the legislation in the same Memphis church where King had given his last speech the day before he was assassinated. Clinton's pulpit speech demonstrated the tremendous shift in racial politics. King had used that pulpit to support poor Black maintenance workers as they attempted to unionize; Clinton used it to ask Black people to support expanding the death penalty. Clinton claimed to be using the words he assumed King would say if he were alive to deliver the speech himself: "I fought to stop white people from being so filled with hate that they would wreak violence on black people. I did not fight for the right of black people to murder other black people with reckless abandonment."[76] It was an awful statement, devoid of any facts or historical context of how public policy had nurtured urban divestment for the better part of the twentieth century and by doing so had actually encouraged crime, violence, and drug use. This was the prevailing logic of the time. Even civil rights activist Jesse Jackson Sr., who had run presidential campaigns in 1984 and 1988 on a broad left platform, contributed to the "tough on crime" recriminations. He did not support the crime bill, but he made a comment that contributed to the political climate that legitimized it: "There is nothing more painful to me at this stage in my life than to walk down the street and hear footsteps and start thinking about robbery—then look around and see somebody white and feel relieved."[77]

Black people living in drug-ravaged communities were desperate for help, but billions for imprisonment and streets filled with police would not address the very real issues of crime in poor and working-class Black communities. Having supported Reagan's War on Drugs, congressional Black Democrats were now reluctant to endorse the crime bill. The growing prison population and its impact on Black communities were already coming into focus. Many in the caucus suggested focusing on crime-prevention measures and even introduced legislation that would allow nonwhite death-row inmates to use statistics demonstrating racial bias as a defense. Black Democrats had leverage; Republicans had threatened to block the bill because it included gun-control measures. But Black mayors, including the mayors of Detroit, Atlanta, and Cleveland, pressured the CBC to vote for the legislation. They wrote the chair of the caucus, Kweisi Mfume, urging him to support the legislation with or without the "racial justice" provision.[78] John Lewis, who had been a leader in the civil rights movement, did not vote for the legislation, but participated in a procedural motion that allowed the bill to advance to the House of Representatives.[79] In the end, the majority of the CBC voted for the bill, including liberal luminaries like John Conyers and former Black Panther Bobby Rush. By the end of Clinton's term, Black incarceration rates had tripled and the United States was locking up a larger proportion of its population than any other country on earth. Black communities continue to suffer from these policies—even as the rate of Black imprisonment slowly recedes. In 2015, Bill Clinton admitted the horrible damage created by his crime legislation—damage widely predicted by the bill's progressive opponents: "We have too many people in prison. And we wound up . . : putting so many people in prison that there wasn't enough money left to educate them, train them for new jobs and increase the chances when they came out that they could live productive lives."[80]

The point here is not to simply assign blame to Black elected officials for the catastrophic conditions in Black communities, but to note that these examples are the fruition of a strategy that centered electoral politics as the "realistic" alternative to the grassroots freedom struggle. As money and power exerted greater influence on the outcome of elections, the capacity to raise funds and attract lucrative suitors distorted the political objectives of infusing "soul" into the political process. By the turn of the twenty-first century the CBC could make no claims on being the "conscience" of the Congress; its members, like every politician in Washington, line up at the trough for corporate money. They have accepted donations from a "who's-who" of corporate interests, including BP, Chevron, ExxonMobil, Shell, Texaco, General Motors, Ford, Nissan, DaimlerChrysler, Anheuser-Busch, Heineken USA, Philip Morris, R. J. Reynolds, and Coca-Cola. The *New York Times* said the CBC "stood alone" in its fundraising "prowess" while documenting how it doubled its donations between 2001 and 2008.[81] As the economy soured and its most deleterious effects took hold, the CBC continued to rake in donations from corporate America. The largest donations to the CBC Foundation, its nonprofit wing, have come from the likes of Walmart and McDonald's.[82] The foundation has also accepted up to $2 million from the American Legislative Exchange Council (ALEC), even while ALEC was spearheading voter-identification laws aimed at suppressing the Black vote.[83] Individual CBC members have collected money from an array of insurance, pharmaceutical, and defense corporations. These corporate donations have ensured that the CBC is no more than a marginal player in campaigns against foreclosures and evictions and for fair wages in the low-wage worker movement.

It also at least partially explains CBC members' reluctance to participate in responding to the murders of Mike Brown, Eric Garner, and the many other victims of police brutality. CBC members are usually good for allowing working-class and poor Black people to come and vent about racist police or unjust housing policies, but rarely do those toothless hearings turn into policies that curb the activity being protested. In the midst of the rebellion in Ferguson, Elijah Cummings, a Democratic representative from Maryland and a leader in the CBC, argued that the coming midterm elections were the next step for the movement: "People need to be reminded that the 2014 elections are very, very, very important. One election could be the determining factor to what kind of legislation we're able to get through."[84] Even as a movement against police brutality unfolded, Black elected officials' gazes were so trained on electoral politics that they could only articulate political gains through the calculus of elections.

After forty years of this electoral strategy, Black elected officials' inability to alter the poverty, unemployment, and housing and food insecurity their Black constituents face casts significant doubt on the existing electoral system as a viable vehicle for Black liberation. Moreover, their complete complicity with and absorption into the worst, most corrupt aspects of American politics, including accepting donations from the most notorious corporations in the country, is not just a simple case of "selling out" for the sake of money and access. It isn't that if they knew better, they would perform differently. This complicity is the price of admission into the ranks of the political establishment. The Black political elite has no *fundamental* political differences with the status quo in the United States insofar as it does not directly impede their ability to participate freely in the nation's governing and business institutions. There are also the "new,"[85] "post-Black," or "third wave"[86] Black elected officials who brandish their distance from the freedom struggle. President Barack Obama is the most visible of this cohort, who are described as having "equal fluency in black and white settings; broad, multiracial fundraising networks; and tenuous ties to black protest politics—[which] might also serve as liabilities as they seek higher office."[87] *Washington Post* columnist Eugene Robinson refers to these adherents of "postracial politics" as the "Transcendents": a new crop of Black political operatives who represent "a small but growing cohort with the kind of power, wealth, and influence that previous generations of African Americans could never have imagined."[88] Robinson describes them as "generally in their forties . . . indeed too young to have lived through Jim Crow. They are not too young to know what it was, and certainly not too young to believe as passionately as their elders in the need to keep fighting in advance the unfinished project of Black uplift."[89]

The difficulties of managing cities today have only drawn even more attention to the distance between ordinary Blacks and the politicians—of the old or new variety—who claim to represent them. In Chicago, during the winter and spring of 2015, a hotly contested mayoral runoff election had candidates Rahm Emanuel and Jesús "Chuy" García, both Democrats, scrambling for the support of Black voters. Emanuel was the incumbent whose first four-year term as mayor had been nothing short of catastrophic for Black people. In total defiance of community pleas and protests, Emanuel closed more than fifty public schools, almost exclusively in Black and Latino neighborhoods, not only harming Black students but displacing hundreds of Black teachers. (In 2000, 40 percent of Chicago Public School teachers were African American; in 2015 they make up only 23 percent.[90]) Since coming into office, Emanuel has championed privatization schemes that undermine public institutions while redistributing tax money to businesses connected to him. In an attempt to recoup the revenue lost from corporate tax relief, Emanuel has inundated city residents with fines and fees at every turn, squeezing money out of the poor and working class.

These policies have directly contributed to the city having the highest rate of Black unemployment among the five most populous cities (the others being New York, Los Angeles, Houston, and

Philadelphia).[91] Despite his dismal record, Emanuel had the support of the Chicago City Council Black Caucus. Alderman Howard Brookins rationalized the caucus's support for one of Emanuel's most dreaded programs, which places "red-light cameras" at intersections throughout the city: "How do we make up that $300 million in revenue and won't that hurt people we're being unfair to? People who can slow down or stop will now be asked to pay higher sales, property or gas taxes or we'll have to cut programs that help those people out."[92] Perhaps Brookins never considered that the $100 citations for running red lights were "hurting people." More likely, he was thinking of the financial support he and several other aldermen received from Emanuel's $2 million "super PAC" (political action committee).[93]

Black politicians embrace programs that fleece and harm working-class African Americans because of the pressures of governing in the era of austerity budgets. Today's Black elected officials are beholden to the same logic as their predecessors. As cities are thrust into competition with each other to attract capital, there is a race to the bottom to cut taxes and shove out those in need of social services. Census data from 2010 showed that more than 181,000 Blacks had left Chicago over the course of a decade.[94] It is not possible to separate that stunning figure from the relentless attack on the public infrastructure, which began under the regime of Richard M. Daley but has continued under Emanuel. When elected officials like Alderwoman Lona Lane refer to "young African-American men walking around with their pants hanging down" as being "like a lost generation,"[95] it excuses the racist justifications that are often used for cutting budgets of programs that disproportionately impact Black people. Focusing on individual failure and lapsed morality—instead of structural inequities—justifies the budget cuts and the shrinking of the public sphere that Black political elites help facilitate. What African Americans in cities around the country need, according to this narrative, is personal transformation, not expanded social services—and the converse is that the poor behavior and attitude of young Blacks explains why their neighborhoods lack resources. These elites' vision for Black liberation seems to be limited to "increasing black business subcontracts and . . . expanding the percentages of blacks in management . . . and cultural integration into the mainstream of white America"[96]—which, of course, is no vision at all.

Black people's progress has always been propelled by the strength of the movements of the mass of ordinary Black people. Not only did the Black struggle of the 1960s transform the lives of African Americans, it was the pivot upon which all progressive movements in that era turned. It was the Black insurgency that created the conditions that allowed Black elected officials to become viable politically. But the more the movement on the streets waned, the greater the distance between ordinary Black people and the elected officials claiming to represent them. Added to that dilemma were the constraints of governing in a time of budget cuts and austerity that compelled Black officials to act in fiscally conservative ways—just as their base was in desperate need of robust spending and resources. The conflict between the Black political establishment and ordinary Blacks, however, has been driven not only by budget constraints but also by contempt for the Black poor and a dramatically narrowed vision for what constitutes Black liberation. Complaining about sagging pants or characterizing low-income Black people as "thugs and criminals" during an uprising legitimizes the racialization and criminalization of Black people. It explains the hardships of African Americans in such a way as to rationalize the poor conditions and lack of resources that pervade working-class communities of color. It is difficult for white conservatives to get away with such blanket stereotypes, but for Black politicians they have become a default position, a way to deflect attention from their incompetence—and sometimes malfeasance. Arriving in the heat of a Ferguson summer only to bellow on about the criticality of midterm elections demonstrated that Black members of Congress did not understand the watershed nature of the uprising. Perhaps this should not be surprising: not only did the Ferguson rebellion expose the racism and brutality of American policing, it also exposed Black elected officials' inability to intervene effectively on behalf of poor and working-class African Americans.

CHAPTER FOUR

The Double Standard of Justice

The white cop in the ghetto is as ignorant as he is frightened, and his entire concept of police work is to cow the natives. He is not compelled to answer to these natives for anything he does; whatever he does, he knows that he will be protected by his brothers, who will allow nothing to stain the honor of the force. When his working day is over, he goes home and sleeps soundly in a bed miles away—miles away from the niggers, for that is the way he really thinks of black people.

—James Baldwin, *No Name in the Street*, 1972

I want to live until I'm 18. . . . You want to get older. You want to experience life. You don't want to die in a matter of seconds because of cops.

—Aniya, age thirteen, marching in
Staten Island, New York, 2015

At the turn of the twentieth century, African Americans began their long transition from living largely in rural areas to living predominantly in urban ones. In that time, there have been many changes in Black life, politics, and culture, but the threat and reality of police surveillance, scrutiny, violence, and even murder has remained remarkably consistent. The daily harm caused by the mere presence of police in Black communities has been a consistent feature of Black

urban history and, increasingly, Black suburban history. Police brutality has been a consistent badge of inferiority and second-class citizenship. When the police enforce the law inconsistently and become the
agents of lawlessness and disorder, it serves as a tangible reminder of
the incompleteness of formal equality. You cannot truly be free when
the police are able to set upon you at will, for no particular reason at all.
It is a constant reminder of the space between freedom and "unfree-
dom," where the contested citizenship of African Americans is held.

The racism of the police is not the product of vitriol; it flows from
their role as armed agents of the state. The police function to enforce the
rule of the politically powerful and the economic elite: this is why poor
and working-class communities are so heavily policed. African Americans are overrepresented among the ranks of the poor and the working
class, so police overwhelmingly focus on those neighborhoods, even as
they direct their violence more generally against all working-class people, including whites. But the police also reflect and reinforce the dominant ideology of the state that employs them, which also explains why
they are inherently racist and resistant to substantive reform. In other
words, if the task of the police is to maintain law and order, then that
role takes on a specific meaning in a fundamentally racist society. Policing has changed over time as the nature and needs of the American
state have changed, but it has also remained incredibly consistent as a
thoroughly racist institution trained on Black communities. The racism of the police, historically, has also overlapped with the economic
needs of business and the state to create a racialized political economy
that is particularly burdensome on Black communities.

Race, Class, and the Police

The political economy of the modern policing state was created in the
opening moments of Black freedom. Historians have identified multiple
origins of the modern American police, including nineteenth-century
slave patrols. After emancipation, the purpose of racism, like the purpose of the police, was transformed. Biologically inflected ideological
explanations, no longer necessary to justify enslavement, were deployed
instead to justify the surveillance and control of Black people, especially
Black workers. "Black Codes," a series of laws, rules, and restrictions

imposed only on African Americans, criminalized poverty, movement, and even leisure. Blacks could be arrested for vaguely worded or innocuous "crimes" such as vagrancy and sentenced to "hard labor" in slavery-like conditions as punishment. Law enforcement officials could also "hire out" Black vagrants to white employers to "work off" their sentences. African Americans had to produce labor contracts to prove they were not vagrants or be hurled back into conditions intimately resembling slavery. It was an effort to re-create slavery "by another name."[1] The police were deployed to enforce these codes, as agents of states still largely controlled by a white planter class that had been militarily defeated but not quite economically and politically destroyed.

Racism and modern policing were thus mutually constitutive in reinforcing the subjugated status of Blacks. The Black Codes conflated Blackness with criminality, as this example from St. Landry's Parish in Louisiana, passed immediately after the end of the Civil War, shows:

SECTION 1. *Be it ordained by the police jury of the parish of St. Landry*, That no negro shall be allowed to pass within the limits of said parish without a special permit in writing from his employer. Whoever shall violate this provision shall pay a fine of two dollars and fifty cents, or in default thereof shall be forced to work four days on the public road, or suffer corporeal punishments as provided hereinafter.

SECTION 2. *Be it further ordained*, That every negro who shall be found absent from the residence of his employer after 10 o'clock at night, without a written permit from his employer, shall pay a fine of five dollars, or in default thereof, shall be compelled to work five days on the public road, or suffer corporeal punishments as provided hereinafter.

SECTION 3. *Be it further ordained*, That no negro shall be permitted to rent or keep a house within said parish. Any negro violating this provision shall be immediately ejected and compelled to find an employer; and any person who shall rent, or give the use of any house to any negro, in violation of this section, shall pay a fine of five dollars for each offence.

SECTION 4. *Be it further ordained*, That every negro is required to be in the regular service of some white person, or former owner, who shall be held responsible for the conduct of said negro. But said employer or former owner may permit said negro to hire his own time by special permission in writing, which permission shall not extend over seven days at any one time. Any negro violating the provisions of this section shall be fined five dollars for each offence, or in default of the payment thereof shall be forced to work five days on the public road, or suffer corporeal punishment as hereinafter provided.

SECTION 5. *Be it further ordained,* That no public meetings or congregations of negroes shall be allowed within said parish after sunset; but such public meetings and congregations may be held between the hours of sunrise and sunset, by the special permission in writing of the captain of patrol, within whose beat such meetings shall take place. This prohibition, however, is not intended to prevent negroes from attending the usual church services, conducted by white ministers and priests. Every negro violating the provisions of this section shall pay a fine of five dollars, or in default thereof shall be compelled to work five days on the public road, or suffer corporeal punishment as hereinafter provided.

SECTION 6. *Be it further ordained,* That no negro shall be permitted to preach, exhort, or otherwise declaim to congregations of colored people, without a special permission in writing from the president of the police jury. Any negro violating the provisions of this section shall pay a fine of ten dollars, or in default thereof shall be compelled to work ten days on the public road, or suffer corporeal punishment as hereinafter provided....

SECTION 11. *Be it further ordained,* That it shall be the duty of every citizen to act as a police officer for the detection of offences and the apprehension of offenders, who shall be immediately handed over to the proper captain or chief of patrol.[2]

All white citizens were expected to police the activities of African Americans, but it was ultimately the responsibility of law enforcement officers to make arrests. These laws make it clear that policing was more than simply racist: the police worked with those in power to provide a regular labor force to replace the labor that had been disrupted by slavery's end. This was cloaked in the rhetoric of law and order, but after slavery, the white elite in the South used the law to control and manipulate newly freed African Americans.[3]

The period of Reconstruction after the Civil War held promise that Black citizenship might be fulfilled; in that context, the Thirteenth Amendment in 1865 and the Civil Rights Act of 1866 expressly banned practices such as Black Codes that could be considered a badge or emblem of slavery.[4] There was, however, a loophole in the Thirteenth Amendment that allowed for the incarcerated to be treated like slaves, and "convict leasing" was born.

Over the course of the nineteenth century and into the twentieth, convict leasing became a new way for Southern employers to manipulate the law and resolve a perpetual labor shortage. The desperate need for labor seemed insatiable; it turned all Black people into potential suspects and justified surveillance and scrutiny. Convict leasing was lucrative for employers compared to slavery, since it involved lower overhead expenses. As one observer put it, "Before the war we owned the Negroes. If a man had a good nigger, he could afford to take care of him; if he was sick get a doctor. He might even put gold plugs in his teeth. But these convicts: we don't own 'em. One dies, get another."[5] The police were the linchpin to this new arrangement.

Frederick Douglass, writing on convict leasing, explained:

> To have Negro blood in the veins makes one unworthy of consideration, a social outcast, a leper, even in the church. The second reason our race furnishes so large a share of the convicts is that the judges, juries and other officials of the courts are white men who share these prejudices. They also make the laws. It is wholly in their power to extend clemency to white criminals and mete severe punishment to black criminals for the same or lesser crimes. The Negro criminals are mostly ignorant, poor and friendless. Possessing neither money to employ lawyers nor influential friends, they are sentenced in large numbers to long terms of imprisonment for petty crimes. The *People's Advocate*, a Negro journal, of Atlanta, Georgia, has the following observation on the prison showing of that state for 1892. "It is an astounding fact that 90 per cent of the state's convicts are colored; 194 white males and 2 white females; 1,710 colored males and 44 colored females. Is it possible that Georgia is so color prejudiced that she won't convict her white law breakers? Yes, it is just so, but we hope for a better day."[6]

In some Southern states, convict leasing was critical to the economy. In 1898 almost 73 percent of total revenue in Alabama was derived from convict leasing in coal mines.[7]

The rampant exploitation of Black labor was contingent on the denigration of Black humanity. Assumptions of Black criminality became seamlessly integrated into collective common sense of what constituted "the Negro." Historian Khalil Muhammad argues that "crime itself was not the core issue. Rather the problem was racial criminalization:

the stigmatization of crime as 'black' and the masking of crime among whites as individual failure. The practice of linking crime to blacks, as a racial group, but not whites . . . reinforced and reproduced racial inequality."[8] It was not only "racial criminalization," in other words, but criminalization in the name of securing a stable workforce. Race did not take on a life of its own. It was consciously invoked to rationalize the debased status of Blacks. Muhammad argues that statistics, particularly rates of Black incarceration, were woven together by the mainstream media, the Southern political and economic elite, and the emergent field of social science to build a narrative of post–Reconstruction Black criminality.

Some of the Black elite contributed to this discourse of Black criminality as a way to distinguish themselves from poorer Blacks. As William S. Scarborough, a professor at the historically Black Wilberforce College, said at the turn of the century, "The criminal negro is one of the heaviest burdens that the race has to carry today."[9] He elaborated on his complaints:

> There are *negroes* and *negroes*, crude, cultured, shiftless, thrifty, grotesque, urbane; immoral and grossly debased; clean and living the life of the spirit. The Vardamans of the world [James K. Vardaman was then governor of Mississippi] know no distinctions, make no discriminations, brand us all alike as a lower order of creature. Therefore Negro criminality cannot be ignored by us.[10]

Elite Black observers admitted that "white oppression was largely to blame," but their acceptance of the conflation of Blackness and crime lent legitimacy to the draconian law-and-order regime. As historian Evelyn Higginbotham Brooks argues, "Black leaders argued that 'proper' and 'respectable' behavior proved blacks worthy of equal civil and political rights. Conversely, nonconformity was equated with deviance and pathology and was often cited as a cause of racial inequality and injustice."[11]

Certainly, by the twentieth century, the criminality and inferiority of Black people constituted a type of racial logic and common sense. As Muhammad explains, "For white Americans of every ideological stripe—African American criminality became one of the most widely accepted bases for justifying prejudicial thinking, discriminatory treatment, and/or acceptance of racial violence as an instrument of public safety."[12] The Supreme Court's 1896 *Plessy v. Ferguson* decision nationalized the "separate but equal" paradigm while also codifying Black inferiority at the highest levels of the American government. These perceptions, and the widespread acceptance of theories of eugenics, were not confined to the South but became a national phenomenon, especially as African Americans began to move into Northern cities, creating panic among elites.[13] In the summer of 1917, the *Chicago Tribune* ran a screaming headline: "Half a Million Darkies from Dixie Swarm to the North to Better Themselves."[14]

Racism was stoked, in part, by Northern employers' cynical use of newly arrived African Americans as strikebreakers in the late 1910s and early 1920s.[15] Tensions also rose because cities generally lacked the housing and infrastructure needed to support the waves of immigrants and Southern Blacks. Blacks' housing choices were strictly limited, no matter how many thousands continued to make their way to cities across the Northeast and Midwest. Landlords fully exploited the segregated housing market, charging Black tenants more for inferior housing and refusing to maintain their properties because Black tenants had no housing alternative outside of overcrowded Black areas. In 1917 the Chicago Real Estate Board amended its bylaws to warn that it would discipline any real-estate agent who introduced a minority resident into a racially homogenous neighborhood.[16]

Housing segregation was important because the physical separation of people allowed heinous stereotypes about African Americans to flourish. This was a product of ignorance and also of the material impact segregation had on Black living spaces. Overcrowding led to rapid deterioration of the housing stock, while an overabundance of refuse resulted in rat infestations and health problems. Whites blamed these conditions on Black people's inferior hygiene instead of the racist manipulation of the housing market.

The concentration and effects of Black poverty provided a constant pretext for police incursions, arrests, and violence, which fueled the antagonistic relationship between the police and African Americans. As early as the 1920s, patterns of police abuse that would be recognizable today contributed to Blacks' growing disillusionment with the police and the supposed freedoms of the North. Police harassment and violence blurred the distinctions between the supposed "land of hope" in the North and the Jim Crow apartheid of the South. In 1925 the *Detroit Independent* reported "repeated police assaults on Negroes. Fifty-five blacks had been shot by policemen in the first half of the year alone. A few of them had been executed—there was no other word for it."[17] It was a "common practice" for Detroit police to "stop Black men at random and subject them to searches, often at gunpoint, and those taken into custody sometimes spent days in jail just waiting to be charged with a crime."[18] Compounding the physical deterioration of Black areas, officials allowed vices, including drugs, illegal alcohol, and prostitution, to flourish in order to keep them out of white areas. According to Muhammad, "estimates from Chicago and other cities suggest that from 80 to possibly 90 percent of vice businesses were owned by nonblacks." The cops knew, "but they didn't care unless they saw a colored man walking in the company of a white woman. Then they ran him in."[19] One investigator at the time observed that "uniformed police officers, prostitutes and the hold-up men divide the money between them in this court."[20]

A larger police presence did not mean greater protection for African Americans in an era of raging white mob violence. White police displayed their contempt for Black communities in multiple ways, including failing to intervene when white mobs attacked African Americans. In many cases the police joined in. In Chicago in 1919, for example, police stood by while racist whites rampaged through Black areas in anger after a Black teenager, Eugene Williams, violated the informal rules of segregation at a local beach. Williams was murdered. Even when his killer was identified, white police refused to arrest him.[21]

In 1943, bubbling tensions would boil over again. African Americans' rising incomes and expectations clashed with whites' sense of dominion over urban space. Black and white workers competed over the use of "schools, playgrounds, parks, beaches" and housing in the city, with conflicts breaking out right at the height of the war effort.[22] In 1943 there were "242 racial riots in 47 cities, the worst of them in Los Angeles, Beaumont, Texas, Mobile, Alabama, Harlem and Detroit."[23] In Harlem that year, rebellion was sparked again when a white police officer murdered an unarmed Black veteran. In Detroit, a violent confrontation between Black and white workers erupted over competition for gainful employment as well as housing. This race riot was frightening as well as shocking to the establishment. Here was the most important industrial city in the country, with some of the highest living standards among ordinary Black and white workers, socially combusting in a way that resulted in the deaths of dozens and millions of dollars in property damage. Elites worried that there could be a "succession of Detroits." While police violence was not the direct cause of this explosion, it was certainly a contributing factor. This was not peculiar to Detroit. As one Black woman said of white violence, including that of police: "There ain't no North anymore. Everything now is South."[24]

African Americans were questioning all of the existing order, including the police function of "maintaining order." The vast majority of police in the United States were white, uneducated, working class, and completely consumed with racism. The racialization of crime and the haggard conditions in Black neighborhoods made them susceptible to great surveillance. It also contributed to the greater rates of poverty and unemployment among Blacks, as stereotypes about Black criminality and lawlessness rendered growing numbers of Black men unemployable or marginally employable. This mark of inferiority also isolated Black women in low-paying jobs. Nevertheless, American cities were increasingly combustible as Black citizens' expectations grew, bringing greater attention to the incongruence between inequality and the promises of US democracy. Police brutality was the most egregious example.

Postwar Policing

In the middle of the 1960s, hundreds of thousands of African Americans participated in urban rebellions to protest and confront racism, police brutality, and injustice. In cities as different as Detroit, Tampa, Houston, Chicago, Philadelphia, and Prattville, Alabama, the rebellions raised basic questions about American democracy. The widespread and continuous nature of the riots turned them from episodic outbreaks of discontent into a force that transformed politics. The issues that defined the urban crisis—poor housing, police brutality, poor schools, and unemployment, among many others—went from being politically peripheral to what President Lyndon Johnson termed "the nation's most urgent task." Black rebellions are usually seen as the dysfunctional cousin to the civil rights movement: while the civil rights movement is universally lauded as successful because of its strategic emphasis on nonviolence, the riots are universally condemned because of their inherent violence. A *New York Times* editorial written only a few weeks after the 1967 Detroit riots captured this argument: "The riots, rather than developing a clamor for great social progress to wipe out poverty, to a large extent have had the reverse effect and have increased the crises for use of police force and criminal law."[25] Yet what ignited the riots was almost always an incident of police brutality.

After the deadly riots in Detroit and Newark in the summer of 1967, Lyndon Johnson impaneled the Kerner Commission, discussed in chapter 1, which reported that

> to some Negroes police have come to symbolize white power, white racism and white repression. And the fact is that many police do reflect and express these white attitudes. The atmosphere of hostility and cynicism is reinforced by a widespread belief among Negroes in the existence of police brutality and in a "double standard" of justice and protection—one for Negroes and one for whites—a deep hostility between the police and ghetto . . . was a primary cause of the riots.[26]

The report really did not capture the absolute hatred Black communities held for the police. James Baldwin more perfectly summarized the feeling in an essay titled "A Report from Occupied Territory":

> Now, what I have said about Harlem is true of Chicago, Detroit, Washington, Boston, Philadelphia, Los Angeles and San Francisco—is true of every Northern city with a large Negro population . . . the police are simply the hired enemies of this population. They are present to keep the Negro in his place and to protect white business interests, and they have no other function. They are, moreover—even in a country which makes the very grave error of equating ignorance with simplicity—quite stunningly ignorant; and, since they know that they are hated, they are always afraid. One cannot possibly arrive at a more surefire formula for cruelty. This is why those pious calls to "respect the law," always to be heard from prominent citizens each time the ghetto explodes, are so obscene. The law is meant to be my servant and not my master, still less my torturer and my murderer. To respect the law, in the context in which the American Negro finds himself, is simply to surrender his self-respect.[27]

One 1968 poll found that 52 percent of Blacks blamed "police brutality" as a "major cause of disorder" compared to only 13 percent of whites, though 63 percent of everyone polled believed that "until there is justice for minorities there will not be law and order."[28]

In 1965, in the months before the explosive Watts Rebellion in South Central Los Angeles, the Johnson administration formed the Commission on Law Enforcement and the Administration of Justice to investigate "law and order" and policing. The central focus of the commission was improving policing in Black communities by actually transforming the profession, including recruiting more Black officers. Its report concluded that "a major, and most urgent, step in the direction of improving police-community relations is recruiting more, many more, policemen from minority groups."[29] It blamed tensions between African Americans and the police on white officers' "lack of understanding of the problems and behaviors of minority groups" and inability to "deal successfully with people whose way of thought and action are unfamiliar. . . . In order to gain the general confidence and acceptance of a community . . . personnel within a police department should be representative of the community as a whole." Officials also focused on "professionalizing" the police, whose profession at this point was not highly regarded. The average salary for the police in small cities in the late 1960s was $4,600, lifting them just above the poverty line. In 1965, only four states mandated *any* police training, and more than twenty states did not have minimum education and literacy requirements. There was so little training that "barbers and beauticians, on average, were required to train more than and three times as long as the average American cop." In Detroit, for example, most cops came from the bottom 25 percent of their high-school class; as Parenti noted, "This was not a unique situation."[30]

While this effort got under way, there was a simultaneous effort to describe postwar racial civil unrest as a problem of Black lawlessness. The commission also argued,

> We must identify and eliminate the causes of criminal activity whether they lie in the environment around us or deep in the nature of individual men. This is a major purpose of all we are doing in combatting poverty and improving education, health, welfare, housing, and recreation. All these are vital, but they are not enough. Crime will not wait while we pull it up by the roots. We must arrest and reverse the trend toward lawlessness.[31]

This was an effort to recast the riots as simple criminal activity, not rebellions against racial discrimination and systematic exclusion from the bounty of the ongoing economic expansion. In reality, as Naomi Murakawa has written, "The U.S. did not confront a crime problem that was . . . racialized; it confronted a race problem that was . . . criminalized."[32] Characterizing Black anger at discrimination and segregation as criminal helped to explain Black Power and independent Black politics as crime, creating a pretext for yet more policing, arrests, and repression of the movement in general. This coincided with an intensification of the "culture of poverty" rhetoric described in chapter 1.

As Black mayors and other managers of city and urban affairs gained prominence during the 1970s and 1980s, so did the demand to diversify local law enforcement. The most successful result was the dramatic transformation from "the virtually all-white, virtually all-male departments of the 1950s and 1960s . . . to departments with large numbers of female and minority officers, often led by female or minority chiefs. Openly gay and lesbian officers, too, are increasingly commonplace. Today's Los Angeles Police Department is not the homogeneous workplace celebrated on *Dragnet*—and neither is the police."[33] In 1970, Blacks composed 6 percent of sworn officers in the 300 largest police departments in the country; by 2006 that figure had grown to 18 percent. By the twenty-first century, in cities with populations over 250,000, 20 percent of officers were Black and 14 percent were Latino. In New York City in 2005, for the first time in history, a majority of the new officers graduating from the NYPD Police Academy were members of racial minorities. In some cities the increases in minority officers has been even more dramatic. In Detroit, more than 60 percent of the police force is Black, compared to less than 10 percent in the 1960s. In Washington, DC, minorities constitute almost 70 percent of the police today, whereas in the 1960s there were fewer than 20 percent.[34]

These dramatic changes in composition and professionalization have not had the effect of mitigating the tensions between police and Black communities, as Johnson's crime commission predicted. Some studies have shown that "black officers shoot just as often as white officers"; "black officers arrest just as often as white officers"; "black officers are often prejudiced against black citizens"; "that black officers are just as likely, or even more likely, to elicit citizen complaints and to be the subject of disciplinary actions."[35] Though there is a popular perception that more nonwhite police can help ease tensions with nonwhite populations that are patrolled, perhaps more compelling is the fact that the explosion of the incarceration of Black men, women, and children took place *after* the years-long effort to "professionalize" and diversify the police.[36] The most diverse police forces in American history have not altered more than a century's worth of violent, racially discriminatory, and unfair policing.

Policing in the Modern Era

There have been three distinct periods of policing in the post–civil rights era, each building upon the previous: Reagan's War on Drugs, Clinton's crime regime, and the era of the "War on Terror." These over-lapping periods have culminated in the phenomenon of "mass incarcer-ation," including increased scrutiny, surveillance, policing, and impris-onment of all working-class people, but especially African Americans. As cities have become more financially independent from the federal infusions of money and have been forced to generate their own sources of income, the police have also become agents of gentrification and municipal revenue collection. This transformation illustrates the de-gree to which law enforcement is an armed extension of the state, reg-ularly wielded in the interests of the rich and powerful.

It is well known today that the United States houses 25 percent of the world's prisoners even though it only accounts for 5 percent of the world's population. In 1971 there were fewer than 200,000 inmates in the United States. Since then the prison population has risen by 700 percent, bringing the number of the incarcerated to 2.4 million, "with another nearly five million under an increasingly restrictive system of correctional control in lieu of or after incarceration."[37] The prison popu-lation began to rise in the 1970s when Richard Nixon began the first it-eration of the War on Drugs.[38] Beginning in the mid-1970s, state prison populations grew at an unprecedented rate, nearly quadrupling between then and now. By the 1980s, rates of incarceration had taken a qualita-tive leap forward: the US prison population had quadrupled by 2013.[39] This was not only fueled by the War on Drugs, as noted in chapter 3: "incarceration rates for violent, property and other crimes . . . increased dramatically as well."[40] The consequences of the bipartisan demand for "law and order" were a massive expansion of police forces, prison and jail construction, the criminal code, and the criminal justice system as a whole. These events coincided with bleak economic prospects for most Americans and significant cuts to the already weak social welfare state.

Former Nixon advisor Kevin Phillips said of the 1980s that "no parallel upsurges of the era of the riches had been seen since the late 19th century, the era of the Vanderbilts, Morgans and Rockefellers."[41] Ronald Reagan reduced the federal income tax rate for the very rich from 70 percent to 28 percent, but this was only the tip of the iceberg.[42] The 1990s produced an even greater concentration of wealth in fewer hands: "By 2000, the United States could be said to have a plutocracy."[43] It was easy for the rich to pay attention to rising crime rates while ignoring the massive gutting of social services and the poverty and insecurity of the bottom ranks.

Even before Bill Clinton became president, he showed that he would not be outflanked on the right by accusations of being "soft on crime." In 1992, Clinton famously left the campaign trail to personally oversee the execution of a mentally disabled Black man who was so unaware of his pending death that he asked to have his dessert after his execution. Clinton went on to make crime-fighting a centerpiece of his presidency.[44]

In the months before his election, the Los Angeles Rebellion ignited South Central once again. Clinton and the Democrats responded by seizing the opportunity to make crime-fighting a core party value. Within two years, Clinton would champion and eventually have voted into law the Violent Crime Control and Law Enforcement Act of 1994. The $30 billion Crime Bill, as noted in chapter 3, provided for 100,000 more police to be hired, expanded the death penalty by creating sixty new offenses for which a person could be executed, expanded construction of new prisons, created "three-strikes" provisions, and ended inmate education. These policies were only the beginning. The Clinton administration also created financial incentives for states to not only imprison more people but keep them in prison longer, under "truth in sentencing" provisions.[45] There was no question that these policies were directed at African American communities, where a gutted welfare state and the introduction of crack cocaine and the drug war had prompted a rise in crime.

In 1996, Clinton championed the Anti-Terrorism and Effective Death Penalty Act, intended to strengthen the Crime Bill by further restricting prisoners' ability to challenge their sentences. By the end of the Clinton presidency in 2000, Black incarceration rates had tripled. Clinton's other legacy was "ending welfare as we know it" in 1996. The consequences of this war on poor people would be borne out during the recession of the early 2000s and the economic collapse of 2008. Resistance to the growing criminal justice system increased at the end of the 1990s, but the attacks on September 11, 2001, eclipsed most of the political spaces in which those critiques were developing. The political establishment united around the expansion of the "security state" with the passage of the USA PATRIOT Act and a host of other new tools that increased the power of the state in the name of fighting terrorism. The "War on Terror" legitimized concentrating greater surveillance, scrutiny, and power in the hands of all law enforcement—not to mention weapons.

During the Clinton administration, the Pentagon was authorized to donate surplus military equipment to local police departments. According to one report, "in the first three years after the 1994 law alone, the Pentagon distributed 3,800 M-16s, 2,185 M-14s, 73 grenade launchers, and 112 armored personnel carriers to civilian police agencies across America. Domestic police agencies also got bayonets, tanks, helicopters and even airplanes."[46] After September 11, elected officials actively promoted the notion that the War on Terror had to be fought on the home front—and that the police were on the front lines of this new "war." In 2006, the Pentagon distributed "vehicles worth $15.4 million, aircraft worth $8.9 million, boats worth $6.7 million, weapons worth $1 million and 'other' items worth $110.6 million" to local police agencies."[47] In 2012, the military transferred a record $546 million worth of property to local police departments.[48] The process of transforming police into soldiers in the inner city exacerbated existing problems, as one former police chief described:

> An emphasis on "officer safety" and paramilitary training pervades today's policing. . . . Police in large cities formerly carried revolvers holding six .38-caliber rounds. Nowadays, police carry semi-automatic pistols with 16 high-caliber rounds, shotguns and military assault rifles, weapons once relegated to SWAT teams facing extraordinary circumstances. Concern about such firepower in densely populated areas hitting innocent citizens has given way to an attitude that the police are fighting a war against drugs and crime and must be heavily armed.[49]

The federal government also provided grants allowing departments to purchase armored personnel carriers, even in places that could hardly be considered potential terrorist targets, like Alabama and Idaho.

This growth has had its greatest impact in African American communities. For more than thirty years, the War on Drugs has been waged in Black communities. The perception of African Americans as responsible for drug-related violence has been fostered by a range of actors, from elected officials in both parties to the mainstream media to popular culture. It has contributed to a general suspicion of African Americans as criminals deserving of extra scrutiny. But the wider the policing net grows, the greater its propensity to entangle those previously able to avoid it. For example, from 2000 to 2009, incarceration rates for African Americans actually dropped—not surprising, given how historically high the rate had climbed—while the rate of imprisonment for whites and Latinos increased over the same period, rising 47.1 percent for white women and 8.5 percent for white men.[50] The overarching aims of the War on Terror at home legitimized the "criminalization creep" throughout American society.

Twenty-First-Century Policing

The rebellion in Ferguson led to deeper investigations into policing there, which found that African Americans were overrepresented among those stopped for traffic violations: they are 67 percent of the population but account for 89 percent of traffic stops. Blacks also accounted for 92 percent of arrests that originated with a traffic stop.[51] Ferguson's policing practices became the subject of national scrutiny, but according to a USA Today investigation, "Blacks are stopped, searched, arrested and imprisoned at rates higher than people of other races" nationwide: "When it comes to racially lopsided arrests, the most remarkable thing about Ferguson, Missouri, might be just how ordinary it is."[52] The report found that 1,581 other police departments arrested Black people at "rates even more skewed than in Ferguson, including cities like Chicago and San Francisco. At least 70 police departments arrested Black people at a rate 10 times higher than non-Blacks."[53] These numbers do not include information from all police departments across the country, but African Americans are generally more likely to be arrested than whites.

Curiously, the policing state has expanded even as crime rates have fallen precipitously, as the *Atlantic* notes:

> Over the past 25 years, the tide of crime and violence seemed to simply recede. Crime is about half of what it was at its peak in 1991. Violent crime plummeted 51 percent. Property crime fell 43 percent. Homicides are down 54 percent. In 1985, there were 1,384 murders in New York City. Last year there were 333. The country is an undeniably safer place. Growing urban populations are one positive consequence.[54]

There is little to no consensus on the cause of the drop in crime rates in the United States, but most experts agree that it had little to do with Clinton's draconian sentencing practices. Many elected officials from the late 1980s and throughout the 1990s hinged their careers on clamoring loudly for "tough-on-crime" policies, but "it turns out that increased incarceration had a much more limited effect on crime than popularly thought. We find that this growth in incarceration was responsible for approximately 5 percent of the drop in crime in the 1990s."[55]

But after thirty years building up the policing state, the temptation to use it is overwhelming. "Nuisance crimes" and other "quality of life" offenses have become the new frontier of American policing, which has little to do with fighting crime. Instead, agents of law enforcement police poverty while instilling fear in and monitoring oppressed populations. As municipalities and state legislatures cut social services and critical aspects of the public sector intended to mitigate the worst aspects of poverty, the police are deployed to "clean up" the consequences.

Crime—where it is actually a problem—is treated as moral depravity instead of the product of poverty or social injustice, relieving the state of any obligation to address poverty; instead, it concentrates even more resources into policing. The starkest example of this is that jails have become the predominant destination for those who commit crimes of mental health. This is because of the dearth of mental healthcare, including treatment facilities that would be more appropriate destinations. Chicago mayor Rahm Emanuel closed half of the city's twelve mental health clinics, leaving those without private insurance struggling to find help. Those who cannot are often arrested. Emanuel cried fiscal poverty as an excuse for closing the clinics, even as he gave the police raises and tens of millions of dollars in overtime.[56] Cook County sheriff Tom Dart has said that one-third of the county jail's ten thousand inmates are mentally ill, even higher than that national average among the incarcerated, 17 percent.[57] Across the country, mental healthcare systems have been devastated by $4.53 billion in state-level budget cuts since 2009. It is hardly surprising, then, that at least half of the people killed by police since 2000 were suffering from some form of mental illness.[58]

The social consequences of austerity budgets have effectively made the police stormtroopers for gentrification, as cities compete to attract businesses and young white professionals with disposable incomes. This is obvious from the new rules, ordinances, and laws that criminalize public displays of poverty. In more than half of the cities in the United States, it is a crime to sit on the sidewalk. In 18 percent it is a crime to sleep in a public place. Seventy-six percent ban soliciting for money or begging in public. Thirty-three percent ban loitering in entire public jurisdictions, while 65 percent ban loitering in particular places. Fifty-three percent prohibit lying down in particular public places. In 43 percent of cities, it is illegal to sleep in a car. In a growing trend, 9 percent of cities have banned sharing or giving food to the homeless.[59] So-called quality of life offenses include victimless "crimes" like loitering, public urination, or begging in public. These offenses have multiplied as jobs and programs to aid the working poor have been cut to the bone or eliminated.

This approach to policing is broadly informed by the "broken windows" theory, popularized by New York City police chief William Bratton in the 1990s. "Broken windows" was the creation of conservative social scientists James Q. Wilson and George L. Kelling, who argued that stopping low-stakes or "nuisance" crimes, such as subway fare evasion, public drinking, or graffiti, would prevent more serious crimes. There is no empirical evidence for its effectiveness, but it has created a pretext for aggressive policing of poor and working-class people, who are more likely to been seen engaged in such "nuisance" activities because their neighborhoods are more likely to be patrolled. Bratton described George Kelling as a mentor, and when Rudolph Giuliani was elected mayor in 1993, he hired Bratton to implement "broken windows" policing in real life. Bratton introduced CompStat, the software that is still used to track stops and arrests across New York City and generate crime statistics for each precinct on a daily basis. An internal NYPD bulletin described the way CompStat organizes their police work:

> In the past, crime statistics often lagged events by months, and so did the sense of whether crime control initiatives had succeeded or failed. Now there is a daily turnaround in the "CompStat" numbers, as crime statistics are called, and NYPD commanders watch weekly crime trends with the same hawk-like attention private corporations pay to profits and loss. Crime statistics have become the department's bottom line, the best indicator of how police are doing precinct-by-precinct and nationwide.[60]

The New York approach to policing, combining "broken windows" and CompStat, was adopted across the country in the 1990s. By 2013, 58 percent of large police departments (a hundred or more officers) were using or planning to use CompStat.[61] Part of the CompStat method involves praising individual cops for showing up in the statistics as a way to encourage them to keep their numbers up. The opposite is also true. As Kelling put it, "If commanders make bad decisions or allow their subordinates to perform poorly, they should not be protected from humiliation."[62] This atmosphere has certainly contributed to the skyrocketing use of "stop-and-frisk" among New York City police—they search for criminal activity in the hope of boosting precinct numbers.

The 1999 police killing of Amadou Diallo first raised questions about the NYPD's practice of race-based stops. From 1998 through 1999, police stopped 175,000 New Yorkers. Even though Blacks make up only 26 percent of New York's population, they accounted for 51 percent of police stops. Latinos, with 24 percent of the population, accounted for 33 percent of stops.[63] By 2011 the number of stops had mushroomed to 684,000, the vast majority of whom were Black and Brown men. According to the Center for Constitutional Rights, between 2004 and 2012 more than four million people were stopped, and in less than 6 percent of those stops was an arrest made. More than 80 percent of those four million people were African American or Latino. Representatives of those communities filed a federal lawsuit, arguing that stop-and-frisk was codified racial profiling.[64]

NYPD officer Pedro Serrano testified during the lawsuit proceedings that he had received direct orders to engage in stop-and-frisk. He also recorded his precinct commanders threatening officers with reassignment to an unfavorable task if they did not stop "the right people at the right time in the right location." If there was any confusion as to who the "right people" were, the commander clarified, "Male blacks. And I told you that at roll call, and I have no problem telling you this: male blacks 14 to 20."[65]

Kelling and Wilson admitted that "broken windows" would turn police into "the agents of neighborhood bigotry." For them, this was the price of doing business: "We can offer no wholly satisfactory answer to this important question [of abating police discrimination]. We are not confident that there is a satisfactory answer, except to hope that by their selection, training, and supervision, the police will be inculcated with a clear sense of the outer limit of their discretionary authority."[66] At a separate hearing, police commissioner Ray Kelly testified that fear and intimidation were the objectives of stop-and-frisk. New York state senator Eric Adams testified that he personally heard Kelly say that stop-and-frisk should "instill fear in them, every time they leave their home, [that] they could be stopped by the police." Adams clarified that "them" referred to Blacks and Latinos.[67] In the summer of 2013, a US District Court for the Southern District of New York declared the NYPD's use of stop-and-frisk unconstitutional. But this has not stopped the practice from continuing in New York and elsewhere, often under other names. In the spring of 2015, a lawsuit was filed on behalf of six African Americans in Chicago for racial discrimination related to stop-and-frisk practices. After an investigation, the American Civil Liberties Union (ACLU) found that the Chicago Police Department's use of stop-and-frisk was even more pervasive than the NYPD's had been before it was declared unconstitutional. In the summer of 2014, Black Chicagoans were subjected to 182,048 stops, 72 percent of all stops, while only accounting for 32 percent of Chicago's population.[68]

This aggressive policing not only leads to an increasing rate of arrest of African Americans, but every encounter with law enforcement draws working-class and poor Blacks into a matrix of fines and fees. Twenty-first-century municipalities, urban and suburban, increasingly rely on revenue generated by fines and fees that either originate with or are the products of arrests. Because politicians have been reluctant to raise taxes on wealthy individuals or corporations, police are increasingly responsible for municipal revenue. As a result, fees as a percentage of state and local revenue have increased over the last several years. The rebellion in Ferguson uncovered how the local government was literally extorting the Black population, to such a degree that monies derived from these fines and fees were the second largest source of revenue. The town issued 33,000 minor-crime arrest warrants for a population of 21,000, mostly for traffic violations—and overwhelmingly to Black residents. Whites, who are 29 percent of the population, accounted for only 12.7 percent of stops.[69] Throughout Missouri, this process of legal extortion is considered a perfectly acceptable practice.

According to a report from Better Together, a nonprofit group, Ferguson does not even rank among the top twenty municipalities in St. Louis County that rely on fines and fees as the central source of their operating budgets. The small city of Edmundson, five miles away, brings in nearly $600 a year for every resident in court fines, more than six times the amount in Ferguson.[70] In the nearby town of Bel-Ridge, a traffic light was rigged so that police could change it as people entered the intersection, boosting their city budget by 16 percent.[71] Local officials, including African American officials, defend this exploitative method as an important source of revenue. "You don't dismantle the whole house in order to kill one bug," said Mayor Patrick Green of Normandy, who is Black. He said that his police force had issued more citations since state agencies asked it to help patrol Interstate 70, and that the money had been used to pay for public safety. "Everyone's saying, 'Oh, no, that's cities just taking advantage of the poor,'" he said. "When did the poor get the right to commit crimes?"[72]

The fees and fines, however, are only the beginning of the ways that the criminal justice system traps poor and working-class people. Nearly a third of US states jail people for not paying off their debts, including court-related fees.[73] This is a completely illegal practice. A 1983 Supreme Court decision ruled that people cannot be jailed for being too poor to pay a fine, fee, or debt, but it takes money to challenge illegal practices throughout the criminal justice system. Shifting the tax burden from those with higher incomes to the poor and working class is regressive at best, exploitative and predatory at its worst. When these fees are not paid, they create a legal odyssey from which it can be difficult, if not impossible, for ordinary people to emerge with their finances intact. Forty-eight states have either increased criminal and civil court fees or added new ones.[74] The number of Americans with unpaid fees and fines grows every year. As National Public Radio notes, "In 2011, in Philadelphia alone, courts sent bills on unpaid debts dating back to the 1970s to more than 320,000 people—roughly 1 in 5 city residents. The median debt was around $4,500. And in New York City, there are 1.2 million outstanding warrants, many for unpaid court fines and fees."[75] More fees and fines are incurred as punishment for late payment. The government then has the right to seize property. Eventually there is the threat of arrest—which, of course, results in a new round of fees and fines. According to DOJ statistics, 66 percent of the incarcerated "owed court-imposed costs, restitution, fines and fees," up from 21 percent in 1991.[76]

Alabama has tried to make up for lost revenue by imposing fees, such as $35 for posting bail, and by charging a 30 percent collection fee for debts. There are currently half a dozen lawsuits that contend that local courts in Alabama perpetuate a cycle of fines for minor offenses and jail for those who cannot pay. Florida allows private debt collectors to add a 40 percent surcharge to the original debt. Some Florida counties also use what are called "collection courts," where debtors can be jailed but do not have a right to a public defender. In at least forty-three states, poor people can be billed for using a public defender— meaning that poor defendants may be priced out of legal counsel.[77] In forty-one states, inmates can be charged "room and board" for jail and prison stays. Texas and Wyoming treat truancy as a criminal offense: in Texas, children ages twelve to eighteen can be tried in criminal court for truancy. Ten unexcused absences in six months automatically generate a citation. Children arrested for truancy in Texas are seen as adults in the eyes of the court, meaning that their parents cannot intervene on their behalf. Said one judge, "I realize that some people believe that there should be [court-appointed] representation. Right now the process doesn't provide for that." In 2013 Texas charged 115,782 children with "failure to attend school," generating $16 million in court fees and other fines. A remarkable yet unsurprising 83 percent of those charged were Black or Latino.[78]

§ § §

When New York mayor Bill DeBlasio tepidly criticized police for choking Eric Garner to death in July 2014, the NYPD declared a work slowdown. The slowdown revealed the extent to which the city depends on the police, not only to protect private property but also to expropriate money and property from ordinary citizens. In 2014, New York City handed out roughly 16,000 parking tickets, bringing in $10.4 million a week.[79] The city makes almost a billion dollars a year in court, criminal, and administrative fines for "quality of life" offenses. These effectively amount to a "race tax," as it is nonwhite populations who bear the disproportionate burden of being overpoliced.

Although budget cuts to social programs fuel aspects of the new policing state, the police force appears to be the only public institution that does not have to worry about budget cuts. Even as cities across the country pay out hundreds of millions of dollars to settle lawsuits alleging police brutality, police continue to operate with impunity.[80] In 2014, cash-strapped Chicago paid more than $50 million to settle misconduct suits (not including the $63 million paid to the lawyers litigating the cases).[81] Over the last decade, the city has paid more than half a billion dollars to settle police brutality suits. This does not include the recent $5 million settlement paid to those who survived police torture in the 1970s and 1980s.[82]

Chicago is not alone. In ten years, New York City has paid, on average, $100 million a year—to the tune of $1 billion—to settle police misconduct cases. The Los Angeles Police Department, celebrated by some as an exemplary reformed police department, paid $54 million in 2011 alone to settle lawsuits against brutality and misconduct.[83] Since 1990, the city of Oakland has spent $74 million to settle 417 such lawsuits. Minneapolis has doled out $21 million since 2003.[84] Philadelphia, whose African American police chief, Charles Ramsey, was handpicked by President Barack Obama to lead a national study on reforming policing, has paid out $40 million during Ramsey's tenure to settle lawsuits involving wrongful shooting deaths, illegal searches, and excessive force complaints. As one lawyer who successfully sued the city explained about Philly police, "The rank and file have no expectation that their behavior is ever going to be subject to any real, meaningful review. . . . That becomes admissible evidence that shows the city is not properly supervising and disciplining officers."[85]

Astronomical sums of taxpayer money to settle police brutality and misconduct cases are apparently a given as one of the costs of running a city. Most other public institutions responsible for this kind of debt and malfeasance—hospitals, clinics, libraries, schools—are either privatized or suffer deep budget cuts that threaten their ability to function properly. When the Chicago Public Schools were facing a $1 billion deficit in 2013, Mayor Rahm Emanuel shuttered fifty-four public schools despite the pleas of thousands of parents. Yet rarely, if ever, are police rebuked for costing cities millions of desperately needed public dollars. Instead, they are universally lauded by public officials and shielded from any consequences—including for killing or brutalizing civilians. The free rein of police is a critical component of urban governance today.

This lack of culpability gives some insight into why police default so quickly to killing. American police kill like no other law enforcement agencies in the so-called First World. In only seven years, according to the Bureau of Justice Statistics, the police have killed 7,427 people. It is a stunning number. The same study found that the police were killing an average of 928 people a year.[86] Consider that only fifty-eight American soldiers were killed in Iraq in 2014.[87] In Canada in 2014, seventy-eight people were killed by law enforcement. From 2010 to 2014, police in England killed four people. German police killed no one in 2013 and 2014. China, with a population four and half times the size of the United States, recorded twelve police killings in 2014.[88]

The enormous body count is only a partial picture of the lethality that infuses American law enforcement. Authorities dramatically under-report police killings, when they are even reported at all. According to the *Wall Street Journal*, hundreds of police killings between 2007 and 2012 were never reported to the FBI.[89] The investigation found that, in the 105 largest police agencies, more than 550 police killings were missing from the record. Incredibly, the federal government does not require that police departments report the number, race, or ethnicity of the people they shoot or kill, thus making it impossible to piece together a full picture of the problem. For example, Florida has not reported police killings to the FBI since 1997; New York City has not done so since 2007.[90]

Without accurate tracking, it is impossible to know who exactly is being killed by police. We do know, however, that the disproportionate contact Black men, women, and children have with law enforcement means that they are most likely bearing the brunt of these killings. One 2005 simulation study showed that a group of mostly white male officers in Florida were "more likely to let armed white suspects slip while shooting unarmed black suspects instead."[91] In real life, as well, the police are more likely to shoot or kill Black men more than anyone else. According to a ProPublica study, from 2010 to 2012, young Black men ages fifteen to nineteen were twenty-one times more likely than their white peers to be killed by the police. Police advocates attacked the study, claiming its sample size was too small to make definitive statements about police killings. When the authors went back to measure a wider sample, they discovered that the disparity of police killing young Black men to young white men was getting worse over time. From 2006 to 2008, the risk ratio was 9 to 1. By 2010, it had risen to 17 to 1; by 2012 it had risen to the study's original finding of 21 to 1.[92]

If the estimates of the number of Black people killed by police in the last decade are true, then police have also murdered hundreds of Latinos and thousands of white people. Not only does this constitute a crisis, it also establishes an objective basis upon which a multiracial movement against police terrorism can be organized. The overwhelming racist nature of American policing obscures the range of its reach, but it is in the interests of anti–police brutality activists to point out the specific *and* the generalized nature of police terror.

Conclusion

On March 2, 2015, after ninety days of investigation, President Obama's Task Force on Twenty-First-Century Policing delivered its findings. Obama hastily organized the committee in the heat of the first national waves of protest the previous December to create the appearance that the federal government was responsive to the demands of popular protest—and as a way to get demonstrators off the streets. He met with youth activists and even put some of them on the commission to give it an air of legitimacy. The commission made fifty-eight recommendations, including ending "racial profiling," expanding "community policing," "better training," and "revamping the entire criminal justice system."[93] Its report also called for "independent investigations" into police killings, seeming to ignore that in the cases of Michael

Brown and Trayvon Martin, "independent" investigations had quietly ended with no punishment for the accused. Moreover, "the report did not discuss how to pay for many of these proposals," nor did it clarify which mechanisms would be invoked to make 18,000 law-enforcement agencies comply. Perhaps most tellingly, some 29 days after the report was delivered, the police had already killed another 111 people, 33 more people than had been killed the month before. Also that month, the brutal murder of Walter Scott was captured on video. Scott had been pulled over because of a defective taillight. Fearing arrest, he took off running, only to be shot in the back eight times by white police officer Michael Slager. Slager was arrested and charged with murder, but Scott's death revealed an entrenched pattern.[94] In June 2015, the *Guardian* reported that US police had killed more than 489 people, including 138 African Americans, since January.[95]

Violence and brutality have always defined the police's relationship to African Americans. There is no "golden age" of policing to which elected officials can point, and there is little reason for optimism that American police can truly be reformed. Thus, the Obama administration's examples of "reformed" police departments reveal the poverty of the concept. In May 2015, Obama traveled to Camden, New Jersey, to tout the city as a "symbol of promise for the nation."[96] Obama was not referring to economic health or stability; he was referring to its approach to policing. In 2013, Camden eliminated its 250-officer police force because of malfeasance, corruption, and the expense of unionized cops and replaced it with a force directed by the county. Freed from the police union contract, Camden hired 411 police officers and 120 "civilian clerks" who act as "analysts in a new operations and intelligence center, monitoring 121 surveillance cameras and the gunshot-mapping microphones."[97] Camden's version of community policing has involved more police on foot patrol, with the objective of having a closer relationship with the people in the neighborhoods they are patrolling.

In other respects, Camden is the perfect example of what "police reform" actually looks like. While the politicians and pundits celebrate falling crime rates, they ignore the unsavory underbelly. Over the first year of the "new and improved" approach to policing, Camden had the most complaints of "excessive force" against the police of any municipality in the entire state of New Jersey. According to the ACLU, the number of complaints "exceeded the combined totals reported by the departments in Newark and Jersey City, the two biggest cities in the state with hundreds more officers."[98] Camden police have also fully embraced "broken windows" policing. Summonses for riding a bike without a helmet increased from 3 to 339; summonses for disorderly conduct increased 43 percent, from 1,766 to 2,521; summonses for failure to adequately maintain lights or reflectors in a vehicle increased 421 percent, from 495 to 2,579; and summonses for tinted car windows increased 381 percent, from 197 to 948. The dispersal of tickets has increased the caseload of the Camden Municipal Court by 29 percent—and the fines and fees have begun to flow.[99] What have not changed or been reformed are Camden's depressed economy, its unemployment rate, and its failed housing market. Camden is 95 percent Black and Latino, 42 percent of the city's population lives below the poverty line, and between 30 and 40 percent of the population is unemployed. The median income in Camden is $26,000 a year, compared to $71,000 annually in the rest of New Jersey. The city of 77,000 people is pockmarked with more than 4,000 abandoned properties. The new focus on fees, fines, citations, and arrests for frivolous crimes threatens to increase poverty and unemployment. President Obama, then, said more than he probably even knew when he lauded Camden as a "national symbol."

American policing has changed as policing has become professionalized and better funded, but these changes have not resulted in better or more just policing. There has also been a frightening continuity of racism, exploitation, and abuse, even as police forces across the country have become more diverse and reflective of the communities they patrol. The police function primarily as agents of social control in a society that is fundamentally unequal, which means that they largely operate in poor and working-class communities. Because African Americans have historically been overrepresented in these neighborhoods, they are often the targets of policing. This is even truer today, as the consequences of policing include hundreds of deaths, hundreds of thousands of arrests, and millions of ruined futures when interactions with law enforcement lead to unemployment, criminal records that create chronic unemployability, and all of the social disorder that follows as a result. It is not surprising, then, that policing is always a focal point of Black social protest.

CHAPTER FIVE

Barack Obama:
The End of an Illusion

When an assault rifle is aimed at your face over nothing more than a refusal to move, you don't feel like the American experience is one that includes you. When the president your generation selected does not condemn these attacks, you suddenly begin to believe that this system is a fraudulent hoax—and the joke is on you. Racism is very much alive in America, but as a president with so much melanin in his skin, you seem to address it very bashfully.

—Tef Poe, "Dear Mr. President: A Letter
from Tef Poe," December 1, 2014

For more than a hundred days, a patchwork group of ordinary people-turned-activists had kept Mike Brown's name alive and held out hope that their protests would result in the indictment of Darren Wilson. Within a matter of minutes those hopes vanished into the November night, as the grand jury's decision not to indict Wilson was announced. One week later while the fires were still smoldering and the bitterness still lingered, hip-hop artist and St. Louis native Tef Poe sent an open letter to President Obama that spoke for a generation of young, Black people who had believed deeply in the promise of the president. He wrote,

I speak for a large demographic of us that has long awaited our Black president to speak in a direct tone while condemning our murders. From our perspective, the statement you made on Ferguson completely played into the racist connotations that we are violent, uneducated, welfare-recipient looters. Your remarks in support of the National Guard attacks upon us and our community devoured our dignity.[1]

Yes We Can?

The hope and optimism that coursed through Black America in anticipation of Obama's victory as the first Black president in 2008 seemed a million miles away. Even while Black people endured the effects of the 2008 economic crisis, particularly the continuation of home foreclosures and double-digit unemployment, there was optimism that Obama's election could change the course. Even before Obama was elected, there had been great optimism about what a Black presidency could mean for American racial politics. National Public Radio hosted a roundtable titled "A New, 'Post-Racial' Political Era in America" several months before the 2008 election.[2]

President Obama turned out to be very different from candidate Obama, who had stage-managed his campaign to resemble something closer to a social movement. In the heated race for the Democratic nomination, Obama distinguished himself from establishment candidate Hillary Clinton by campaigning clearly against the war in Iraq and vowing to shut down the Guantánamo military internment camp. He spoke of economic inequality and connected with young people who were underwhelmed at the prospect of voting for yet another old, white windbag in John McCain. Black people's enthusiasm for the Obama campaign cannot be reduced to racial solidarity or recrimination. Obama electrified his audiences:

> We've been asked to pause for a reality check. We've been warned against offering the people of this nation false hope. But in the unlikely story that is America, there has never been anything false about hope. For when we have faced down impossible odds, when we've been told we're not ready or that we shouldn't try or that we can't, generations of Americans have responded with a simple creed that sums up the spirit of a people: Yes, we can. Yes, we can. Yes, we can.

It was a creed written into the founding documents that declared the destiny of a nation: Yes, we can. It was whispered by slaves and abolitionists as they blazed a trail towards freedom through the darkest of nights: Yes, we can. It was sung by immigrants as they struck out from distant shores and pioneers who pushed westward against an unforgiving wilderness: Yes, we can. It was the call of workers who organized, women who reached for the ballot, a president who chose the moon as our new frontier, and a king who took us to the mountaintop and pointed the way to the promised land: Yes, we can, to justice and equality.

Yes, we can, to opportunity and prosperity. Yes, we can heal this nation. Yes, we can repair this world. Yes, we can.[3]

In March 2008 Obama finally gave a comprehensive speech on race, in which he pulled off the feat of addressing the concerns of African Americans while calming the fears of white voters. That he broached the topic at all meant his speech was wildly misinterpreted by liberals and the mainstream media alike as further left of center than it actually was. For example, David Corn, writing for *Mother Jones*, described Obama's speech as "trying to show the nation a pathway to a society free of racial gridlock and denial. . . . Obama was not playing the race card. He was shooting the moon."[4] Obama had been pressured for weeks to rebuke his pastor, the Reverend Jeremiah Wright, who had delivered a sermon titled "God Damn America," referring to the wrong the United States had committed in the world. Obama's political enemies had unearthed the sermon and tried to attribute Wright's ideas to Obama. Obama used his platform in Philadelphia to distance himself from Wright, whom he described as "divisive" and with a "profoundly distorted view of this country." He went on to contextualize Wright's angry comments and condemnations as based on his coming of age in a United States where

> legalized discrimination—where blacks were prevented, often through violence, from owning property, or loans were not granted to African-American business owners, or black homeowners could not access FHA mortgages, or blacks were excluded from unions or the police force or the fire department—meant that black families could not amass any meaningful wealth to bequeath to future generations.[5]

No one running for president of the United States had ever spoken so directly about the history of racism in government and society at large. Yet Obama's speech also counseled that a more perfect United States required African Americans "taking full responsibility for our own lives . . . by demanding more from our fathers, and spending more time with our children, and reading to them, and teaching them that while they may face challenges and discrimination in their own lives, they must never succumb to despair or cynicism; they must always believe that they can write their own destiny." Obama couched his comments in the language of American progress and the vitality of the American dream, but the speech was remarkable nonetheless in the theater of American politics, where cowardice and empty rhetoric are the typical fare. In that sense Obama broke the mold, but he also established the terms upon which he would engage race matters—with dubious evenhandedness, even in response to events that required decisive action on behalf of the racially aggrieved. He spoke quite eloquently about the nation's "original sin" and "dark history," but has repeatedly failed to connect the sins of the past to the crimes of the present, where racism—albeit often without epithet or insult—thrives when police stop-and-frisk, when subprime loans are reserved for Black buyers, when public schools are denied resources, and when double-digit unemployment has become so normal that it barely registers a ripple of recognition. A healthy cynicism runs especially deep among young African Americans: In 2006, 52 percent of Black youth (ages eighteen to twenty-five) described the US government as "unresponsive" to Black needs, while 61 percent said they had experienced discrimination when looking for work and 54 percent believed that Black youth receive a "poorer education" than white youth.[6]

Before Ferguson, Obama's Philadelphia speech was as close as he had ever come to speaking truthfully about racism in the United States, even though he presented himself as an interested observer, a thoughtful interlocutor between African Americans and the nation as a whole, rather than a US senator with the political influence to effect the changes of which he spoke. Obama would continue in his role as "informed observer" even as president. We are led to believe that a man who can direct drone strikes in the mountains of Pakistan and Afghanistan, who can mobilize resources to any corner of the world in the name of American foreign policy, is powerless to champion legislation and the enforcement of existing laws and rights in the interest of racial justice.

In the context of the 2008 election, eight years after the Republicans stole the White House by disenfranchising Black voters in Florida and three years after Hurricane Katrina, Obama's reluctant candor on race matters felt like a sea change. Political scientist Cathy Cohen identified Hurricane Katrina as a radicalizing event in the lives of Black youth, similar to the impact of the Rodney King beating on the previous generation.[7] The federal government's absence in New Orleans as thousands of Black people drowned dramatically pierced its post-9/11 declarations of national unity in the face of terrorism. While the American government had moved heaven and earth to rain war across the Middle East against an "axis of evil," its shocking indifference to Black suffering inside the United States was a stark reminder of how little had actually changed. As actor Danny Glover so poignantly said, "When the hurricane struck the Gulf and the floodwaters rose and tore through New Orleans, plunging its remaining population into a carnival of misery, it did not turn the region into a Third World country, as it has been disparagingly implied in the media; it revealed one. It revealed the disaster within the disaster; grueling poverty rose to the surface like a bruise to our skin."[8]

Shortly after Katrina struck, tens of thousands of mostly Black college students marched in the small town of Jena, Louisiana, to protest a racist attack on Black high school students there. Their activism did not mark the beginning of a movement, but they uncovered the persistence of racial inequality. Since September 11, wars and occupation had foreclosed the space for protest or even for articulating inequality, but Katrina exposed to the world that the United States was still the same old racist empire. Jena helped to revive a tradition of marching and protesting that had been decidedly muted. As Cohen argues, "For many in black communities, mobilization around the Jena Six reignited the hope that black politics—as it is often imagined and conceptualized: that is extrasystemic, collective, movement politics— is still alive among the younger generation of black Americans."[9]

Generation O

The themes of "hope" and "change" tapped into optimism that the future could be different and better. Hip-hop artist Young Jeezy lyricized,

"Obama for mankind, we ready for damn change so y'all let the man shine!" Khari Mosely, a Democratic Party ward chair in Pittsburgh, described Obama's effect on the "so-called 'lost' generation of inner-city youth . . . young guys with the oversized baseball caps, low-hanging pants and colorful sneakers . . . who, through him, have rediscovered a sense of purpose in themselves and of faith in this nation."[10] Jay-Z linked Obama's run to a longer narrative of Black struggle: "Rosa sat so Martin could walk; Martin walked so Obama could run; Obama is running so we all can fly!"[11] Rap mogul Sean Combs said, "I'm not trying to be dramatic, but I just felt like, Martin Luther King, and I felt the whole civil rights movement, I felt all that energy, and I felt my kids. It was all there at one time. It was a joyous moment."[12]

Black voters' enthusiasm for Obama was spelled out in the election returns. An unprecedented number, across all ages and genders, voted to put Obama in the White House. There were two million more Black voters in 2008 than in 2004.[13] Overall, 64 percent of eligible Black voters voted in the 2008 presidential election, including 68 percent of eligible African American women voters, produced the highest turnout in a presidential election since 1968.[14] But it was young Black voters who put Obama over the top. According to the Pew Research Center, the Black youth vote created the highest turnout among young voters from any ethnic group in US election history. Black millennials had the highest voter turnout "in the nation's history."[15] "I feel happy and optimistic when I see Barack and Michelle. They give me hope, and the kids I teach hope, for something better," said one woman.[16] By 2012, for the first time ever, the percentage of Black voter turnout eclipsed that of white voter turnout in a presidential election, 66 percent compared to 64 percent.

The excitement about Obama turned into postelection euphoria. That was certainly the feeling in Chicago on election night, when a cross-section of the city converged in Grant Park to hear the country's first Black president-elect address the nation. It was a rare, almost strange scene to see a multiracial crowd gathered in Chicago, one of the most segregated cities in the United States. That was the power of Obama's calls for hope and change. On the eve of President Obama's inauguration, 69 percent of Black respondents told CNN pollsters that Martin Luther King's vision had been "fulfilled."[17] In early 2011, asked whether they expected their children's standard of living to be better or worse than their own, 60 percent of Blacks chose "better," compared with only 36 percent of whites.[18] This was not just blind hope: it was the expectation that things would, in fact, be better. One researcher described the broader context: "Certainly, the Obama presidency has fueled euphoria in black circles. But even before Obama came on the scene, optimism was building—most notably among a new generation of black achievers who refused to believe they would be stymied by the bigotry that bedeviled their parents. Obama's election was, in effect, the final revelation—the long awaited sign that a new American age had arrived."[19] "Now we have a sense of future," said Yale sociologist Elijah Anderson. "All of a sudden you have a stake. That stake is extremely important. If you have a stake, now there's risk—you realize the consequences of compromising an unknowable future."[20] Almost 75 percent of African Americans in the South said that Obama would help America rid itself of racial prejudice.[21] *Forbes* ran an enthusiastic editorial opinion in December 2008 titled "Racism in America Is Over."[22]

Shots Ring Out

In the first hours of the new year, just weeks before Obama was to be inaugurated as the next president, shots rang out. It was a reminder that, as bright as the future seemed, the past was never far behind. An armed transit officer named Johannes Mehserle shot an unarmed twenty-two-year-old Black man who lay face down in handcuffs on a public transportation platform. His name was Oscar Grant. Dozens of witnesses, many of whom were returning to Oakland after New Year's Eve celebrations, watched in horror as Grant was murdered in cold blood. His murder was captured on several smartphone video cameras. Black Oakland exploded in palpable anger, with hundreds, then thousands of people taking to the streets, demanding justice.

Perhaps this outcry would have happened under any circumstance, but the brutality of Grant's murder in the few weeks before the nation's first Black president was to take office felt like a shock of cold water. Police brutality and even murder had been a long fact of life in Oakland, California. But the United States was supposed to have entered into a postracial parallel universe. A local movement, led by Grant's family and friends, unfolded across the Bay Area to demand that prosecutors charge and try Mehserle. Protests, marches, campus activism, public forums, and organizing meetings sustained enough pressure to force local officials to charge Mehserle with murder. It was the first murder trial of a California police officer for a "line-of-duty" killing in fifteen years. In the end, Mehserle spent less than a year in prison, but the local movement foreshadowed events to come.

Obama's surprising electoral victory was beginning to lose its luster in the twilight of his first term. Obama has and will always poll high among African Americans, but that should not be mistaken for blind support for him or the policies he champions. As long as members of the Republican Party treat Obama in a brazenly racist manner, Black people will defend him because they understand that those attacks against Obama serve as a proxy for attacks on them. Early in his administration, however, with the full effects of the recession still pulsing in Black communities, conflict between the Black president and his base could be detected. Black America was in the midst of an "economic free fall" and with it the disappearance of Black wealth. As Black unemployment was climbing into the high double digits, civil rights leaders asked Obama if he would craft policies to address Black joblessness. He responded, "I have a special responsibility to look out for the interests of every American. That's my job as president of the United States. And I wake up every morning trying to promote the kinds of policies that are going to make the biggest difference for the most number of people so that they can live out their American dream."[23] It was a disappointing response, even if that disappointment did not manifest in his approval ratings. In 2011, with Black unemployment above 13 percent, 86 percent of Blacks approved of the overall job the president was doing, but 56 percent expressed disappointment in the "area of providing proper oversight for Wall Street and the big banks."[24] Only half of Blacks said Obama's policies had improved the nation's economic condition. For African Americans, Obama's presidency had been largely defined by his reluctance to engage with and directly address the ways that racial discrimination was blunting the impact of his administration's recovery efforts.

Obama has not shown nearly the same reticence when publicly chastising African Americans for a range of behaviors that read like a handbook on anti-Black stereotypes, from parenting skills and dietary choices to sexual mores and television-watching habits. These public admonishments work to close off the political space within which African Americans can express legitimate grievances about an economic recovery that has offered material relief to bankers and auto executives but only moral uplift to Black people. Their cries for relief have been met with quips that Obama is "not the president of Black America." Vann Newkirk, a self-described member of "Generation O," spoke for many when he wrote, "The Great Recession left us saddled with debt, deprived of savings, overeducated and underemployed, and deeply dissatisfied with the dissonance between American ethos and reality. Even now, in the midst of a recovery, we make up 40 percent of all unemployed individuals, still have a double-digit unemployment rate, and struggle with savings and debt."[25]

There is something disingenuous in focusing on poor and working-class Blacks without any discussion about the ways that the criminal justice system has "disappeared" Black parents from the lives of their children. When Obama talks about absentee Black fathers, he never mentions the disparity in arrests and sentencing that is responsible for the disproportionate number of missing Black men. Few media discussions about Obama's candidacy mentioned curbing the nation's criminal justice system's voracious appetite for Black bodies, but the scars of "law and order" were all over the Black body politic: a million African Americans incarcerated; 10 percent of the Black formerly incarcerated prevented from voting; and one in four of Black men (in the age group twenty to twenty-nine) are under control of the criminal justice system. "Postracial" America was disappearing under an avalanche of disparities throughout the criminal justice system.

Over the course his first term, Obama paid no special attention to the mounting issues involving law enforcement and imprisonment, even as Michelle Alexander's *The New Jim Crow* described the horrors that mass incarceration and corruption throughout the legal system had inflicted on Black families. None of this began with Obama, but it would be naive to think that African Americans were not considering the destructive impact of policing and incarceration when they turned out in droves to elect him. His unwillingness to address the effects of structural inequality eroded younger African Americans' confidence in the transformative capacity of his presidency. As Newkirk put it:

The jubilation that I felt: the jumping for joy; the tears. They were not just my own but those of people who'd marched before me. The experience was spiritual.

But that idealism soon eroded. What we didn't expect was the false dream of blind post-race would supplant and masquerade as the dream of post-racism. . . . The alternating currents of willful ignorance of racial issues and virulent racist responses to the president frustrated many black millennials, especially those indoctrinated on Obama's progressive ideal of hope. We were left struggling to find a way to voice our concerns when the momentum of the campaign ended.[26]

The American Spring

There was one moment when Black America collectively came to terms with Barack Obama's refusal to use his position as president to intervene on behalf of African Americans. Troy Davis was a Black man on death row in the state of Georgia. It was widely believed that he had been wrongfully convicted, and in the fall of 2011 he was facing execution for a crime he had not committed. Davis's cries of innocence were not a voice in the wilderness: for years he and his sister, Martina Davis-Corriea, had joined with anti-death-penalty activists to fight for his life and exoneration. By September 2011, an international campaign was under way to have him removed from death row. The protests grew larger and more frantic as the death date crept closer. There were protests around the world; support from global dignitaries rolled in as the international movement to stop Davis's execution took shape. The European Union and the governments of France and Germany implored the United States to halt his execution, as did Amnesty International and former FBI director William Sessions. A Democrat in the Georgia Senate, Vincent Fort, called on those charged with carrying out the execution to refuse: "We call on the members of the Injection Team: Strike! Do not follow your orders! Do not start the flow of the lethal injection chemicals. If you refuse to participate, you make it that much harder for this immoral execution to be carried out."[27] As Davis's execution drew near on the evening of September 20, people from around the world waited for Obama to say or do something—but, in the end, he did nothing. He never even made a statement, instead sending press secretary Jay Carney to deliver a statement on his behalf, which simply noted that it was not "appropriate" for the president to intervene in a state-led prosecution. In the end, the Black president succumbed to states' rights.[28] One Black observer captured the disappointment: "President Obama gives opinions on everything that's safe and what he thinks America wants to hear, but he straddles the fence on issues important to African Americans."[29] It was a moment of awakening for Generation O—and of newfound understanding of the limits of Black presidential power, not because Obama could not intervene, as his handlers insisted, but because he refused to do so. Johnetta Elzie, one of the best known of the Ferguson activists, told a reporter that Davis's execution "hurt me . . . that was the first time I'd ever been hurt by something happening to a stranger."[30]

The Troy Davis protests were certainly not in vain. The day after the state of Georgia murdered Davis, Amnesty International and the Campaign to End the Death Penalty called for a "Day of Outrage" in protest. More than a thousand people marched, eventually making their way to a small encampment on Wall Street that was calling itself "Occupy Wall Street." The Occupy encampment had begun a week or so before Davis was killed, but it was in its fledgling stages. When the Troy Davis activists converged with the Occupy activists, the protestors made an immediate connection between Occupy's mobilization against inequality and the injustice in the execution of a working-class Black man. After the march, many who had been activated by the protests for Davis stayed and became a part of the Occupy encampment on Wall Street. Thereafter, a popular chant on the Occupy marches was "We are all Troy Davis."[31]

Protests to save the life of death-row inmate Troy Davis and the electrifying Occupy Wall Street protests in 2011 seemed to signify the beginning of the "American Spring." Obama's refusal to intervene for Davis and the Republican victories in the 2010 midterm elections signaled that the progressive window many activists believed had been opened by the 2008 electoral victories had now slammed shut. The protest movement lost and Davis was executed.

The Occupy movement, by contrast, would develop into the most important political expression of the US class divide in more than a generation. The slogan "We are the 99 percent" and the movement's articulation of the divide between the "1 percent" and the rest of us offered a materialist, structural understanding of American inequality. In a country that regularly denies the existence of class or economic inequality, this was a critical step toward making sense of the limited reach of the American dream. Occupy's close proximity to the protests for Troy Davis highlighted the entanglement of racial and economic inequality. Support for Occupy was higher among Blacks than among the general population, with 45 percent expressing a "positive" view of Occupy and another 35 percent saying the movement had been good for the American "political system."[32] Despite the movement's difficulties in coherently expressing the relationship between economic and racial inequality, its focus on government's bailouts for private enterprise while millions of ordinary people bore the weight of unemployment, foreclosures, and evictions addressed some of the most important issues affecting African Americans. It was hard to ignore that Black homeowners had been left to fend for themselves.

The media seized on descriptions of Occupy as "white," which diminished hard-fought and sometimes successful efforts to bring more African Americans into the movement. The Occupy movement was mostly white, overall, and at one point various currents within it debated whether or not the police should be considered a part of the "99 percent." However, the movement varied from city to city. In some cities there were very few Blacks, Latino/as, and other people of color involved, but Oakland activists named their encampment after Oscar Grant, and Atlanta activists named theirs after Troy Davis. Occupy Wall Street in New York had a "people of color working group" whose entire purpose was to organize around antiracist issues with the intent of drawing more Blacks and other people of color into the movement. Occupy Chicago organized teach-ins called "Racism in Chicago," "Our Enemies in Blue," and "Evictions and Foreclosures."

Most significantly, Black Occupy activists organized "Occupy the Hood," whose goal was to raise the profile of the Occupy movement in communities of color across the country and widen the range of people involved. Some "Occupy the Hood" organizers had also been involved in organizing against "stop-and-frisk." Thus, not only did Occupy popularize economic and class inequality in the United States by demonstrating against corporate greed, fraud, and corruption throughout the finance industry, it also helped to make connections between those issues and racism. The public discussion over economic inequality rendered incoherent both Democratic and Republican politicians' insistence on locating Black poverty in Black culture. While it obviously did not bury the arguments for culture and "personal responsibility," Occupy helped to create the space for alternative explanations within mainstream politics, including seeing Black poverty and inequality as products of the system. The vicious attack and crackdown on the unarmed and peaceful Occupy encampments over the winter and into 2012 also provided a lesson about policing in the United States: the police were servants of the political establishment and the ruling elite. Not only were they racist, they were also shock troops for the status quo and bodyguards for the 1 percent.

From Trayvon to the Future

The murder of Trayvon Martin in Sanford, Florida, in the winter of 2012 was a turning point. Like the murder of Emmett Till nearly fifty-seven years earlier, Martin's death pierced the delusion that the United States was postracial. Till was the young boy who, on his summer vacation in Mississippi in 1955, was lynched by white men for an imagined racial transgression. Till's murder showed the world the racist brutality pulsing in the heart of the "world's greatest democracy." To emphasize the point, his mother, Mamie, opted for an open-casket funeral to show the world how her son had been mutilated and murdered in the "land of the free." Martin's crime was walking home in a hoodie, talking on the phone and minding his own business. George Zimmerman, now a well-known menace but then portrayed as an aspiring security guard, racially profiled Martin, telling the 911 operator, "This guy looks like he's up to no good, or he's on drugs or something."[33] The "guy" was a seventeen-year-old boy walking home from a convenience store. Zimmerman followed the boy, confronted him, and eventually shot him in the chest, killing him shortly thereafter. When the police came, they accepted Zimmerman's account. Martin was Black and the default assumption was that he was the aggressor—so they treated him as such. They tagged him as a "John Doe" and made no effort to find out if he lived in the neighborhood or was missing. But the story began to trickle through the news media and, as more details became public, it was clear that Martin had been the victim of an extrajudicial killing. Trayvon Martin had been lynched.

Within weeks, marches, demonstrations, and protests bubbled up across the country. The demand was simple: arrest George Zimmerman for the murder of Trayvon Martin. The anger was fueled, in part at least, by the overwhelming double standard: if Martin had been white and Zimmerman Black, Zimmerman would have faced immediate arrest, if not worse. Instead, the case showed the deadly consequences of racial profiling and of the alternating fear and disgust of Black boys and men that allowed the police to try to sweep the matter under the rug. The protests were national, as they had been for Troy Davis, but they were much more widespread. This was the impact of Occupy, which had relegitimized street protests, occupations, and direct action in general. Many of the Occupy activists who had been dispersed by police repression the previous winter found a new home in the growing fight for justice for Martin. Protests in Florida and New York City reached into the thousands, with smaller protests in cities across the country.

The legal inaction around Martin's murder on the local, state, and federal levels demonstrated the racist hysteria that prevailed throughout American society. Martin was not a suspect because he had actually done anything suspicious; he was just Black. For weeks, President Obama deflected questions, commenting only that it was a local case. It took more than a month for Obama to finally speak publicly about the case, famously saying, "If I had a son, he'd look like Trayvon. . . . When I think about this boy, I think about my own kids." But he also said, "I think every parent in America should be able to understand why it is absolutely imperative that we investigate every aspect of this, and that everybody pulls together—federal, state and local—to figure out exactly how this tragedy happened."[34]

Obama could not come out and say the obvious, but the fact that he spoke at all was evidence of the growing momentum of the street protests that had been building for weeks. Martin's murder was a national and international embarrassment. Black people may have understood that Obama could not lead a social movement against police brutality as the president, but how could he not use his seat to amplify Black pain and anger? Though everyone applauded his personal touch, Obama was signaling that the federal government would stay out of the "local" matter. But it was exactly for moments like these that Black people had put Obama in the White House. "We had hope riding—we got Barack Obama elected and got him reelected, but this is still happening. That's kind of like saying, you knew the system hated you, and now, whatever speculation you had about it, even though Barack's in office, you have to check yourself," said poet Frankiem Nicoli.[35]

It is impossible to know or predict when a particular moment is transformed into a movement. Forty-five days after George Zimmerman murdered Trayvon Martin in cold blood, he was finally arrested. It was the outcome of weeks of protests, marches, and demonstrations, many of which had been organized through social media, beyond the conservatizing control of establishment civil rights organizations. Parents, families, and friends of others killed by police, like Alan Blueford, Ramarley Graham, James Rivera, Danroy "DJ" Henry, and Rekia Boyd, fought alongside local activists to bring attention to the murders of their children and loved ones.

I wrote that summer of the gathering tension over unpunished killings by police:

> If the police continue to kill Black men and women with impunity, the kind of urban rebellions that shook American society in the 1960s are a distinct possibility. This isn't the 1960s, but the 21st century—and with a Black president and a Black attorney general serving in Washington, people surely expect more. Meanwhile, in a matter of a few days in late July, near-riots broke out in Southern California and Dallas after police, growing more brazen in their disregard for Black and brown life, executed young men in broad daylight, out in the open for all to see. . . . There's a growing feeling of being fed up with the vicious racism and brutality of cops across the country and the pervasive silence that shrouds it—and people are beginning to rise against it.[36]

In the summer of 2013, more than a year after his arrest, George Zimmerman was found not guilty of the murder of Trayvon Martin. His exoneration crystallized the burden of Black people: even in death, Martin would be vilified as a "thug" and an aggressor, Zimmerman portrayed as his victim. The judge even instructed both parties that the phrase "racial profiling" could not be mentioned in the courtroom, let alone used to explain why Zimmerman had targeted Martin.[37]

President Obama addressed the nation, saying, "I know this case has elicited strong passions. And in the wake of the verdict, I know those passions may be running even higher. But we are a nation of laws, and a jury has spoken. We should ask ourselves, as individuals and as a society, how we can prevent future tragedies like this. As citizens, that's a job for all of us."[38] What does it mean to be a "nation of laws" when the law is applied inequitably? There is a dual system of criminal justice—one for African Americans and one for whites. The result is the discriminatory disparities in punishment that run throughout all aspects of American jurisprudence. George Zimmerman benefited from this dual system: he was allowed to walk free for weeks before protests pressured officials into arresting him. He was not subjected to drug tests, though Trayvon Martin's dead body had been. This double standard undermined public proclamations that the United States is a nation built around the rule of law. Obama's call for quiet, individual soul-searching was a way of saying that he had no answers.

For Generation O, this response illustrated the limits of Black political power. FM Supreme, a young Black hip-hop and spoken-word artist from Chicago, described the meaning of Zimmerman's exoneration:

> When they announced it, it felt like a movie. . . . I just was like, man, this is fucked up. Are you kidding me? I wasn't really surprised, but I wasn't prepared for that. Overall, the decision that was made reinforces that the United States of America has no value for the life of Black people. . . . How they demonized Trayvon Martin, how they were prodding his dead body to see if he had drugs in his system—they don't value us. They didn't check to see if George Zimmerman had drugs in his system. . . . We gotta move. We've got to take action. Specifically, we've got to holler at Stand Your Ground. We need to address racism in America. We need to hit them economically. And so we have to come up with a strategy. We need to recall Emmett Till and how after his death, there was Rosa Parks and the bus boycotts.[39]

Almost two years after Zimmerman was acquitted, the DOJ quietly announced it would file no federal charges against him. Martin's mother, Sybrina Fulton, said, "What we want is accountability, we want somebody to be arrested, we want somebody to go to jail, of course."[40]

The acquittal did not spell the end of the movement; it showed all the reasons it needed to grow.[41] Out of despair over the verdict, community organizer Alicia Garza posted a simple hashtag on Face-book: "#blacklivesmatter." It was a powerful rejoinder that spoke di-rectly to the dehumanization and criminalization that made Martin seem suspicious in the first place and allowed the police to make no effort to find out to whom this boy belonged. It was a response to the oppression, inequality, and discrimination that devalue Black life every day. It was everything, in three simple words.[42] Garza would go on, with fellow activists Patrisse Cullors and Opal Tometi, to transform the slogan into an organization with the same name: #BlackLivesMat-ter. In a widely read essay on the meaning of the slogan and the hopes for their new organization, Garza described #BlackLivesMatter as "an ideological and political intervention in a world where Black lives are systematically and intentionally targeted for demise. It is an affirma-tion of Black folks' contributions to this society, our humanity, and our resilience in the face of deadly oppression."[43]

Zimmerman's acquittal also inspired the formation of the import-ant Black Youth Project 100 (BYP 100), centered in Chicago. Charlene Carruthers, its national coordinator, said of the verdict, "I don't believe the pain was a result, necessarily, of shock because Zimmerman was found not guilty . . . but of yet another example . . . of an injustice being validated by the state—something that black people were used to."[44] In Florida, the scene of the crime, Umi Selah (formerly known as Phillip Agnew) and friends formed the Dream Defenders; for thirty-one days they occupied the office of Florida governor Rick Scott in protest of the verdict. Selah said, "I saw George Zimmerman celebrating, and I remember just feeling a huge, huge, huge . . . collapse. . . . I'll never for-get that moment . . . because we didn't even expect that verdict to come down that night, and definitely didn't expect for it to be not guilty."[45] Selah quit his job as a pharmaceutical salesman to organize full time.[46]

No one knew who would be the next Trayvon, but the increas-ing use of smartphone recording devices and social media seemed to quicken the pace at which incidents of police brutality became public. These tools being in the hands of ordinary citizens meant that families of victims were no longer dependent on the mainstream media's interest: they could take their case straight to the public. Meanwhile, the forma-tion of organizations dedicated to fighting racism through mass mobili-zations, street demonstrations, and other direct actions was evidence of a newly developing Black left that could vie for leadership against more established—and more tactically and politically conservative—forces. The Black political establishment, led by President Barack Obama, had shown over and over again that it was not capable of the most basic task: keeping Black children alive. The young people would have to do it themselves.

CHAPTER SIX

Black Lives Matter:
A Movement, Not a Moment

What happened to my daughter was unjust. It was unjust. It was re-
ally unjust. I've been through all the range of emotions that I can go
through, concerning this. But I will not stop, as all of the rest of the
mothers have said, until I get some answers.

—**Cassandra Johnson**, mother of Tanisha Anderson,
killed by Cleveland police in 2014

Every movement needs a catalyst, an event that captures people's experiences and draws them out from their isolation into a collective force with the power to transform social conditions. Few could have predicted that white police officer Darren Wilson shooting Mike Brown would ignite a rebellion in a small, largely unknown Missouri suburb called Ferguson. For reasons that may never be clear, Brown's death was a breaking point for the African Americans of Ferguson— but also for hundreds of thousands of Black people across the United States. Perhaps it was the inhumanity of the police leaving Brown's body to fester in the hot summer sun for four and a half hours after killing him, keeping his parents away at gunpoint and with dogs. "We was treated like we wasn't parents, you know?" Mike Brown Sr., said. "That's what I didn't understand. They sicced dogs on us. They wouldn't let us identify his body. They pulled guns on us."[1] Maybe it was the military hardware the police brandished when protests against Brown's death arose. With tanks and machine guns and a never-ending supply of tear gas, rubber bullets, and swinging batons, the Ferguson police department declared war on Black residents and anyone who stood in solidarity with them.

Since then, hundreds more protests have erupted. As the United States celebrates various fiftieth anniversaries of the Black freedom struggles of the 1960s, the truth about the racism and brutality of the police has broken through the veil of segregation that has shrouded it from public view. There have been periodic ruptures in the domestic quietude that is so often misinterpreted as the docility of American democracy: the brutal beating of Rodney King, the sodomy of Abner Louima, the execution of Amadou Diallo. These beatings and murders did not lead to a national movement, but they were not forgotten. As Ferguson protestor Zakiya Jemmott said, "My first protest was in 1999, when Amadou Diallo was murdered by police. I haven't seen any changes and have not changed my perception of police officers."[2]

It is impossible to answer, and perhaps futile to ask, the question "why Ferguson?" just as it's impossible ever to accurately calculate when "enough is enough." The transformation of Mike Brown's murder from a police killing into a lynching certainly tipped the scales. Writer Charles Pierce captured what many felt: "Dictators leave bodies in the street. Petty local satraps leave bodies in the street. Warlords leave bodies in the street. Those are the places where they leave bodies in the street, as object lessons, or to make a point, or because there isn't the money to take the bodies away and bury them, or because nobody gives a damn whether they are there or not."[3] In the hours after Brown's body was finally moved, residents erected a makeshift memorial of teddy bears and memorabilia on the spot where police had left his body. When the police arrived with a canine unit, one officer let a dog urinate on the memorial. Later, when Brown's mother, Lesley McSpadden, laid out rose petals in the form of his initials, a police cruiser whizzed by, crushing the memorial and scattering the flowers.[4] The next evening, McSpadden and other friends and family went back to the memorial site and laid down a dozen roses. Again, a police cruiser came through and destroyed the flowers.[5] Later that night, the uprising began.

The police response to the uprising was intended to repress and punish the population, who had dared to defy their authority. It is difficult to interpret in any other way their injudicious use of tear gas, rubber bullets, and persistent threats of violence against an unarmed, civilian population. The Ferguson police, a 95 percent white and male force, obscured their badges to hide their identities, wore wristbands proclaiming "I AM DARREN WILSON," and pointed live weapons at unarmed civilians engaged in legal demonstrations. The municipality resembled a rogue state, creating arbitrary rules governing public protests and assaulting the media, as both an act of revenge and an attempt to hide the sheer brutality of its operation. In the twelve days following Brown's death, 172 people were arrested, 132 of whom were charged only with "failure to disperse." At one point during the demonstrations, a Ferguson officer pointed his AR-15 semiautomatic rifle in the direction of a group of journalists and screamed, "I'm going to fucking kill you!" When someone asked, "What's your name, sir?" He screamed, "Go fuck yourself!"[6] For a moment, the brutal realities of Black life in Ferguson were exposed for all to see.

Black protestors went on to unmask the kleptocracy at the heart of municipal operations in Ferguson, revealing that the Ferguson police department, directed by the mayor and city council, were targeting the Black population as the major source of revenue for the town (see chapter 4). Black households were inundated with fines, fees, citations, tickets, and arrests to such an extent that the revenues were the town's second leading source of revenue. Court fines deriving from motor-vehicle violations were 21 percent of revenue, accounting for "the equivalent of more than 81 percent of police salaries before overtime."[7] Failure to pay or appear in court to respond to tickets instantly produced an arrest warrant. Emails between city administrators openly called for more. In March 2013, the finance director wrote to the city manager, "Court fees are anticipated to rise about 7.5%. I did ask the Chief if he thought the PD [police department] could deliver 10%. He indicated he could try."[8] By December 2014, the department had 16,000 outstanding arrest warrants, mostly for minor offenses.[9] Ninety-five percent of traffic stops were directed at Black drivers. As the DOJ report said, "Ferguson law enforcement practices are directly shaped and perpetuated by racial bias."[10] Black people in Ferguson were living under the near complete domination of the police.

Indeed, as the daily protests went on, the Ferguson police's escalating brutality and lawlessness seemed to arise out of frustration that they could not make the Black men and women of Ferguson submit. Quentin Baker, a nineteen-year-old from St. Louis, observed that "all of these things happen after the police provoke it. What they want to do is impose their will."[11] Just as residents rebuilt the memorials for Mike Brown within hours every time the police tried to destroy them, the same dynamic held for the protests. Every night the police used tear gas and rubber bullets to disperse the crowd; the next day, the crowds would reemerge. Ferguson activist Johnetta Elzie described how the protestors were changing even in the face of "unthinkable" police violence:

> I became less of a peaceful protester and more of an active one. Using my voice to chant loudly along with other protesters seemed to be enough but it wasn't. Instead, I decided to yell directly at the police. I decided to dare the police to look at the faces of the babies and children their dogs were so ready to chase down. As more people began to look directly at the police and yell their grievances, the more aggravated they became.[12]

Protestor Dontey Carter said, "I've been down here since the first day. . . . We all had the same pain and anger about this. We all came together that day. . . . They're killing us, and it's not right."[13]

Carter's words addressed the urgency of a summer that had turned into a killing season. Just weeks before Mike Brown was shot, the world had watched video of New York City cop Daniel Pantaleo choking the life out of Eric Garner. Four days before Brown was killed, the police struck in a suburb of Dayton, Ohio. John Crawford III, a twenty-two-year-old, unarmed African American man, was killed in the aisle of a Walmart while he talked on the phone with the mother of his children. Crawford had been holding a toy gun. Even though Ohio is an "open carry" state where citizens are allowed to carry unconcealed guns, local police opened fire on Crawford with little to no warning, killing him.[14] Two days after Brown's murder, police in Los Angeles shot unarmed Ezell Ford three times in the back as he lay face down on the sidewalk. The following day, elsewhere in California, Dante Parker, a thirty-six-year-old African American man, was detained by police and tasered multiple times before dying in police custody.[15] The

Ferguson rebellion became a focal point for the growing anger in Black communities across the country.

For almost the entire fall, the Ferguson movement focused on winning an indictment of Darren Wilson. Prosecutors worked to drag out the grand jury proceedings as long as possible, believing that colder weather would edge the movement off the streets. Undoubtedly, given the level of repression, the intensity of the August protests was not sustainable over time. But when that level of intensity waned, the *persistence* of the protests kept the movement alive. Activists and others from around the country were also important in helping sustain the local movement. In late August 2014, Darnell Moore and Patrisse Cullors of #BlackLivesMatter organized a "freedom ride" to bring people from all around the country to the suburb in solidarity with the local movement. Moore described the breadth of the mobilization:

> More than 500 people traveled from across the United States and Canada to provide various forms of support to the activists on the ground in Ferguson. Those who traveled with us represented a new and diverse contingent of black activists. We weren't all the same age, nor did we share the same political viewpoints. We weren't all heterosexual or documented or free from past involvement with the criminal justice system. Some of us were transgender, disabled or bisexual.[16]

Local activists held vigils, picketed the Ferguson police department, and blocked traffic on Interstate 70, which runs through Ferguson, in a dogged effort to maintain pressure on local officials to indict Wilson. Continued police harassment was also critical to sustaining the movement. In late September, Mike Brown's memorial was doused with gasoline and ignited. The flames revitalized the protests: more than two hundred people gathered in an angry protest that saw five people arrested.[17]

When local officials began to speculate that the grand jury decision would be made public in October, local activism picked up. A multiracial protest erupted in the solidarity song "Which Side Are You On?" during a performance of the St. Louis Symphony. When the protestors marched out, chanting "Black lives matter," many in the audience—including symphony musicians—applauded. On October 8, an off-duty St. Louis police officer fired at Black teenager Vonderrit Myers seventeen times, hitting him with eight bullets and killing him. Days after Myers's death, two hundred students marched from Myers's neighborhood, called Shaw, to join hundreds more students in an occupation of St. Louis University (SLU). For several days more than a thousand students occupied the campus, harkening back to the days of the Occupy movement.[18] The occupation of SLU coincided with Ferguson October, in which hundreds of people traveled to Ferguson—in solidarity with the local movement, but also to register their own protest. As protestor Richard Wallace from Chicago put it, "Everybody here is representing a family member or someone that's been hurt, murdered, killed, arrested, deported."[19] Ferguson officials continued to stall in announcing Wilson's fate, but the resilience of the Ferguson movement was inspiring people far beyond the Midwest. Historian Donna Murch wrote,

> I have no words to express what is happening in Ferguson. In the name of Michael Brown, a beautiful black storm against state violence is brewing so dense it has created a gravity of its own, drawing in people from all over the U.S., from centers of wealth and privilege to this city whose most prosperous years were a century ago. It looks explicitly not only to St. Louis city and county police and other municipal law enforcement, but also to the imperial wars in the Middle East as sites of murder and trauma. The call repeated over and over is Stokely Carmichael's: "Organize, Organize, Organize." And this growing youth movement has all the ancestral sweetness of kinship. In the words of a local hip-hop artist/activist, "Our grandparents would be proud of us."[20]

Changing of the Guard

A battle over the meaning of Ferguson between activists, civil rights leaders, elected officials, and federal agents was under way. For the activists and Black people of Ferguson, the point of the struggle was to win justice for Mike Brown, which meant keeping the protests alive. Winning an indictment against Wilson would vindicate their strategy and tactics, which often came into noisy conflict with establishment figures who made repeated calls for "calm" and often seemed more intent on criticizing the people in the streets than the conditions that compelled them to act in the first place.

The civil rights establishment, members of Congress, and federal agents were on hand for a variety of reasons. Members of the CBC appeared most concerned with increasing the voter rolls through registration campaigns and trying to transform the anger in the streets into a midterm-election turnout that would favor the Democratic Party. The civil rights establishment had overlapping and competing goals. The NAACP, whose reputation had been in decline, was looking to rehabilitate its image by trying to lead and direct events in Ferguson. Jesse Jackson Sr., as a leading figure in civil rights lore, had been politically adrift and marginalized because he was not in the orbit of the Obama White House. He had been supplanted by the Reverend Al Sharpton as the new national face of the civil rights establishment. For years, families had called upon Sharpton to bring attention and resources to their children's murder by the police. Sharpton could and did provide both—and enhanced his reputation as a conduit into the Black community. He arrived in Ferguson shortly after Mike Brown's death. Barely a week after Sharpton's arrival came the DOJ, led by former attorney general Eric Holder. Sharpton and Holder worked in tandem to reestablish the legitimacy of "law and order" and of the federal government as a respectable arbiter in local situations that could not otherwise be resolved.

But by the time Sharpton arrived in Ferguson, it was too late. Young Black people had already endured two standoffs with police that had ended with tear gas and rubber bullets. People were furious. These bullying tactics had transformed the marches into much more than a struggle for Mike Brown. The battle in the Ferguson streets was also fueled by the deep grievances of the town's young people, whose future was being stolen by the never-ending cycle of fines, fees, warrants, and arrests. They were fighting for their right to be on the street and to be freed from the vice grip of the Ferguson police. They had experienced their own collective power and were drawing strength from outlasting the police. They were losing their fear. And they were not about to stand down or move aside to accommodate Sharpton's arrival as the spokesperson for a local movement already firmly in place.

The conflict was almost immediate. Sharpton convened a meeting the day he arrived. His first speech blamed protestors for the violence that had been the central theme of the mainstream media. He told the group, "I know you are angry. . . . I know this is outrageous. When I saw that picture [of Brown lifeless on the ground], it rose up in me in outrage. But we cannot be more outraged than his mom and dad. If they can hold their heads in dignity, then we can hold our heads up in dignity." He added, "To become violent in Michael Brown's name is to betray the gentle giant that he was. Don't be a traitor to Michael Brown."[21]

Even though Sharpton had just arrived in town, he was describing Mike Brown's character and personality to his friends and peers. It was condescending and presumptuous. Sharpton's words also lent legitimacy to Ferguson officials' accounts, which blamed violence on protestors even as police blatantly violated their rights to assemble. But Sharpton's plan transcended events in Ferguson: if he could quell the fires of Ferguson, his political value would increase exponentially. This was an important case for the Obama administration, given the growing national focus on police brutality. Holder's presence in Ferguson confirmed this. When the protests continued despite Sharpton's arrival, he amplified his criticism of "violent" protestors by trying to draw a sharp line between them and "peaceful" demonstrators.

As Sharpton delivered the eulogy at Brown's funeral, he reserved his harshest words for the young Black protestors who had stood up to police violence and provocations. Brown's parents, he said,

> had to break their mourning to ask folks to stop looting and rioting. . . . You imagine they are heartbroken—their son taken, discarded and marginalized. And they have to stop mourning to get you to control your anger, like you are more angry than they are. . . . Blackness was never about being a gangster or a thug. Blackness was no matter how low we was pushed down, we rose up anyhow. . . . Blackness was never surrendering our pursuit of excellence. It was when it was against the law to go to some schools, we built black colleges. . . . We never gave up. . . . Now, in the 21st century, we get to where we got some positions of power. And you decide it ain't black no more to be successful. Now you want to be a nigger and call your woman a ho. You've lost where you've come from. We've got to clean up our community so we can clean up the United States of America.[22]

In one fell swoop, Sharpton not only condemned the young people of Ferguson but invoked stereotypes to do so. It confirmed a sense among the new activists that Sharpton and those like him were out of step. There was a lingering, if unspoken question: What gave Sharpton or

Jackson or the NAACP or the Justice Department the authority to tell protestors how they should respond to the violence of the Ferguson police? What, really, did any of them know about the daily harassment local residents experienced? What had any of these officials ever done to stop police murder and brutality?

A New Civil Rights Movement?

The young people of Ferguson had great reverence and respect for the memory of the civil rights movement, but the reality is that its legacy meant little in their everyday lives. "I feel in my heart that they failed us," Dontey Carter said of contemporary civil rights leaders. "They're the reason things are like this now. They don't represent us. That's why we're here for a new movement. And we have some warriors out here."[23] When Jesse Jackson Sr. arrived in Ferguson, he was confronted by a local activist, who said, "When you going to stop selling us out, Jesse? We don't *want* you here in St. Louis!"[24] Other activists did not go that far, but they did note that young Black people had been thrust into leadership on the ground in Ferguson because they were the ones under attack. Johnetta Elzie recognized that: "The youth leading this movement is important because it is our time. For so long the elders have told us our generation doesn't fight for anything, or that we don't care about what goes on in the world. We have proved them wrong."[25]

This division between the "old guard" and the "new generation" grew deeper as the movement began to take form. During a "Ferguson October" forum, tensions threatened to boil over when the organizers asked representatives of the civil rights establishment who had not been on the streets or at any of the daily protests to discuss the state of the movement. As NAACP president Cornell William Brooks gave a speech, several young people in the audience stood and turned their backs. Hip-hop artist Tef Poe informed the gathering, "This ain't your grandparents' civil rights movement." He described the real movement as being made up of the young men in the streets with bandanas and young women who were supposed to be in school but were on the front lines instead. He said to the NAACP and the others assembled on the stage, "Y'all did not show up. . . . Get off your ass and join us!"[26]

Part of Sharpton's appeal for the political establishment has been his ability to keep protests narrowly fixed on the specifics of a given case, or at least on the narrow issue of "police accountability." But the deepening conflict between the young activists and the establishment was exacerbated as Ferguson officials dragged out the decision of whether or not to indict Wilson. For the young people, this meant escalating the pressure, while the "old guard" continued to counsel patience and allowing the process to play out. But there were other tensions. The young activists were beginning to politically generalize from the multiple cases of police brutality and develop a systemic analysis of policing. Many began to articulate a much broader critique that situated policing within a matrix of racism and inequality in the United States and beyond. Millennials United in Action activist Ashley Yates recognized that

> the youth knew something very early in that the older generation didn't. We knew that the system had already failed even before they began to show their hand publicly. We knew that not only was the murder of Mike Brown unjustified, it was another example of how the systems in place made it acceptable to gun us down. We are the generation that was ignited by Trayvon Martin's murder and placed our faith in a justice system that failed us in a very public and intentional manner.[27]

Elzie also observed, "Thanks to Twitter, I had been able to see photos of Gaza weeks before, and feel connected to the people there on an emotional level. I never thought the small county of Ferguson, this little part of Greater St. Louis, would become Gaza."[28]

There was truth to the generational divide, as there often is when a new generation of activists emerges and is not weighed down by earlier defeats or habituated to a particular method of organizing or thinking. They bring new ideas, new perspectives, and often, new vitality to the patterns and rhythms of activism. In general, as the movement has developed, there has been an impulse by some activists to celebrate the youth and denigrate age and experience. Generational tensions do not mean that movements and organizing in general cannot be multigenerational. Civil rights icon Ella Baker was significantly older and more experienced than the young activists she worked alongside in forming the Student Non-Violent Coordinating Committee (SNCC), yet she commanded tremendous respect because of the respect she had for the young people she organized with. In a well-known essay that described some of her conceptions of organizing and leadership during the sit-in movement in 1960, she wrote

> [The] desire for supportive cooperation from adult leaders and the adult community was . . . tempered by apprehension that adults might try to "capture" the student movement. The students showed willingness to be met on the basis of equality, but were intolerant of anything that smacked of manipulation or domination. This inclination toward *group-centered leadership*, rather than toward a *leader-centered group pattern of organization*, was refreshing indeed to those of the older group who bear the scars of the battle, the frustrations and the disillusionment that come when the prophetic leader turns out to have heavy feet of clay.[29]

Despite the constant clamor of "generational divide" today, there is much fluidity between the youth and older African Americans, who are often the parents of the young people being killed by the police. Where the generational divide expressed itself most forcefully today is over the developing politics of the movement. The tactical and strategic flexibility of the youth activists flowed from a developing politics that could not be constrained by a narrow agenda of voter registration or a simple electoral strategy. In Ferguson, these emerging politics were embodied by the emergence of young Black women as a central organizing force.

Black Women Matter

Most murders of Black people at the hands of the state go unnoticed by the public and unreported by the mainstream media. The few cases—compared to the significantly larger number of people killed—that do come into the public spotlight often involve Black men or boys. This was certainly true in Ferguson and Baltimore. This is not entirely surprising since, when police shoot to kill, they are usually taking aim at African American men. But Black women who are partnered with, have children with, or parent Black men and boys also suffer the effects of violence against them. The erasure of this particular way that Black women experience police violence minimizes the depth and extent of the harm caused by the abusive policing state. Black men falling under the control of the criminal justice system has a deleterious impact on their families and neighborhoods. Ex-convict status increases rates of poverty and unemployment, and the formerly incarcerated are banned from access to federal programs intended to blunt the worst effects of poverty, including housing vouchers, student loans, and other forms of financial aid. These policies affect not only Black men but also Black women who have Black men in their lives.

Black women, however, are also the victims of the policing state, including police violence and imprisonment. While Trayvon Martin became a household name, most people are not familiar with the case of Marissa Alexander, a Black woman who was a victim of domestic violence. After using a firearm to keep her abuser at bay, Alexander invoked Florida's "stand your ground" statute as a defense. Although George Zimmerman, who killed Martin, succeeded in using this defense, Alexander was sentenced to twenty years in prison. Even though Alexander would eventually be released from jail, the contrast was a stark reminder of the dual system of justice in the United States.

The police also kill Black women. The names of Rekia Boyd, Shelly Frey, Miriam Carey, and Alberta Spruill are less familiar than those of Mike Brown or Eric Garner, but their killings were motivated by the same dehumanizing factors. Police also view Black women's lives with suspicion and ultimately as less valuable, making their death and brutalization more likely, not less. It is hardly even newsworthy when Black women, including Black transwomen, are killed or violated by law enforcement—because they are generally seen as less feminine or vulnerable. Consider the case of Tulsa, Oklahoma, police officer Daniel Holtzclaw, who was convicted of raping thirteen Black women while on duty. Holtzclaw is believed to have targeted Black women because they were of "lower social status," meaning that they were less likely to be believed and fewer people would care.[30] Indeed, Holtzclaw's crimes barely made a ripple in the national news.

Even though Black women have always been susceptible to violence from the police and the criminal justice system, where organizing and struggle have emerged, they have, for the most part, had a male face. For cases that develop a national profile, a male lawyer or reverend or civil rights leader—such as Al Sharpton—is usually the most visible face. Of course, mothers and other women in the lives of the (typically male) victims are heard from, but the activism has been seen as male-led and organized—until Ferguson.

In fact, the media have been particularly cognizant of the "women of Ferguson" as central to turning "a string of protests into a movement, by seamlessly shifting between the roles of peace-keepers, disrupters, organizers and leaders."[31] Indeed, the women who played an indispensable role in keeping the Ferguson movement together through the summer until the early winter were also aware of their role. As Brittney Ferrell points out,

> The media has left out that if it were not for Black women, there would be no movement. We have seriously carried this to where it is now, not to say there are no men out here doing their thing because there are. What I am saying is that women have been here since day one, we are willing to lay our lives on the line to keep up the good fight without the support from anyone or any organization, hence why we built our own.[32]

To ask why Black women have played such a central role in this movement is to assume that they have played a lesser role in other movements. It should go without saying that Black women have always played an integral role in the various iterations of the Black freedom struggle. Whether it was Ida B. Wells, who risked her life to expose the widespread use of lynching in the South, or the mothers of the wrongfully accused Scottsboro Boys, who toured the world to build the campaign to free their sons, Black women have been central to every significant campaign for Black rights and freedom. Black women, including Ella Baker, Fannie Lou Hamer, Diane Nash, and countless and unknown others, were critical to the development of the civil rights movement, but that movement is still primarily known by its male leaders.

Today, though, the face of the Black Lives Matter movement is largely queer and female. How has this come to be? Female leadership may actually have been an outcome of the deeply racist policing Black men have experienced in Ferguson. According to the US Census Bureau, while there are 1,182 African American women between the ages of twenty-five and thirty-four living in Ferguson, there are only 577 African American men in this age group. More than 40 percent of Black men in both the 20–24 and 35–54 age groups in Ferguson are missing.[33]

It's not just Ferguson. Across the United States, 1.5 million Black men are "missing"—snatched from society by imprisonment or premature death. To put it starkly, "More than one out of every six Black men who today should be between 25 and 54 years old have disappeared from daily life."[34] This does not mean that, if the 40 percent of Black men missing from Ferguson were present, they would be playing the same role that women have played in building, organizing, and sustaining the movement, but it does provide a concrete example of the impact of the hyperaggressive, revenue-generating approach to policing in Ferguson. It is more likely that these women have stepped into leadership roles because of the absolutely devastating impact of policing and police violence in Black people's lives in general. But whatever the reasons, their presence has contributed more than just gender balance.

The Black women leading the movement against police brutality have worked to expand our understanding of the broad impact of police violence in Black communities. Sometimes this is articulated through the straightforward demand that society as a whole recognize that the police victimize Black women. "The media is excluding the fact that the police brutality and harassment in our communities impacts the women just as much as the men," says Zakiya Jemmott, adding, "They're highlighting black male lives and pushing the black female lives lost to police violence to the side. I want for the media to understand that *all* black lives matter."[35] But Black women have also made a much more deliberate intervention to expose police brutality as part of a much larger system of oppression in the lives of all Black working-class and poor people. Charlene Carruthers of Black Youth Project 100 explains,

> It's important because we are really serious about creating freedom and justice for all black people, but all too often black women and girls, black LGBTQ folks, are left on the sidelines. And if we're going to be serious about liberation we have to include all black people. It's really that simple. And it's been my experience that issues of gender justice and LGBT justice have been either secondary or not recognized at all.[36]

The Black women who created the hashtag #BlackLivesMatter—Patrisse Cullors, Opal Tometi, and Alicia Garza—articulate most clearly the overlapping oppressions confronting Black people in the struggle to end police violence and win justice. In an essay that captures the expansive nature of Black oppression while arguing that the movement cannot be reduced only to police brutality, Alicia Garza writes,

It is an acknowledgment Black poverty and genocide is state violence. It is an acknowledgment that 1 million Black people are locked in cages in this country—one half of all people in prisons or jails—is an act of state violence. It is an acknowledgment that Black women continue to bear the burden of a relentless assault on our children and our families and that assault is an act of state violence. Black queer and trans folks bearing a unique burden in a hetero-patriarchal society that disposes of us like garbage and simultaneously fetishizes us and profits off of us is state violence; the fact that 500,000 Black people in the US are undocumented immigrants and relegated to the shadows is state violence; the fact that Black girls are used as negotiating chips during times of conflict and war is state violence; Black folks living with disabilities and different abilities bear the burden of state-sponsored Darwinian experiments that attempt to squeeze us into boxes of normality defined by White supremacy is state violence.[37]

The focus on "state violence" strategically pivots away from a conventional analysis that would reduce racism to the intentions and actions of the individuals involved. The declaration of "state violence" legitimizes the corollary demand for "state action." It demands more than the removal of a particular officer or the admonishment of a particular police department, but calls attention to the systemic forces that allow the individuals to act with impunity. Moreover, these organizers are "intersectional" in their approach to organizing—in other words, they start from the basic recognition that the oppression of African Americans is multidimensional and must be fought on different fronts. The analytic reach of these organizers is what really underlies the tension between the "new guard" and the "old guard." In some ways, it demonstrates that today's activists are grappling with questions similar to those Black radicals confronted in the Black Power era, questions bound up with the systemic nature of Black oppression in American capitalism and how that shapes the approach to organizing.

Placing police brutality into a wider web of inequality has largely been missing from the more narrowly crafted agendas of the liberal establishment organizations, like Sharpton's National Action Network (NAN), which have focused more on resolving the details of particular cases than on generalizing about the systemic nature of police violence. This has meant that mainstream civil rights organizations tend to focus on legalistic approaches to resolve police brutality, compared to activists who connect police oppression to other social crises in Black communities. Of course, that approach has not been fully supplanted; a significant focus of the Ferguson movement was voter registration and increasing the presence of African Americans in local governing bodies. But the movement in Ferguson has also validated those who embraced a much wider view by showing how the policing of African Americans is directly tied to the higher levels of poverty and unemployment in Black communities through the web of fees and fines and arrest warrants trapping Black people in a never-ending cycle of debt. The gravity of the crisis confronting Black communities, often stemming from these harmful encounters with the police, legitimizes the need for a more encompassing analysis. It allows people to generalize from police violence to the ways that public funding for police comes at the expense of other public institutions, and creates the space to then ask why. Not only do the "new guard's" politics stand in sharp contrast to those of the "old guard" but so does their approach to organizing. Beyond being led by women, the new guard is decentralized and is largely organizing the movement through social media. This is very different from national organizations like the NAACP, NAN, or even Jackson's Operation PUSH, whose mostly male leaders make decisions with little input or direction from people on the ground. This strategy is not simply the product of male leadership, but of an older model that privileged leveraging connections and relationships within the establishment over street activism—or using street protests to gain leverage within the establishment. The newness of the Ferguson movement and the incipient movement against police violence have temporarily prevented that kind of political shortcut.

From Moment to Movement

On November 24, 2014, a grand jury in Ferguson decided not to indict Darren Wilson for the murder of Mike Brown. Angry protests ripped through the suburb in the dead of night when the decision was announced. Rows of riot police protected City Hall and the police department while the commercial section of Black Ferguson was allowed to burn. There was little surprise about the decision not to indict, but there was anger at the completion of a legal lynching. President Obama returned to the airwaves to counsel patience and respect for the law. He reminded his audience that "we are a nation built on the rule of law," a concept rendered hollow and meaningless by months of witnessing the lawlessness of the Ferguson police department.[38] Obama implored protestors to channel their concerns "constructively" and not "destructively," but the split screens of several networks showed the president's words were falling on deaf ears as fires burned through the night in Ferguson. This was not, however, a revival of the previous August, when the fires were igniting a new movement against police brutality; these were the flames of resignation and exhaustion.

As happened so often in 2014, at the moment when it appeared that the momentum of activism had swung back in the other direction, there was a new death at the hands of the police, like kindling on a fire. Two days before the Wilson decision was announced, young Tamir Rice, only twelve, was shot and killed by police in a playground in Cleveland, Ohio. Rice had been playing with a toy gun. Police shot and killed the boy within two seconds of their arrival—so quickly that the police car had not even stopped. Nine days earlier, Tanisha Anderson, also of Cleveland, had been killed when an officer performed a "judo" move to take her to the ground and in the process slammed her head into the concrete.[39] Days later, a Staten Island grand jury returned a decision not to indict Daniel Pantaleo, the officer who choked Eric Garner to death. Where the Ferguson decision seemed like an endpoint to the months-long struggle for justice there, these deaths and the Garner decision opened up an entirely new chapter. The continuation of the protests, however, was fraught with the tensions of going from "moment to movement."[40]

Obama quickly organized a meeting of some of the more visible activists from Ferguson and around the country to discuss police violence. James Hayes from the Ohio Student Union was one of the participants. "We appreciate that the president wanted to meet with us, but now he must deliver with meaningful policy," Hayes reported. "We are calling on everyone who believes that Black lives matter to continue taking to the streets until we get real change for our communities."[41] That such a meeting ever convened was proof alone that this was no longer just about Ferguson. The nation's political establishment was concerned about containing the movement.

This was no ordinary meeting; it included the president and vice president of the United States as well as the attorney general. But just as they were attempting to get in front of the anger over Ferguson, two days later the decision not to indict Pantaleo produced even larger protests than those that had greeted the Wilson decision. Tens of thousands of people across the United States clogged the streets in disgust, if not rage, over the refusal to punish another white police officer for the death of an unarmed Black man. In Garner's case, the evidence was incontrovertible. Hundreds of thousands of people had watched the video of him pleading for his life and repeating, eleven times, "I can't breathe" while Pantaleo squeezed the life out of his body. Yet the grand jury found no fault. In the aftermath of the Garner decision Obama shelved the talk about "a nation of laws" and announced the formation of a new task force charged with creating "specific recommendations about how we strengthen the relationship between law enforcement and communities of color and minority communities that feel that bias is taking place."[42]

Activists were not waiting. As waves of protests washed across the United States, the first national protests against police brutality were called for the following week: one in New York City and one in Washington, DC. The march in New York was organized on Facebook by activists, the Washington march by Sharpton's NAN. The emergence of the national movement was immediately confronted by the reemergence of the political tensions that had surfaced in Ferguson. Sharpton had intended to stage-manage the entire affair, featuring himself as keynote speaker. Activists from Ferguson had traveled to Washington, but were dismayed to see the stage filled with people who had no organic connection to the movement. In fact, security guards were demanding VIP badges to gain access to the stage, where the opening rally of the march would commence. Johnetta Elzie was infuriated: "When we first got there, two people from NAN told us that we needed a VIP pass or a press pass to sit on the ledge," she said. "If it is a protest, why do you need to have a VIP pass?"[43] When Sharpton finally made his way to the stage, he ripped the Ferguson activists, who were demanding to address the crowd, as "provocateurs." The breach between Sharpton and the Ferguson-hardened activists was not simply about stage passes or other perceived slights, however. One young organizer named Charles Wade observed, "I think part of it is people just don't connect with his leadership. . . . We've been excluded by the traditional groups, so we've started our own thing."[44] Both marches were wildly successful, bringing tens of thousands of people onto the streets and giving the movement its first profile as a national phenomenon, but the different paths forward were becoming clearer.

Days after the march, Sharpton wrote an article that revealed as much about the tremendous pressure he was under as it did his extremely vague view of how the movement would "reform [the] system":

> 10 or 25 years from now, it won't matter who got the most publicity or the most applause at a rally. . . . Let us not give in to pettiness and emotion, for true change is at our doorstep. You could see on the faces of those marching and chanting on Saturday, and you can see it in Washington as our elected officials are taking steps to reform a system that has failed far too many for too long. . . . You can literally feel it in the air—permanent change is on the horizon. Now we must seize it, and this moment, as we record history together.[45]

It was a far cry from his arrogant saunter into Ferguson. But Sharpton's mentions of "publicity" and "applause" showed that these were things that were on his mind. His vision of "big change" did not look like much: the two "major" reforms he named were body cameras for police and independent prosecutors to investigate police misconduct.

The smallness of his demands perfectly distilled the difference between the "old guard" and the growing youth rebellion. He made no mention of racism, mass incarceration, or any of the broader issues for which younger activists were arguing much more aggressively. Jesse Jackson also weighed in on this question: "To go from protesting to power, you need demonstrations, legislation and litigation. . . . Sprinters burn out real fast. These young people need to be in it for the long run. And it must be an intergenerational coalition. A movement that's mature requires clergy and lawyers and legislators. The struggle is never a one-string guitar."[46] Jackson was certainly less offensive than Sharpton, but his comments reflected a different conception of what the movement should focus on and look like. Moreover, it perpetuated the assumption that the new organizers were against "old people," which has never been demonstrated to be true. As Alicia Garza clarified in an interview, "We learned by making mistakes and from our elders who are brave enough to share with us all that they've learned. I think it's about having courageous conversations about the world we want to build and how we think we can get there, and calling people out when we see things that are problematic."[47] Jackson's coalition of "clergy, lawyers and litigators" has failed miserably over the last forty years. Counseling the youth to pick up the tools of a failed strategy only served to reinforce the perception that the old guard was out of touch and out of its element. Sharpton's frustration at the questioning of his leadership and his role as the conduit to Black America eventually boiled over. Weeks after the December marches, Sharpton compared the "new guard" to "pimps" and to the people following them as "hoes." He went on:

> And while they got y'all arguing about old or young in Ferguson, they running an election and y'all ain't got a candidate in the race. Cause you're busy arguing with your mommy and daddy when they re-electing a mayor, and re-electing a prosecutor. They got you arguing about who going to lead a march—the old or the young—when they cutting up the city budget. You can't be that stupid! . . . It's the disconnect that is the strategy to break the movement. And they play on your ego. "Oh, you young and hip, you're full of fire. You're the new face." All the stuff that they know will titillate your ears. That's what a pimp says to a ho.[48]

Sharpton's stunning rant confirmed all of the concerns about his continuing role as the self-anointed leader of Black America.

In the days after the big December protests, Ferguson Action, the central body of the various activist formations located in and inspired by Ferguson, released a statement that included some of the activists who had been barred from speaking in Washington. It was titled "About This Movement" and, in its breadth and optimism, it made Sharpton's tantrum seem even pettier:

> This is a movement of and for ALL Black lives—women, men, transgender and queer. We are made up of both youth AND elders aligned through the possibilities that new tactics and fresh strategies offer our movement. Some of us are new to this work, but many of us have been organizing for years. We came together in Mike Brown's name, but our roots are also in the flooded streets of New Orleans and the bloodied BART stations of Oakland. We are connected online and in

the streets. We are decentralized, but coordinated. Most importantly, we are organized. Yet we are likely not respectable negroes. We stand beside each other, not in front of one another. We do not cast any one of ours to the side in order to gain proximity to perceived power. Because this is the only way we will win. We can't breathe. And we won't stop until Freedom.[49]

Black Lives Matter

In December and January, "Black Lives Matter" was the rallying cry from every corner. A week after the Garner decision, several hundred congressional aides, most of them Black, walked off the job in protest.[50] Black professional athletes wore T-shirts adorned with the slogan "I Can't Breathe." Soon after, high school and college students began wearing the shirts as well. Thousands of college, high school, and even middle school students began organizing and participating in die-ins, walkouts, marches, and other forms of public protest.[51] At Princeton University, more than four hundred students and faculty participated in a die-in. The protest included mostly African American students, but a number of white, Latino/a, and Asian students participated in the direct action. Students at Stanford blocked the San Mateo Bridge across San Francisco Bay. Students at seventy medical schools organized die-ins under the slogan "White Coats for Black Lives."[52] Public defenders and other lawyers organized their own actions, including die-ins.[53] Protests were sweeping the nation and politicians raced to keep up. Presidential hopeful Hillary Clinton, who had never publicly mentioned Mike Brown's name, was forced to say "Black Lives Matter" when she spoke in New York three days after the march.[54]

Even Obama began to change his tune. When talking about young African Americans, he was speaking less about morality and "instead focused on African American concerns about unfair treatment and called them part of the American family—which makes it awfully hard to single them out as the problem child in need of some tough love."[55] Garza of #BlackLivesMatter spoke to the significance of the actions: "What's happening right now is that a movement is growing. We are building relationships and connections, exercising new forms of leadership, new tactics, and learning lessons from our elders—people like Bayard Rustin, Diane Nash, Linda Burnham, Assata Shakur and Angela Davis—who have been part of social movements before us."[56]

With the momentum clearly on the side of the movement, its leaders now had to articulate a way forward. Sharpton and the establishment had provided a convenient foil against which to contrast their politics, strategies, and tactics. It was easy to focus on the differences, but how did the new organizers, like those who penned the Ferguson Action document, envision the movement forging ahead? In the aftermath of Sharpton's meltdown and with "Black Lives Matter" absorbed into the daily banter of African Americans, they now had the country's attention. The sharp contrast between the intersectional, grassroots organizing of the "new guard" and the top-down control of the civil rights establishment had helped to obscure important differences that existed *among* the new organizers. For example, some embraced building organizations like Black Youth Project 100 (BYP 100), #BLM, Dream Defenders, Million Hoodies, and Hands Up United, while others saw little need for that, instead embracing social media as the best way to organize the movement. Two of the most high-profile and influential activists in the movement, Johnetta Elzie and DeRay McKesson, were less committed to building an organization.

Ferguson Action's statement echoed this sentiment when it described the movement as "coordinated" and "organized" but "decentralized." In some sense, the futility of organization had been confirmed by their wild success in organizing protests and demonstrations on the fly. For months, Twitter and other social media platforms *were* successful in organizing large and influential protests. The December 13 march in New York City was organized by two relatively novice activists on Facebook; within hours thousands of people had "liked" it and committed to attending. Upward of fifty thousand people actually showed up for the rally. But how would the movement go from direct action, die-ins, highway closures, and walkouts to ending police brutality without dedicated spaces to meet, strategize, and engage in democratic decision-making? Considering the demands and "vision" that Ferguson Action put forward, everything from ending racial profiling to full employment and ending mass incarceration, it is impossible to imagine any of this happening only online.

These debates over organization resemble some of the hostility to organization that emerged in the Occupy movement from 2011. In both cases, the absence of formal structures and formal leadership was described as "giving everyone a voice." If there is no organization, then no one can take over control. DeRay McKesson acknowledged this when he said, "But what is different about Ferguson . . . what makes that really important, unlike previous struggle, is that—who is the spokesperson? The people. The people, in a very democratic way, became the voice of the struggle."[57] McKesson is one of the most visible actors in the movement and his insights are influential. He elaborates:

> It is not that we're anti-organization. There are structures that have formed as a result of protest, that are really powerful. It is just that you did not need those structures to begin protest. *You* are enough to start a movement. Individual people can come together around things that they know are unjust. And they can spark change. Your body can be part of the protest; you don't need a VIP pass to protest. And Twitter allowed that to happen. . . . I think that what we are doing is building a radical new community in struggle that did not exist before. Twitter has enabled us to create community. I think the phase we're in is a community-building phase. Yes, we need to address policy, yes, we need to address elections; we need to do all those things. But on the heels of building a strong community.[58]

Protests *are* for everyone—but how do you determine if the protest was successful or not, and how do you draw those who showed up deeper into organizing? Basically, how do you move from protest to movement? Historian Barbara Ransby speaks to this difficulty: "While some forms of resistance might be reflexive and simple—that is, when pushed too hard, most of us push back, even if we don't have a plan or a hope of winning—organizing a movement is different. It is not organic, instinctive, or ever easy. If we think we can all 'get free' through individual or uncoordinated small-group resistance, we are kidding ourselves."[59]

Not everyone rejects the need for organization. The fight against police terror has produced many new organizations and networks. At a forum at the historic Riverside Church in New York City, Asha Rosa of the Black Youth Project 100 spoke passionately on the need to be not only radical but also organized:

Organizations are longer lasting than an action, longer lasting than
a campaign, longer lasting than a moment. Organizations are where
we can build structures that reflect our values, and build communities
that help us sustain ourselves in this work and sustain the work itself.
We saw 60,000 people in the streets in New York City [for the December protest]. . . . I won't be surprised if we don't see 60,000 people
in the streets again until it's warm, and that's okay. . . . There are
phases in these movements. We have to sustain that and make sure
there are organizations for people to get plugged into.[60]

From the BYP 100, Dream Defenders, Hands Up United, Ferguson
Action, and Millennials United to perhaps the most well known of the
new organizations, #BlackLivesMatter (#BLM), this new era has produced an important cohort of activist organizations. Thus far, #BLM
has become the largest and most visible group, with at least twenty-six
chapters. #BLM describes itself as "a decentralized network aiming
to build the leadership and power of black people." Patrisse Cullors
describes its members as working "within the communities where they
live and work. They determine their goals and the strategies that they
believe will work best to help them achieve their goals. . . . We are
deliberately taking a cautious and collaborative approach at developing
a national Black Lives Matter strategy because it takes time to listen,
learn and build."[61] #BLM has reinvigorated the Occupy method of
protest, which believes decentralized and "leaderless" actions are more
democratic, essentially allowing its followers to act on what they want
to do without the restraint of others weighing in. But at a time when
many people are trying to find an entry point into anti-police activism
and desire to be involved, this particular method of organizing can be
difficult to penetrate. In some ways, this decentralized organizing can
actually narrow opportunities for the democratic involvement of many
in favor of the tightly knit workings of those already in the know.

These are issues #BLM will have to resolve, but as the largest and
most influential organization in the movement, its example is critical
and has wider implications. Organizational autonomy and decentral-
ization raise questions of how actions will be coordinated and the concentrated weight of the entire movement brought to bear on targeted
institutions. Different locations have different issues: how are local
actions woven into a coherent social movement, not just a series of

disparate demonstrations with no relationship to each other? If every city, organization, and individual does whatever it/she/he feels empowered to do in the name of the movement, how will we ever transform a series of effective local actions into a national movement? There have been situations where multiple groups have been able to coordinate: the #SayHerName campaign to highlight the effects of police violence on Black women stands out as a prime example. But the larger the movement grows, the more need there will be for coordination.

The Revolution Will Not Be Funded

If the success of the movement can be judged by the greater awareness it has created across the United States of police violence and brutality, it can also be measured by the amount of financial support some movement organizations have commanded. Some organizations involved in movement organizing have nonprofit status, while others do not but are still able to generate funding from influential foundations and wealthy individuals. The Black Lives Matter movement more generally has captured the attention of the nonprofit funding and philanthropy galaxy. This includes the Soros and Ford Foundations, but also Resource Generation, described as an "organization of wealthy people under 35 who support progressive movements."[62] In fact, there are philanthropic networks that exist for the sake of pressuring other foundations into donating resources to various social-justice movements. When the organizations connected to the Black Lives Matter movement were convening for a summer conference, the National Committee for Responsible Philanthropy made an appeal to other funders: "A profound transformation of the social, economic and political fabric that for decades has marginalized our Black communities is possible. The Movement for Black Lives convening will be a major step in that transformation. Any foundation that is committed to achieving real equity and contributing to the dismantling of racism has an opportunity and a responsibility to participate."[63] The appeal went on to thank "funders like the Evelyn and Walter Haas, Jr. Fund, the Levi Strauss Foundation, the Barr Foundation" for making "investing in leadership development a priority."

These facts alone do not cast aspersions on the many organizations that receive these funds. Virtually all of the leading organizations of the civil rights movement received foundation funding, including SNCC, CORE, and SCLC. The Highlander Folk School—where many civil rights activists, including Rosa Parks and Martin Luther King Jr., were trained in civil disobedience and other protest techniques—received much of its funding from the Field Foundation. Social justice organizations rely on any number of sources to finance their important work. But while activists may only be in search of precious dollars to continue organizing, it's doubtful that multibillion-dollar foundations are donating for purely altruistic reasons. Indeed, historian Aldon Morris recounts funders' dubious collusion with agents of the state in a collective effort to undermine civil rights organizing:

> SNCC's financial situation improved in the summer of 1962, when it received some funds from the Taconic Foundation, the Field Foundation, and the Stern Family Fund. Those foundations worked in close conjunction with the Kennedy Administration and shared the Administration's view that black activists should channel their energies aimed at acquiring the vote for Southern blacks. . . . Following the tumultuous Freedom Rides, the Kennedy Administration made overt attempts to funnel the efforts of all the civil rights organizations into voter registration activities rather than disruptive protest movements. Indeed, the Kennedy Administration was adamant in opposing wide-scale civil disobedience.[64]

Morris goes on to quote James Farmer, a leader of SNCC, on how "the Kennedy administration attempted to 'cool out' the demonstrations": "Bobby Kennedy called a meeting of CORE and SNCC, in his office . . . and he said, 'Why don't you guys cut out all that shit, freedom riding and sitting-in shit, and concentrate on voter education . . . if you do that I'll get you a tax exemption.'"[65] Organizations that depend on outside funding can face problems if their funders develop political critiques of their work. "The nonprofit system is set up for foundations to have an inordinate amount of power and control over what grassroots organizations do," cautions Umi Selah, executive director of Dream Defenders. A former employee of a major funder for progressive Black causes also points out that many donations come "with a set of rules typically about how a funder wants to see things on the ground."[66]

Some groups have taken to collecting dues from their members and taking donations from the general public as way to offset dependence on outside funders. It is very early to understand fully the role that funders and the "nonprofit-industrial complex" will have on this movement, but they are certainly a factor, one that makes fully independent movement groups all the more necessary.[67] For example, the Ford Foundation seeks to play an important role in funding movement organizations, but despite its espoused intentions, it has played a historic role in subverting movements inside and outside the United States. Arundhati Roy writes of its deleterious impact in India in her book *Capitalism: A Ghost Story*:

> The Ford Foundation has a very clear, well-defined ideology and works extremely closely with the US State Department. Its project of deepening democracy and "good governance" is very much a part of the Bretton Woods scheme of standardizing business practice and promoting efficiency in the free market. . . . It is through this lens that we need to view the work that the Ford Foundation is doing with the millions of dollars it has invested in India—its funding of artists, filmmakers and activists, its generous endowment of university courses and scholarships.[68]

Perhaps the largest issue with the foundations and funders is that these organizations also attempt to politically shape the direction of the organizations they fund. The Ford Foundation, like many other funders, offers grants, but also produces "white papers," seminars, and conferences where it puts forward political perspectives and strategies aimed at directing the organizations it is funding.

Political scientist Megan Francis, describing the relationship between the NAACP and the American Fund for Public Service, also known as the Garland Fund, suggests that not only did the Garland Fund provide enormous financial resources to the NAACP in the 1950s, it also used its influence to redirect the NAACP's organizing focus:

> So why did the NAACP move from a racial-violence focused agenda to one that centered on education? In one word: money. The Garland Fund had so much sway over the NAACP's agenda because the Garland Fund had so much to offer the cash-strapped NAACP. In the negotiation of a grant, it quickly became apparent that the NAACP's black leadership favored a civil rights program with an explicit focus on racial violence. . . . Faced with the possibility of losing a critical funding source, the NAACP begrudgingly complied with the

Garland Fund's requests. In the coming years, the NAACP relegated issues of racial violence to the margins and adopted a focus on education, for which it was known for the rest of the 20th century.[69]

Ultimately, funders and other philanthropic organizations help to narrow the scope of organizing to changing "policy" and other measures within the existing system.

Foundation money also "professionalizes" movements in a way that promotes careerism and the expectation that activism will be externally funded. In fact, most activism is volunteer-based, with fundraising a collective effort of the participants, not the particular expertise of grant writers. The important work of many grassroots organizations in the movement has been obscured by more financially stable organizations. Much smaller, local committees have sprung up around particular cases or to make specific demands that are tied to local situations in cities across the country.

For example, in Madison, Wisconsin, the group Young, Gifted and Black has been organizing for justice for Tony Robinson, a young Black man killed by the police in the spring of 2015. In Cleveland, community activists, including clergy, academics, and the Council on American-Islamic Relations, have come together to demand the arrest of the two officers who killed Tamir Rice.[70] In Chicago, a newly formed organization called We Charge Genocide traveled to Geneva, Switzerland, to call on international officials to compel the American government to stop police murder and brutality against African Americans. In Philadelphia, through the winter of 2014 and much of 2015, a citywide group called the Philly Coalition for REAL Justice brought together as many as sixty people twice a week to organize against police brutality. The coalition has organized thousands of people over the last year.[71] In Dallas, Texas, Mothers Against Police Brutality has not only helped to organize the important fight against police brutality but has actively tried to organize solidarity between the anti-police-brutality movement and the immigrant-rights movement. In the days before a May Day rally, marchers from both movements converged holding signs proclaiming "Black Lives Matter" and chanting "Down, down deportation; up, up immigration!"[72] These types of organizing efforts, often viewed by funders as "unprofessional," exist around the country and are an entry point for ordinary people who want to be involved in movements.

The Demands: This Is What We Want

The absence of an independent movement organization has meant that the actual demands of the movement have been muddled. Some of this arises from the difficulty of the task itself. Police violence is a part of the DNA of the United States. As I have argued earlier, there has been no golden age of policing in which violence and racism were not central to the job. But that does not mean that nothing can be done to rein in the policing state. The Ferguson Action website has compiled the most comprehensive list of movement demands, including demilitarizing the police, passing anti-racial-profiling legislation, and collecting data documenting police abuse, among other measures.[73] Hands Up United, based in Ferguson and St. Louis, has called for the "immediate suspension without pay of law enforcement officers that have used or approved excessive use of force."[74] #BLM has called on the attorney general to release the names of police who have killed Black people over the last five years "so they can be brought to justice—if they haven't already."[75]

The demands of different organizations in the movement overlap, but what is the mechanism for acting on these demands when they are disconnected from any structure coordinated through the movement? How can we pay systematic attention to the progress made in achieving these demands or determining whether or not the demands have to be recalibrated? Connecting police violence to the vast effects of institutional racism is a strength of the current movement, but there is also a danger of submerging reforms that are attainable now into a much broader struggle to transform the very nature of American society. In other words, fighting around the demand to be "free" does not clarify the steps it will take to achieve that goal.

Demanding everything is as ineffective as demanding nothing, because it obscures what that struggle looks like on a daily basis. It can also be demoralizing, because when the goal is everything, it is impossible to measure the small but important steps forward that are the wellspring of any movement. This is not an argument for thinking small or abandoning the struggle to completely transform the United States; it is an argument for drawing a distinction between the struggle for reforms that are possible today and the struggle for revolution, which is a longer-term project. To be sure, there is definitely a relationship between the two. The struggle to reform various aspects of our existing society makes people's lives better in the here and now; it also teaches people how to struggle and organize. Those are the building blocks that can lead to larger and more transformative struggles. In the process, people in the movement develop politically, gain experience and expertise, and become leaders. It is impossible to conceive of leaping from inactivity to changing the world in a single bound.

For example, many Black people in the South who were radicalized in the 1950s in the struggle against Jim Crow would probably not have recognized themselves ten years later. Many people whose politics began with narrow demands to end Jim Crow eventually concluded that a government invested in racism could never achieve justice for Black people. Consider the experiences of the activists who made up SNCC, who in 1964 arrived at the Democratic National Convention in Atlantic City with the hope of seating Black delegates from their Mississippi Freedom Democratic Party as the delegation from Mississippi. The point was to expose and embarrass the national party for allowing the all-white Democratic Party to seat its delegation, knowing full well that Black people in Mississippi were violently disenfranchised. The SNCC activists believed if they were successful, they could break the grip of the Dixiecrats—the white Democratic Party of the South—on the electoral process throughout the South. But there was no way that Lyndon Johnson and the national Democratic Party were going to risk Southern white votes by acquiescing to the demands of civil rights activists. In the end, Johnson forced a deal down the activists' throats that left the convention and the white supremacist wing of the Democratic Party basically intact. James Forman, the executive director of SNCC, spelled out the meaning of the defeat:

> Atlantic City was a powerful lesson. . . . No longer was there any hope . . . that the federal government would change the situation in the Deep South. The fine line of contradiction between the state governments and the federal government, which we had used to build a movement, was played out. Now the kernel of opposites—the people against both the federal and state governments was apparent.[76]

Narrowing the demands of the movement in order to retain focus does not mean narrowing its reach. The brilliance of the slogan "Black Lives Matter" is its ability to articulate the dehumanizing aspects of anti-Black racism in the United States. The long-term strength of the movement will depend on its ability to reach large numbers of people by connecting the issue of police violence to the other ways that Black people are oppressed.

This process is already under way, as "new guard" activists have worked to make those connections. The best example of this involves the struggle of low-wage workers to raise the minimum wage to $15 an hour. Twenty percent of fast-food workers are Black and 68 percent of them earn between $7.26 and $10.09 an hour.[77] In Chicago, fast-food restaurants employ 46 percent of Black workers—in New York it's 50 percent.[78] Twenty percent of Walmart's 1.4 million workers are African American, making it the largest employer of Black Americans. There is a logical connection between the low-wage workers' campaigns and the Black Lives Matter movement. The overrepresentation of African Americans in the ranks of the poor and working class has made them targets of police, who prey on those with low incomes. Black and Latino/a workers are also more likely to suffer the consequences of the mounting fees and fines discussed in chapter 4. Mwende Katwiwa of the BYP 100 in New Orleans explains the relationship between economic and racial justice:

> Too often Black youth are trapped in a singular narrative about their lived experience that does not address the structural and social conditions. . . . The #BlackLivesMatter movement goes beyond a call to end police brutality and murder against Black people—it is a recognition that Black life is valuable while it is still being lived. Valuing Black life means Black people should have access to their basic human dignity at their workplace—especially Black youth who are disproportionately impacted by unemployment and are over-represented in low-wage jobs.[79]

The movement today is in a much better position to nurture and develop a relationship with the growing low-wage-worker struggle than has been possible with the civil rights establishment. For years, Walmart and McDonald's have been reliable contributors to the CBC, NAACP, and NAN.[80] At Al Sharpton's sixtieth birthday bash, held at the Four Seasons hotel in New York, corporations were encouraged to make donations to the NAACP at various levels. The phone company AT&T pledged at the "activists level" with a full-page ad in the party program, while Walmart and GE Asset Management only pledged at the

"preacher level," with half-page ads. McDonald's and Verizon pledged
at the "track suit" level with a back page ad. Sharpton would not say
how much each level was worth, but he did say that NAN reached its
goal of raising $1 million and that "we have no new liens. . . . We'll be
operating in the black this year. The biggest debts have already settled,
and the party . . . was the second big fund-raiser."[81] Is it any wonder
Sharpton and the others have been so quiet about the fight to raise the
minimum wage to $15?

The fight for educational justice in Black communities has also
gained momentum in the last several years and could be another entry point for collaboration between movements. The education justice
movement has focused on three issues that disproportionately affect
Black students: efforts to privatize publicly funded schools, the school-
to-prison pipeline, and high-stakes testing in public schools. There is
a clear relationship between privatization and "zero-tolerance policies"
that cause Black children to encounter law enforcement. Privately run
but publicly financed charter schools have embraced "no excuses" discipline, in which "teachers rigorously enforce an intricate set of behavioral expectations on students. Minor infractions—a hand improp-
erly raised, a shirt untucked, eyes averted—invite escalating punitive
measures: demerits, lost privileges, detention, suspension. The policing
theory that gave us stop-and-frisk now underpins the disciplinary system of the education reform movement."[82]

Zero-tolerance policies embedded in "no excuses" discipline have
rapidly increased the use of suspension and expulsions as the primary
disciplinary tool in public and charter schools. The rate of suspension
has increased for Black students, from 6 percent in the 1970s to 15 percent
today. Removal from school is only one aspect of this; as the impulse
toward suspension has increased so has the presence of police in the halls
of schools. Greater police presence has resulted in the criminalization
of childhood antics that in an earlier era were handled in the principal's office. Black students bear the brunt of the punitive turn in public
education. When hundreds of Seattle high school students walked out
in reaction to the failure to indict Darren Wilson in Ferguson, teacher
Jesse Hagopian drew a connection between Black Lives Matter and
public education: "These students were surely animated by the injustice
in Ferguson, but . . . they have no need to travel across the country to

confront the ferocity of racism. The Seattle Public Schools are under investigation by the federal Department of Education for suspension rates for black students four times higher than white students for the same infractions."[83] Just as corporate money mutes the participation of civil rights organizations in the struggle to raise the minimum wage, it has the same effect on their participation in the fight against corporate education reform and privatization. The NAACP and the Urban League have received *millions* of dollars from the Gates Foundation alone[84]— the project of billionaire Bill Gates to transform education by championing charter schools—which has actually become a cover for attacking teacher unions and pushing standardized testing.

In both of these cases the Black Lives Matter movement has the potential to make deeper connections to and create relationships with organized labor. Black workers continue to be unionized at higher rates than white workers. The reason is simple: Black union workers make far above and beyond what nonunion Black workers make, in salary and benefits. Black workers also tend to be concentrated in the sectors most under attack by the state—federal, state, and local government, including education and other municipal jobs. Throughout the winter of 2015, Black Lives Matter activists all over the country organized actions to "shut it down," including highways, public transportation, shopping establishments—even brunch! Developing alliances with organized labor could lead to workers exercising their power to shut down production, services, and business as usual as pressure for concrete reforms concerning the policing state. The pathway for this has already been trodden. On May 1, 2015, tens of thousands of activists rallied across the country under the banner of Black Lives Matter—and in Oakland, California, the International Longshore and Warehouse Union, Local 10, conducted a work stoppage that halted the flow of millions of dollars' worth of goods and prevented them from being loaded onto cargo ships. This was the first time a major union had initiated a work stoppage in solidarity with the Black Lives Matter movement. The coalition that helped to organize the action said in a statement:

> Labor is one sector of the community that can truly shut this country down. If workers refuse to work, product doesn't get made, and money doesn't exchange hands. The only way this country is going to take us seriously is if we interrupt their commerce and impact their bottom

line. Simply appealing to their humanity doesn't work. If that was the case, the epidemic of Black genocide at the hands of police would have ended decades ago.[85]

Broadening the reach of the movement also belies the notion that the movement is divided between old and young. Collaborating with Black workers, including Black teachers and other trade unionists, cuts across age groups and demonstrates that working-class African Americans of all generations have a vested interest in the success of the movement.

Solidarity

One important frontier of the movement also involves its capacity to develop solidarity with other oppressed groups of people. African Americans have always felt the most punishing aspects of life under American capitalism acutely. This has not meant, however, that Black people are alone in their desire to transform the harshness of society. The oppression of Indigenous people, immigrants, and nonwhite people more generally pervades American society. In profound ways, it is the secret to the conundrum of how the 1 percent can dominate a society where the vast majority has every interest in undoing the existing order. Basic math would seem to indicate that 12 or 13 percent of the population, which is what African Americans constitute, would have no realistic capacity to fundamentally transform the social order of the United States.

The challenge for the movement is transforming the goal of "freedom" into digestible demands that train and organize its forces so that they have the ability to fight for more, the movement must also have a real plan for building and developing solidarity among the oppressed. This means building networks and alliances with Latinos in opposition to attacks on immigrant rights, connecting with Arabs and Muslims campaigning against Islamophobia, and organizing with Native organizations that fight for self-determination within the United States. This is not an exhaustive list; it is only a beginning.

The struggle to build solidarity between oppressed communities, however, is not obvious. For example, when three young Muslims, Deah Barakat, Razan Abu-Salha, and Yusor Abu-Salha, were shot and killed by a white man in Chapel Hill, North Carolina, and activists began the hashtag #MuslimLivesMatter, there was a backlash. Some activists described the hashtag as an "appropriation" of the ongoing Black movement:

> This is not at all to undermine or belittle the injustices that other minority groups in this country deal with every day; in fact, it is quite the opposite. Every community deserves to be able to think critically about their own positions in America, about their own challenges, about their own experiences, and in their own terms. Of course Muslim lives are under fire in our American systems. There is no question about that. However, building off the #BlackLivesMatter trend equates struggles that are, though seemingly similar, drastically different.[86]

It is one thing to respect the organizing that has gone into the movement against police violence and brutality, but quite another to conceive of Black oppression and anti-Black racism as so wholly unique that they are beyond the realm of understanding and, potentially, solidarity from others who are oppressed.

In the contest to demonstrate how oppressions differ from one group to the next, we miss how we are connected through oppression—and how those connections should form the basis of solidarity, not a celebration of our lives on the margins. The American government demonizes its enemies to justify mistreating them, whether it is endless war, internment, and torture or mass incarceration and police abuse. There is a racist feedback loop, in which domestic and foreign policies feed and reinforce each other. This is why US foreign policy in the Middle East has reverberated at home. The cynical use of Islamophobia to whip up support for continued American interventions in Arab and Muslim countries inevitably has consequences for Muslim Americans. And the ever-expanding security state, justified by the "War on Terror," becomes the pretext for greater police repression at home—which, of course, disproportionately affects African Americans and Latino/as in border regions.

In the late 1990s, a movement began to stop racial profiling against Black drivers in police stops. Major class-action lawsuits in Maryland, New Jersey, Pennsylvania, and Florida highlighted the extent to which African Americans were subjected to unwarranted suspicion and harassment on the nation's interstates. New Jersey became a center of anti-profiling activism when, in the spring of 1998 during a routine police stop, an officer fired into a van filled with young African American men. Al Sharpton led a protest of several hundred people, including a five-hundred-car motorcade, onto Interstate 95. That same year, the ACLU filed a class-action lawsuit on behalf of several Black motorists who complained of racially motivated traffic stops on Interstate 95. The widespread suspicion of Blacks and Latino/as contributed to an atmosphere of intimidation and an implicit threat of violence. (This certainly seemed to be the case with the 1999 murder of Amadou Diallo, which touched off a wave of protests and civil disobedience demanding the prosecution of the cops involved.) Then, in March 1999, Republican New Jersey governor Christine Todd Whitman fired the state police superintendent when he said profiling was justified because "mostly minorities" trafficked in marijuana and cocaine.[87]

The movement's momentum however, was dramatically cut short in the aftermath of the terrorist attacks of 9/11. The US government rushed to turn tragedy into a call for national unity in preparation for a new war with Afghanistan in 2001 and later in Iraq. Moreover, federal agents justified racial profiling to hunt down Muslims and Arabs in the aftermath. No longer was this tactic subject to federal investigation and lawsuits. It became a legitimate and widely supported tool in the War on Terror. For example, in 1999, 59 percent of Americans said they believed that the police engaged in racial profiling; of those, 81 percent thought the practice was wrong.[88] Even George W. Bush, several months before 9/11, addressed a joint congressional session on the practice to declare, "Racial profiling is wrong and we will end it in America."[89] However, by September 30, 2001, Black support for racial profiling of Arabs had jumped to 60 percent, compared to 45 percent among the general population.[90] Not only was the developing struggle against racism buried under a wave of jingoism and Islamophobic racism, but the focal point of the antiracist struggle, racial profiling, was now being championed as a necessary tool to protect the United States.

When the movement reflects divisions that the American state actively promotes, it makes all of the movements against racism weaker. This does not mean the movements should paper over actual differences among various groups of people, but it does mean there is a need to understand the commonalities and overlaps in oppression while also coming to terms with the reality that there is a lot more to gain by building unity and a lot more to lose by staying in our respective corners.

Conclusion

Protests can expose these conditions and their relationship to the policing state; protests can draw in larger numbers of people; protests can compel public figures to speak against those conditions. Protests can do many things, but protests alone cannot end police abuse and the conditions that are used to justify it. The movement against police brutality, even in its current inchoate state, has transformed how Americans see and understand policing in the United States. Over the course of a year, Black people from coast to coast have led a struggle to expose the existence of an urban police state with suburban outposts. It has shown the country the depths of the lie that we live in a colorblind or postracial country. Eighty-three percent of Americans say racism "still poses a problem," up 7 percent from 2014. Sixty-one percent of whites and 82 percent of Blacks agree that "there's a need for a conversation about racism in American life."[91] In less than a year, the number of white Americans who view police killings as "isolated incidents" has fallen from 58 percent to 36 percent.[92] At the same time, in July 2015 alone, the police killed an astonishing 118 people, the most that had been killed over the entire year thus far.[93] By mid-August they had killed another fifty-four. On the anniversary of Mike Brown's death, Ferguson police shot and critically injured another Black teenager. In New York City, where there was a vibrant anti-police-brutality movement for years before the most recent iteration of the national movement, liberal mayor Bill DeBlasio has pledged to hire a thousand new police officers. This was surprising, since DeBlasio rode the success of the campaign to end stop-and-frisk into office in 2013. This is only one example of how resilient the police are as an institution, but it also shows elected officials' reluctance to discipline them.

The movement is confronted with many challenges, but it has also shown that it will not go away easily. This has less to do with the organizing genius of organizers than with deep anger among ordinary Blacks who have been beaten, imprisoned, humiliated, and abused, all the while being blamed for their own victimization. The power of ordinary African Americans to push the movement forward was seen in June 2015 in McKinney, Texas, when the police attacked several Black children at a swimming party, including fifteen-year-old Dajerria Becton, who was manhandled by one officer in particular.

In years past, a story like this would have resulted in little if any attention. Instead, a few days later, hundreds of Black and white protestors filled the street of the small suburban development where the children had been set upon, chanting, "We want to go swimming" and "No swimming, no driving." It must have been a powerful scene to everyone who witnessed it—and for different reasons. Many of the suburban white neighbors who supported the police were outraged but could do nothing about it; they had been rendered powerless. The police were undoubtedly intimidated by the action, so much so that the most aggressive cop, who had attacked Becton, was forced to resign days later. Most importantly, though, for the Black children who had been abused and threatened at gunpoint by the police and for their parents, to have hundreds of people show up to insist that their lives mattered must have repaired some part of the damage. For them to see the solidarity of hundreds of white people must have given them some hope that not all whites are racist and that some would even stand up and fight alongside them. The demonstration may have also validated their right to resist and stand up to racism and racist violence and affirmed that they were right to protest from the very beginning.

The Black Lives Matter movement, from Ferguson to today, has created a feeling of pride and combativeness among a generation that this country has tried to kill, imprison, and simply disappear. The power of protest has been validated. For it to become even more effective, to affect the policing state, and to withstand opposition and attempts to infiltrate, subvert, and undermine what has been built, there must be more organization and coordination in the move from protest to movement.

CHAPTER SEVEN

From #BlackLivesMatter to Black Liberation

On April 12, 1865, the American Civil War officially came to an end when the Union Army accepted the unconditional surrender of the Confederacy on the steps of a courthouse in Appomattox, Virginia. The Union Army, led by 200,000 Black soldiers, had destroyed the institution of slavery; as a result of their victory, Black people were now to be no longer property but citizens of the United States. The Civil Rights Act of 1866, the first declaration of civil rights in the United States, stated that

> citizens of every race and color, without regard to any previous condition of slavery or involuntary servitude, shall have the same right, in every State and Territory in the United States . . . to full and equal benefit of all laws and proceedings for the security of person and property, as is enjoyed by white citizens.[1]

There was no ambiguity that the war had buried chattel slavery once and for all. Days after the surrender of the Confederacy, Abraham Lincoln rode into Richmond, Virginia, the former capital of the slaveholders, where he stood upon the stairs of the former Confederate capitol building and told a large gathering crowd of Black people days into their freedom,

In reference to you, colored people, let me say God has made you free. Although you have been deprived of your God-given rights by your so-called Masters, you are now as free as I am, and if those that claim to be your superiors do not know that you are free, take the sword and bayonet and teach them that you are—for God created all men free, giving to each the same rights of life, liberty and the pursuit of happiness.[2]

One hundred and fifty years later, on April 12, 2015, at nine in the morning, 217 miles north of the Appomattox courthouse, Freddie Gray, a twenty-five-year-old Black man, was arrested by the Baltimore police. His only apparent crime was making eye contact with the police and then running away. Freddie Gray was loaded into a van. By the time he emerged forty-five minutes later, his voice box had been crushed, his neck snapped, and 80 percent of his spinal cord severed.

The distance from the end of the Civil War, with the birth of Black citizenship and civil rights, to the state-sanctioned beating and torture of Freddie Gray constitutes the gap between formal equality before the law and the self-determination and self-possession inherent in actual freedom—the right to be free from oppression, the right to make determinations about your life free from duress, coercion, or threat of harm. Freedom in the United States has been elusive, contingent, and fraught with contradictions and unattainable promises—for almost everyone.

Black people were not freed into an American dream, but into what Malcolm X described as an "American nightmare" of economic inequality and unchecked injustice. The full extent of this inequality was masked by racial terrorism. One hundred years after Emancipation, African Americans dismantled the last vestiges of legal discrimination with the civil rights movement, but the excitement of the movement quickly faded as American cities combusted with Black people who were angry and disillusioned at being locked out of accessing the riches of American society. Hundreds of thousands of African Americans participated in the uprisings in search of resolutions to the problems of lead poisoning, rat infestations, hunger and malnutrition, underemployment, poor schools, and persisting poverty. Where liberals and radicals often converged was in the demand that Blacks should have greater political control over their communities. For liberals, Black electoral politics was a sign of political maturity as the movement left the streets for the poll booth, urban governance, and community control. The problem was not "the system," it was exclusion from access to all that American society had to offer. Some radicals were also lured by the possibility of self-governance and community control. Indeed, it was a viable strategy, given that much of Black life was controlled by white elected officials and white-led institutions. The question remained: Could the machinery wielded in the oppression of Blacks now be retooled in the name of Black self-determination?

If freedom had in one era been imagined as inclusion in the mainstream of American society, including admittance to its political and financial institutions, then the last fifty years have yielded a mixed record. Indeed, since the last gasps of the Black insurgency in the 1970s, there are many measures of Black accomplishment and achievement in a country where Black people were never intended to survive as free people. Is there no greater symbol of a certain kind of Black accomplishment than a Black president? For those who consider mastery of American politics and Black political representation as the highest expressions of inclusion in the mainstream, then we are surely in the heyday of American "race relations." Yet, paradoxically, at a moment when African Americans have achieved what no rational person could have imagined when the Civil War ended, we have simultaneously entered a new period of Black protest, Black radicalization, and the birth of a new Black left.

No one knows what will come of this new political development, but many know the causes of its gestation. For, as much success as some African Americans have achieved, four million Black children live in poverty, one million Black people are incarcerated, and 240,000 Black people lost their homes as a result of the foreclosure crisis—resulting in the loss of hundreds of millions of dollars in Black savings. Never before in American history has a Black president presided over the misery of millions of Black people, the denial of the most basic standards for health, happiness, and basic humanity. Entertainer and activist Harry Belafonte Jr., recalled his last conversation with Martin Luther King Jr., in which King lamented, "I've come upon something that disturbs me deeply. . . . We have fought hard and long for integration, as I believe we should have, and I know that we will win. But I've come to believe we're integrating into a burning house."[3]

The aspiration for Black liberation cannot be separated from what happens in the United States as a whole. Black life cannot be transformed while the rest of the country burns. The fires consuming the United States are stoked by the widespread alienation of low-wage and meaningless work, unaffordable rents, suffocating debt, and poverty. The essence of economic inequality is borne out in a simple fact: there are 400 billionaires in the United States and 45 million people living in poverty. These are not parallel facts; they are intersecting facts. There are 400 American billionaires *because* there are 45 million people living in poverty. Profit comes at the expense of the living wage. Corporate executives, university presidents, and capitalists in general are living the good life—*because* so many others are living a life of hardship. The struggle for Black liberation, then, is not an abstract idea molded in isolation from the wider phenomenon of economic exploitation and inequality that pervades all of American society; it is intimately bound up with them.

The struggle for Black liberation requires going beyond the standard narrative that Black people have come a long way but have a long way to go—which, of course, says nothing about where it is that we are actually trying to get to. It requires understanding the origins and nature of Black oppression and racism more generally. Most importantly, it requires a strategy, some sense of how we get from the current situation to the future. Perhaps at its most basic level, Black liberation implies a world where Black people can live in peace, without the constant threat of the social, economic, and political woes of a society that places almost no value on the vast majority of Black lives. It would mean living in a world where Black lives matter. While it is true that when Black people get free, everyone gets free, Black people in America cannot "get free" alone. In that sense, Black liberation is bound up with the project of human liberation and social transformation.

Radical Reconstructions

This book opens with a long quote from an essay Martin Luther King Jr. published in 1969. In it, he writes that the Black struggle "reveals systemic rather than superficial flaws and suggests that radical reconstruction of society itself is the real issue to be faced." What would constitute the "radical reconstruction" of American society? This was a central question confronting the Black movement at the end of the last period of mass struggle. King himself had come to locate the crises confronting the United States in the "triplets" of "racism, materialism and militarism." King and hundreds of thousands of other angry Blacks, whites, and Latino/as across the country were rapidly radicalizing in reaction to the hypocrisy, contradictions, and brutality of capitalism. From the "massive resistance" of white supremacists led by the Democratic Party in the South to the expanding war in Vietnam, to the dense poverty exposed by waves of ghetto rebellions, the US government had become an emperor with no clothes.

This unfolding radicalization was not happening in isolation: it was part of a global rebellion against an old colonial order that was rapidly coming undone. During the course of World War II, Great Britain, the Netherlands, Italy, Japan, and France all lost colonial possessions. After the war, in 1947, England went on to lose the British colony of India, which was partitioned into India and Pakistan. And 1960 became known as the "Year of Africa" when seventeen African countries achieved independence from their colonial overlords. Decolonization was achieved in various ways, from "peaceful" transference of power to armed nationalist struggles. The ensuing debates over the futures of postcolonial societies included arguments over how to transform export-based economies into ones that prioritized the needs of the local population. In several of these countries, the debates revolved around different interpretations of socialism. In many ways these debates were distorted, given the wide influence of the Soviet Union, a country that at one point had been socialist but by this period had been for many years a one-party authoritarian regime. The Soviet model of socialism was based on an extremely narrow, limited definition of "state ownership." But who owned the state was an equally important question. There were other questions generated by those movements, including: how to win state power, political economy, and how all of this would contribute to economic development and self-determination after centuries of colonial ruin. Nonwhite, formerly colonized people around the world hailed socialism (defined in many ways) almost universally as the means for achieving their freedom and reconstructing state power in their own names.

By the end of the 1960s, many Black revolutionaries took for granted that African Americans were a colonized population within the United States. In the book *Black Power*, Carmichael and Hamilton said as much: "Black people in this country form a 'colony,' and it is not in the interest of the colonial power to liberate them. Black people are legal citizens of the United States with, for the most part, the same *legal* rights as other citizens. Yet they stand as colonial subjects in relation to white society."[4] This idea was popular because it seemed an accurate way to describe the relationship between the impoverished, largely Black urban cores in the midst of much whiter, larger metropolitan areas. Colonialism could also explain the financially predatory relationship of business to Black communities, which was almost wholly organized around extraction, with little to no investment. All of these descriptions made sense of Black oppression and exploitation and seemed to fit with what was happening to Black and Brown people all over the globe. As Stokely Carmichael wrote, "Black Power cannot be isolated from the African Revolution. It can only be comprehended within the context of the African Revolution. Thus with Black Power . . . came an intensification as the African Revolution from Watts to Soweto went into the phase of the armed struggle."[5]

It was, however, inaccurate to describe Black Americans' relationship to the United States as colonial, despite these obvious similarities. The profits reaped from the exploitation of Black urban dwellers were not insignificant, but neither were they the important revenue streams back to the American "metropole." The outflow of capital from the inner city worked almost exclusively to the benefit of the layer of business owners directly involved in economically exploitative relationships with the urban ghetto, such as bankers and real-estate agents. This was not a motor of American capitalism compared to the cotton, rubber, sugar, and mineral extraction and trade that had fueled colonial empires for hundreds of years.

Being an oppressed minority population does not necessarily mean being colonial subjects. Calling Black people a colonized people drew the Black struggle into the global rebellion against the "colonial oppressors." Malcolm X spoke to this when he recognized that it was "incorrect to classify the revolt of the Negro as simply a racial conflict of Black against white, or as purely an American problem. Rather, we are seeing today a global rebellion of the oppressed against the oppressor, the exploited against the exploiter."[6] Placing the Black rebellion within

the context of the "African Revolution" defied the idea that Black people were a "minority" population fighting on their own in the belly of
the beast. The identification of the Black struggle with the anticolonial
movement also reintroduced interpretations of socialism back into the
Black movement. There had been thousands of Black socialists, communists, and other anticapitalists in the United States for years, but the
anticommunist witch hunt led by the federal government had largely
destroyed any links between the socialist movement of the 1930s and
the new wave of struggle in the 1960s.

By the end of the 1960s, socialism was once again on the table as
a legitimate alternative to the "evil triplets" King worried about. Most
Black radicals were gravitating toward some conceptualization of socialism. It was easy to see why, considering how exposed the crimes
of capitalism were. The United States had been experiencing years of
economic growth, yet poverty, underemployment, and substandard
housing were still the norm for Black and Brown people. In a speech
Malcolm X gave at the founding of his Organization of Afro-American Unity, he said:

> I'm telling you we do it because we live in one of the rottenest countries
> that has ever existed on this earth. It's the system that is rotten; we have
> a rotten system. It's a system of exploitation, a political and economic
> system of exploitation, of outright humiliation, degradation, discrimi-
> nation—all of the negative things that you can run into, you have run
> into under this system that disguises itself as a democracy. . . . And you
> run around here getting ready to get drafted and go someplace and
> defend it. Someone needs to crack you upside your head.[7]

He would go on to name that system:

> All of the countries that are emerging today from under the shackles
> of colonialism are turning toward socialism. I don't think it's an acci-
> dent. Most of the countries that were colonial powers were capitalist
> countries and the last bulwark of capitalism today is America and it's
> impossible for a white person today to believe in capitalism and not
> believe in racism. You can't have capitalism without racism. And if
> you find a person without racism and you happen to get that person
> into conversation and they have a philosophy that makes you sure
> they don't have this racism in their outlook, usually they're socialists
> or their political philosophy is socialism.[8]

Similarly, King, near the end of his life, connected the "fire" burning down the house of America to the inequities rooted deep in the country's political economy. In 1967, King was reckoning with several questions that pierced the heart of American injustice:

> "Where do we go from here," that we honestly face the fact that the Movement must address itself to the question of restructuring the whole of American society. There are forty million poor people here. And one day we must ask the question, "Why are there forty million poor people in America?" And when you begin to ask that question, you are raising questions about the economic system, about a broader distribution of wealth. When you ask that question, you begin to question the capitalistic economy. And I'm simply saying that more and more, we've got to begin to ask questions about the whole society. We are called upon to help the discouraged beggars in life's marketplace. But one day we must come to see that an edifice which produces beggars needs restructuring. It means that questions must be raised. You see, my friends, when you deal with this, you begin to ask the question, "Who owns the oil?" You begin to ask the question, "Who owns the iron ore?" You begin to ask the question, "Why is it that people have to pay water bills in a world that is two-thirds water?"[9]

Black women were also connecting the system of capitalism to the hardship their families experienced. Black women who had been active in the civil rights movement went on to form the Third World Women's Alliance in 1968. By the early 1970s they published the *Black Women's Manifesto*, which analyzed racism and sexism in the movement and more generally: "The system of capitalism (and its afterbirth . . . racism) under which we all live, has attempted by many devious ways and means to destroy the humanity of black people. This has meant an outrageous assault on every black man, woman and child who resides in the United States."[10] Some of the women involved in the Third World Women's Alliance would also go on to form the Combahee River Collective. They too would link the oppression of Blacks and women to capitalism:

> We realize that the liberation of all oppressed peoples necessitates the destruction of the political-economic systems of capitalism and imperialism as well as patriarchy. We are socialists because we believe that work must be organized for the collective benefit of those who

do the work and create the products, and not for the profit of the bosses. Material resources must be equally distributed among those who create these resources. We are not convinced, however, that a socialist revolution that is not also a feminist and anti-racist revolution will guarantee our liberation. . . . Although we are in essential agreement with Marx's theory as it applied to the very specific economic relationships he analyzed, we know that his analysis must be extended further in order for us to understand our specific economic situation as Black women.[11]

By 1970, the Black Panther Party, an unabashed revolutionary socialist organization, was the largest and most influential Black revolutionary organization, with more than 5,000 members and 45 chapters. In 1971, the Panthers' newspaper, the *Black Panther*, reached its peak circulation at 250,000 papers a week[12]—a reach far beyond their membership. Ordinary Blacks reading the paper would have found the Panthers' outline for Black liberation mapped out with their "Ten-Point Program." Among their many demands were an end "to the robbery by the capitalists of our Black community," "decent housing fit for the shelter of human beings," "an immediate end to police brutality and murder of black people," and "land, bread, housing, education, clothing, justice and peace."[13]

Anticapitalism filtered into every aspect of Black life, including the workplace. In 1968, the Dodge Revolutionary Union Movement, made up of former Black students and Black autoworkers in Detroit, made similar references. An organizer from that group, John Watson, said in 1968,

To struggle in our own interests means that the Black people of the ghetto must struggle to overthrow white capitalism. The struggle against capitalism is world wide [*sic*] and the revolutionary struggle of the ghetto is crucial and essential in the over all [*sic*] world revolution. If the Koreans and Vietnamese can overthrow imperialism in Asia, then Asia will be free. But if the Black Revolution can overthrow capitalism and imperialism in the US, then the whole world will be freed. This, then, is our role.[14]

By the end of the 1960s, there was widespread understanding that the capitalist economy was responsible for Black hardship and that socialism was an alternative way to organize society. Organizations that called for the overthrow of the government, like the Black Panthers, were so popular that in 1969 FBI director J. Edgar Hoover declared that "the Black Panther Party, without question, represents the greatest threat to internal security of the country."[15] The popularity of the Panthers—in concert with successive years of ghetto rebellions—compelled the economic and political elite to create more space for the development of a Black middle class, but for the majority the questions of inequality and injustice remained largely unresolved.

Given the widespread advocacy of socialism, in one form or another, at the end of the last Black insurgency, it is almost odd when socialism is dismissed as incapable of explaining racism or Black oppression. Political commentator Tim Wise published in 2010 a typical critique on his blog:

> Left activists often marginalize people of color by operating from a framework of extreme class reductionism, which holds that the "real" issue is class, not race, that "the only color that matters is green," and that issues like racism are mere "identity politics," which should take a backseat to promoting class-based universalism and programs to help working people. This reductionism, by ignoring the way that even middle class and affluent people of color face racism and color-based discrimination (and by presuming that low-income folks of color and low-income whites are equally oppressed, despite a wealth of evidence to the contrary) reinforces white denial, privileges white perspectivism and dismisses the lived reality of people of color. Even more . . . it ignores perhaps the most important political lesson regarding the interplay of race and class: namely, that the biggest reason why there is so little working-class consciousness and unity in the United States (and thus, why class-based programs to uplift all in need are so much weaker here than in the rest of the industrialized world), is precisely because of racism and the way that white racism has been deliberately inculcated among white working folks. Only by confronting that directly (rather than sidestepping it as class reductionists seek to do) can we ever hope to build cross-racial, class based coalitions. In other words, for the policies favored by the class reductionist to work—be they social democrats or Marxists—or even to come into being, racism and white supremacy must be challenged directly.[16]

Specificity always helps to illuminate the issues, but Wise lumps several categories of people together, only to reduce their ideas and political activity to downplaying or ignoring racism. Folding "the left," "activists," "social democrats," and "Marxists" together and describing them collectively as privileging "white perspectives" while dismissing "the lived reality of people of color" obscures more than it clarifies. For one, there are important distinctions among those with a political analysis and framework for understanding the world and those who show up at demonstrations. There is also an embedded assumption that "the left" is white and effectively ignores racism—a curious assumption, given the clear historical support and affiliation with socialism and socialists among African Americans quoted above. How did socialism go from being the greatest threat to the federal government (as it called the revolutionary socialist Black Panthers) to being perceived as "white" and marginal to the struggles of "people of color"?

To really unpack that history would involve understanding the extent of the repression the federal government exacted against its "internal enemy" as a way to break their influence among ordinary African Americans. It would also involve taking the politics of the Panthers seriously, as well as the political debates that ensued across the revolutionary left of the 1960s and 1970s over where to build their groups, how to build, and among what audience. To be sure, there were deep internecine battles over how to move forward, but the least charitable way to describe these debates is to reduce many differing political viewpoints and organizations into the generic category of "class reductionist left activist." The revolutionary left today *is* mostly white and tiny, but today's reality must be firmly situated in a history of massive repression, including imprisonment and state-sanctioned murder, as well as in intense political debates over strategy, tactics, and political perspectives.

As to the political content of Wise's critique, most revolutionary socialists would agree that the most significant challenge to the development of class consciousness in the United States *is* racism and that, without a struggle against racism, there is no hope for fundamentally changing this country. It is true that the most well-known socialist-identified person in the United States is Vermont senator Bernie Sanders, who exemplifies most of what Wise is criticizing more generally in the left. But Sanders is a United States senator who has spent decades rubbing shoulders with the powerful elite. Sanders is reluctant and almost uncomfortable discussing the specific ways that racism adds another burden onto the existing oppression Black workers and the poor face. Thus, Sanders essentially argues that addressing economic inequality is the best way to combat racism. It is an old argument from the right wing of the socialist movement that was challenged and denounced by its left wing—the wing that became the Communist Party after the Russian Revolution in 1917.

The Russian Revolution gave life to an international communist movement that was much further to the left than the old Socialist Party. The emergence of revolutionary communism in the 1920s and 1930s overlapped with the rapidly developing radicalization of African Americans. Blacks were referring to themselves as "New Negroes," as opposed to the old, victimized Negroes of the Jim Crow South. These "new" Blacks were imbued with the confidence of living in big cities, finally out from under the surveillance and intimidation of Jim Crow. They were emboldened by their brethren having fought in the "Great War," which President Woodrow Wilson described as an American war fought in the name of democracy. They were also embittered by the contradiction that America made public appeals to democracy while racist whites initiated pogroms across the North.

Within this overheating political cauldron, there were different Black political responses. The followers of Marcus Garvey argued that Blacks should triumphantly return to Africa. Black radicalism also flourished. The African Blood Brotherhood was small but influential in its espousal of both socialist and nationalist politics. The Communist Party (CP) also became a political pole of attraction and recruited many of the best Black revolutionaries of the era, who actively transformed the party's political perspective on its work among African Americans. As historian Robin D. G. Kelley has argued, "If the Third International . . . proved more sympathetic and sensitive to the racial nature of American class struggle, it is largely because Black folk made it so . . . advocating a radical fusion of socialism and 'race politics.'"[17] When Black writer and literary giant Claude McKay traveled as a delegate to the Communist International in 1922, he reported:

> In associating with the comrades of America, I have found demonstrations of prejudice on the various occasions when the white and black comrades had to get together, and this is the greatest obstacle that the Communists of America have got to overcome—the fact

that they first have got to emancipate themselves from the ideas they entertained toward Negroes before they can be able to reach the Negroes with any kind of radical propaganda.[18]

The Russian revolutionary Vladimir Lenin directly intervened in the American CP and argued that the party should immediately begin to agitate politically among African Americans.

The shift in orientation was sharp and dramatic. Whereas the founding convention of the CP in 1919 merely stated that the "racial oppression of the Negro is simply the expression of his economic bondage and oppression, each intensifying the other," by 1921, after Lenin's involvement on the question, the CP now declared:

> The Negro workers in American are exploited and oppressed more ruthlessly than any other group. The history of the Southern Negro is the history of a reign of terror—of persecution, rape and murder. . . . Because of the anti-Negro policies of organized labor, the Negro has despaired of aid from this source, and he has either been driven into the camp of labor's enemies, or has been compelled to develop purely racial organizations which seek purely racial aims. The Workers Party will support the Negroes in their struggle for Liberation, and will help them in their fight for economic, political and social equality. . . . Its task will be to destroy altogether the barrier of race prejudice that has been used to keep apart the Black and white workers, and bind them into a solid union of revolutionary forces for the overthrow of our common enemy.[19]

By the early 1940s, thousands of Blacks had joined the CP.

In the period leading up to World War II, the politics of communism became the dominant political framework for most of the non-white world as hundreds of millions of people of color across the globe were inspired by Lenin's writings on the right of oppressed nations to fight for their own freedom. Lenin wrote:

> The proletariat must struggle against the enforced retention of oppressed nations within the bounds of the given state. . . . The proletariat must demand freedom of political separation for the colonies and nations oppressed by "their own" nation. Otherwise, the internationalism of the proletariat would be nothing but empty words; neither confidence nor class solidarity would be possible between the workers of the oppressed and the oppressor nations. . . . On the other hand,

the socialists of the oppressed nation must, in particular, defend and implement the full and unconditional unity, including organizational unity, of the workers of the oppressed nation and those of the oppressor nation. Without this it is impossible to defend the independent policy of the proletariat and their class solidarity with the proletariat of other countries.[20]

Through the period of the Popular Front (the name for the strategy Lenin describes), the CP maintained its popularity among African Americans and many of the oppressed. But over time, the constantly shifting, contradictory positions of the CP and Soviet Union, which were now led by the increasingly tyrannical Josef Stalin, led to a mass exodus from the party after the war. In the United States during the war, the CP had embraced the Democratic Party and called for unity against Hitler at all costs. Its conclusion that American Blacks should therefore downplay the continuing fight against racial inequality would eventually erode the ranks of the CP's Black membership. But the foibles of the CP should not be conflated with the validity of anticapitalism and socialism as political theories that inform and guide the struggle for Black liberation. C. L. R. James, a Black revolutionary from the Caribbean and a collaborator of Russian revolutionary Leon Trotsky, continued to develop Marxist theory and its relationship to the Black struggle when he wrote in 1948—years before the emergence of the civil rights movement—about the dynamics of the Black movement and its impact on the class struggle in general:

We say, number one, that the Negro struggle, the independent Negro struggle, has a vitality and a validity of its own; that it has deep historic roots in the past of America and in present struggles; it has an organic political perspective, along which it is traveling, to one degree or another, and everything shows that at the present time it is traveling with great speed and vigor. We say, number two, that this independent Negro movement is able to intervene with terrific force upon the general social and political life of the nation, despite the fact that it is waged under the banner of democratic rights and is not led necessarily either by the organized labor movement or the Marxist party. We say, number three, and this is the most important, that it is able to exercise a powerful influence upon the revolutionary proletariat, that it has got a great contribution to make to the development of the proletariat in the United States, and that it is in itself a constituent part of the struggle for socialism. In this way we challenge directly any attempt to subordinate or to push to the rear the social and political significance of the independent Negro struggle for democratic rights.[21]

James's observations still resonate, especially in the context of today's movement. The Black movement is an independent force that has its own timing, logic, and perspective based on the history of racism and oppression in this country.

It is also the case that when the Black movement goes into motion, it destabilizes all political life in the United States. King argued that the Black movement "forc[es] America to face all its interrelated flaws—racism, poverty, militarism, and materialism. It . . . expos[es] the evils that are rooted deeply in the whole structure of our society. It reveals systemic rather than superficial flaws."[22] The oppression of Black workers exposes the foundational lie of the United States as a free and democratic society more than that of any other group, with the exception of the Indigenous population. The political activism and rebellion of Black people bring that lie to the surface for all to see, throwing into question the actual nature of US society. White workers have always followed the lead of Black workers. The militant strike wave I described in chapter 2 was certainly influenced by the Black freedom struggle that had provided a powerful example of organizing and resistance for white workers in the union movement to follow. For this reason, far from being marginal to the struggles of Black people, socialists have *always* been at the center of those movements—from the struggle to save the Scottsboro Boys in the 1930s, to Bayard Rustin's role in organizing the 1963 March on Washington, to the Black Panther Party's organizing against police brutality. At the height of McCarthyism, socialists and communists were so identified with the antiracist movement that antiracist organizing was automatically assumed to be the work of communists.

The Political Economy of Racism

Capitalism is an economic system based on the exploitation of the many by the few. Because of the gross inequality it produces, capitalism requires various political, social, and ideological tools to divide the majority—racism is one among many oppressions intended to serve this purpose. Oppression is used to justify, "explain," and make sense of rampant inequality. For example, racism developed under the regime of slavery to explain and justify the enslavement of Africans at a time when the world was celebrating the notions of human rights, liberty, freedom, and self-determination. The dehumanization and subjected status of Black people had to be rationalized in this moment of new political possibilities.

It is widely accepted that the racial oppression of slaves was rooted in the exploitation of the slave economy, but fewer recognize that under capitalism, *wage slavery* is the pivot around which all other inequalities and oppressions turn. Capitalism used racism to justify plunder, conquest, and slavery, but as Karl Marx pointed out, it would also come to use racism to divide and rule—to pit one section of the working class against another and, in so doing, blunt the class consciousness of all. To claim, then, as Marxists do, that racism is a product of capitalism is not to deny or diminish its centrality to or impact on American society. It is simply to explain its origins and persistence. Nor is this reducing racism to just a function of capitalism; it is locating the dynamic relationship between class exploitation and racial oppression in the functioning of American capitalism.

Marx has been criticized for ignoring the issues of race in his own day, but there is evidence that Marx was well aware of the centrality of race under capitalism. He did not write extensively on slavery and its racial impact, but he did write about how European capitalism's emergence was rooted in the pilfering, rape, and destruction of natives, colonial subjects, and Black slaves. He famously wrote that "the discovery of gold and silver in America, the extirpation, enslavement and entombment in mines of the aboriginal population, the beginning of the conquest and looting of the East Indies, the turning of Africa into a warren for the commercial hunting of Black skins, signaled the rosy dawn of the era of capitalist production."[23] Marx also recognized the degree to which slavery was central to the world economy:

> Direct slavery is just as much the pivot of bourgeois industry as machinery, credits, etc. Without slavery you have no cotton; without cotton you have no modern industry. It is slavery that has given the colonies their value; it is the colonies that have created world trade,

and it is world trade that is the pre-condition of large-scale industry. Thus slavery is an economic category of the greatest importance.
Without slavery North America, the most progressive of countries,
would be transformed into a patriarchal country. Wipe out North
America from the map of the world, and you will have anarchy—the
complete decay of modern commerce and civilization. Cause slavery
to disappear and you will have wiped America off the map of nations.
Thus slavery, because it is an economic category, has always existed
among the institutions of the peoples. Modern nations have been able
only to disguise slavery in their own countries, but they have imposed
it without disguise upon the New World.[24]

Thus within Marxism there is a fundamental understanding of the
centrality of slave labor to national and international economies.

But what about race? Marx did not write prolifically on race, but
one can look to his correspondence and deliberations on the American
Civil War to get some idea about his views of racial oppression and
how it operated within capitalism and his opposition to it. For example, in *Black Reconstruction*, W. E. B. Du Bois quotes at length a letter
Marx penned, as head of the International Workingmen's Association,
to Abraham Lincoln in 1864, in the midst of the Civil War:

The contest for the territories which opened the epoch, was it not to
decide whether the virgin soil of immense tracts should be wedded to
the labor of the immigrant or be prostituted by the tramp of the slave
driver? When an oligarchy of 300,000 slave holders dared to inscribe
for the first time in the annals of the world "Slavery" on the banner of
armed revolt, when on the very spots where hardly a century ago the
idea of one great Democratic Republic had first sprung up, whence
the first declaration of the rights of man was issued . . . when on the
very spots counter-revolution . . . maintained "slavery to be a bene-
ficial institution". . . and cynically proclaimed property in man "the
cornerstone of the new edifice". . . then the working classes of Europe
understood at once . . . that the slaveholders' rebellion was to sound
the tocsin for a general holy war of property against labor. . . . They
consider it an earnest sign of the epoch to come that it fell to the lot
of Abraham Lincoln, the single-minded son of the working class, to
lead his country through the matchless struggles for the rescue of the
enchained race and the Reconstruction of a social order.

Marx personally opposed slavery and he furthermore theorized that slavery and the intense racism that flowed from it not only resulted in the oppression of slaves but also threatened the stability of the white working class by creating a downward pressure on wages in general. It was impossible to compete with the free labor of the enslaved.

This did not mean white workers were sympathetic to the cause of the slaves—with a few notable exceptions, they were not. Marx was not, however, addressing the issue of consciousness; he was describing the objective factors that created the *potential* for solidarity. He wrote in *Capital*, "In the United States of America, every independent movement of the workers was paralyzed as long as slavery disfigured a part of the Republic. Labor cannot emancipate itself in the white skin where in the Black it is branded." Marx grasped the modern dynamics of racism as the means by which workers who had common objective interests could also become mortal enemies because of subjective, but nevertheless real, racist and nationalist ideas. Looking at the tensions between Irish and English workers, with a nod toward the American situation, Marx wrote:

> Every industrial and commercial center in England possesses a working class divided into two hostile camps, English proletarians and Irish proletarians. The ordinary English worker hates the Irish worker as a competitor who lowers his standard of life. In relation to the Irish worker he feels himself a member of the ruling nation and so turns himself into a tool of the aristocrats and capitalists of his country against Ireland, thus strengthening their domination over himself. He cherishes religious, social and national prejudices against the Irish worker. His attitude is much the same as that of the "poor whites" to the "niggers" in the former slave states of the USA. The Irishman pays him back with interest in his own money. He sees in the English worker at once the accomplice and stupid tool of the English rule in Ireland. This antagonism is artificially kept alive and intensified by the press, the pulpit, the comic papers, in short by all the means at the disposal of the ruling classes. This antagonism is the secret of the impotence of the English working class, despite its organization. It is the secret by which the capitalist maintains its power. And that class is fully aware of it.[25]

From this we can see a Marxist theory of how racism operated after slavery was ended. Marx was highlighting three things: first, that capitalism promotes economic competition between workers; second, that the ruling class uses racist ideology to divide workers against each other; and, finally, that when one group of workers suffer oppression, it negatively affects all workers and the class as a whole.

White Supremacy for Some, Not Others

If white working-class people do not benefit from capitalist exploitation, then why do they allow racism to cloud their ability to unite with nonwhite workers for the greater good of all working people? The answer requires understanding how a white identity was created as a corollary to the racism directed at African Americans.

One benefit of the North American form of racial slavery to enslavers and the ruling class generally was that it deflected potential class tensions among white men. American freedom for whites was contingent on American slavery for Blacks. Historian Edmund Morgan explains that slavery was

> the primary evil that men sought to avoid for society as a whole by curbing monarchs and establishing republics. But it was also the solution to one of society's most serious problems, the problem of the poor. Virginians could outdo English republicans as well as New England ones, partly because they had solved the problem: they had achieved a society in which most of the poor were enslaved.[26]

The enslaved could not easily rise up; if and when they did, all white men could unite to subjugate them. Whites who were small farmers and those who were big planters had nothing in common except that they were not slaves, and that eased the potential tensions between them.

When slavery ended, an evolving strategy of "white supremacy" functioned in a similar way to blunt the political and economic tensions that existed among white men in the South, as chapter 4 describes. Broadly, "white supremacy" was the response to the supposed threat of "Negro domination"—the idea that the end of slavery and the reforms of Reconstruction would reverse the roles of Blacks and whites. Poor whites were recruited to the "lost cause" of white supremacy in order to preserve their own privileged spot in the hierarchy or risk their own demise with the ever-present threat of "negro domination." But the rallying cry of "white supremacy" was intended to obscure, not elucidate. "White supremacy" was not a coherent strategy "but involved ad hoc responses to chaotic circumstances."[27] In its original iteration it was intended to remove Blacks from political power, without which they would be more vulnerable to economic coercion. Above all, "white supremacy did not mean that whites were to be supreme." Instead, it was a political strategy intended to manipulate racial fears as a means of maintaining class rule for the landed elite of the cotton-rich Black Belt.[28] White supremacy has historically existed to marginalize Black influence in social, political, and economic spheres while also obscuring major differences in experience in the social, political, and economic spheres among white people. Like slavery, this was necessary to maximize productivity and profitability while dulling the otherwise sharp antagonisms between the richest and poorest white men.

What does this have to do with the world today? The political strategy of uniting all whites around white supremacy and a commitment to politically and economically marginalizing or excluding Black people does not exactly resemble the country we live in today. This does not mean that white men are not in an overwhelmingly powerful position in the institutions that control the political and economic destiny of this country. But the actual legacy of the political project of white supremacy expresses itself by obscuring the class antagonism among whites. "White people" are typically regarded as an undifferentiated mass with a common experience of privilege, access, and unfettered social mobility. These perceptions have largely been facilitated by the academic distillation of a "white" identity into an aspirational category of "whiteness."

"Whiteness" is therefore not necessarily embodied in white people; it can apply to anyone—Black, Latino, Asian, and, yes, white people. In some ways, this distinction between whiteness and white people was intended, importantly, to allow for distinction and differentiation. But when "acting white" is invoked to explain the actions of reactionary nonwhite political actors, like Supreme Court justice Clarence Thomas, it is being used to transpose class and race, further distorting the existence of class differences. In this way, "whiteness" is an adaptation of the American left to the myth that the United States is a classless society. Nonwhite people in positions of power are accused of "performing whiteness" instead of exercising their class power—as if Clarence Thomas or Barack Obama are acting in ways they do not wholly intend to. Moreover, it invariably collapses important distinctions among whites into a common white experience that simply does not exist. This has huge implications in the struggle to build solidarity among the oppressed and exploited and in creating the alliances and coalitions that must be built to challenge the plutocracy at the helm of the country.

More than 19 million white Americans fall below the poverty line, nearly double the number of poor Black people. Black people are over-represented among the ranks of the poor, but the sheer number of poor white people also destabilizes assumptions about the nature of American society. The poverty rate among working-class whites has grown from 3 percent to 11 percent since 2000.[29] Even though the recession increased Black poverty, the gap between white and Black poverty has narrowed—not because Blacks are doing better, but because whites are doing worse.[30] In fact, 76 percent of whites have experienced poverty at some time in their lives. Four out of five American adults struggle with "joblessness, near-poverty, or reliance on welfare for at least part of their lives."[31] Despite the ubiquitous "common sense" of "white privilege," most ordinary whites are insecure about the future. Whites' pessimism about the economic future is at a twenty-five-year high, with millions believing that they cannot improve their living standards. This pessimism is rooted in the erosion of their economic situation.[32]

Far and away, African Americans suffer most from the blunt force trauma of the American criminal justice system, but the pervasive character of law-and-order politics means that whites get caught up in its web as well. African Americans are imprisoned at an absurd rate of 2,300 for every 100,000 Black people. White people, on the other hand, are incarcerated at a rate of 450 people per 100,000. The difference speaks directly to the racial disparities that define American criminal justice, but it is worth noting that the rate at which white people in the United States are incarcerated is still higher than the incarceration rates of almost every other country in the world.[33] It's also unquestionable that Blacks and Latino/as experience death at the hands of police at much greater rates than whites, but *thousands* of white people have also been murdered by the police. This does not mean the experiences of whites and people of color are equal, but there is a basis for solidarity among white and nonwhite working-class people.

This more complicated picture of the material reality of white

working-class life is not intended to diminish the extent to which ordinary whites buy into or accept racist ideas about Blacks. It is also true
that, by every social measure, whites do better than African Americans
on average, but that does not say much about who benefits from the
inequality of our society. For example, in a country with four hundred
billionaires, what does it mean that 43 percent of white households make
only between $10,000 and $49,000 a year?[34] Of course, an even larger
number of Black people make this pitiful amount—65 percent—but
when we only compare the average incomes of working-class Blacks and
whites, we miss the much more dramatic disparity between the wealthiest and everyone else.

If it isn't in the interest of ordinary whites to be racist, why do
they accept racist ideas? First, the same question could be asked of
any group of workers. Why do men accept sexist ideas? Why do many
Black workers accept racist anti-immigrant rhetoric? Why do many
Black Caribbean and African immigrant workers think that Black
Americans are lazy? Why do most American workers of all ethnicities
accept racist ideas about Arabs and Muslims? In short, if most people
agree that it would be in the interest of any group of workers to be more
united than divided, then why do workers hold reactionary ideas that
are an obstacle to unity?

There are two primary reasons: competition and the prevalence
of ruling-class ideology. Capitalism creates false scarcity, the perception that need outstrips resources. When billions are spent on war,
police-brutality settlements, and publicly subsidized sports stadiums,
there never seems to be a shortage of money. But when it comes to
schools, housing, food, and other basic necessities, politicians always
complain about deficits and the need to curb spending and cut budgets.
The scarcity is manufactured, but the competition over these resources
is real. People who are forced to fight over basic necessities are often
willing to believe the worst about other workers to justify why they
should have something while others should not.

The prevailing ideology in a given society consists of the ideas that
influence how we understand the world and help us make sense of our
lives—through news, entertainment, education, and more. The political
and economic elite shape the ideological world we all live in, to their benefit. We live in a thoroughly racist society, so it should not be surprising

that people have racist ideas. The more important question is under what circumstances those ideas can change. There is a clash between the prevailing ideology in society and people's lived experience. The media may inundate the public with constant images and news stories that describe Blacks as criminals or on welfare, but an individual's experience with Blacks at work may completely contradict the stereotype—hence the insistence from many whites that they are not racist because they "know Black people." It can be true in that person's mind. People's consciousness can change and can even contradict itself.

This is also true for African Americans, who can harbor racist ideas about other Black people while *simultaneously* holding antiracist ideas. After all, Black people also live in this racist society and are equally inundated with racist stereotypes. The development of consciousness is never linear—it is constantly fluctuating between adhering to ideas that fit a "common sense" conception of society and being destabilized by real-life events that upend "common sense." The Italian Marxist Antonio Gramsci explains the phenomenon of mixed consciousness this way:

> The active man-in-the-mass has a practical activity but has no clear theoretical consciousness of his practical activity which nonetheless involves understanding the world in so far as it transforms it. His theoretical consciousness can . . . be historically in opposition to his activity. One might almost say that he has two theoretical consciousness[es] (or one contradictory consciousness): one which is implicit in his activity and which in reality unites him with all fellow workers in the practical transformation of the real world; and one superficially explicit or verbal, which he has inherited from the past and uncritically absorbed. The person is strangely composite: it contains Stone Age elements and principles of a more advanced science, prejudices of all past phases of history at the local level and intuitions of a future philosophy which will be that of a human race united the world over.[35]

Whether or not a group of workers has reactionary, mixed, or even revolutionary consciousness does not change its objective status as exploited and oppressed labor. The achievement of consciousness is the difference between the working class being a class in itself as opposed to a class for itself. It affects whether or not workers are in a position to fundamentally alter their reality through collective action. As one writer observed, "Only a collective can develop a systematic alternative world view, can overcome to some degree the alienation of manual and mental work that imposes on everyone, on workers and intellectuals alike, a partial and fragmented view of reality."[36]

Just because white workers, to take a specific example, may at times fully accept reactionary ideas about African Americans does not change the objective fact that the majority of the US poor are white, the majority of people without health insurance are white, and the majority of the homeless are white. It is true that Blacks and Latino/as are disproportionately affected by the country's harsh economic order, but this is a reality they share with the majority of white workers. The common experience of oppression and exploitation creates the potential for a united struggle to better the conditions of all. This is obviously not an automatic process, nor is it a given that essentially economic struggles will translate to support or struggle for the political rights of Blacks to be free of discrimination and racism. Political unity, including winning white workers to the centrality of racism in shaping the lived experiences of Black and Latino/a workers, is key to their own liberation.

Tim Wise's observations reduce these real issues to an abstract accusation of "privileging" class over race. But our movement has to have theoretical, political, and strategic clarity to confront challenges in the real world. When, in 2012, Chicago's Black public school CEO Barbara Byrd Bennett was scheming with mayor Rahm Emanuel to close more than fifty schools located exclusively in Black and Latino/a neighborhoods, should Black teachers, students, and parents have united with Bennett, who has certainly experienced racism and sexism in her life and career, but who was also leading the charge to undo public education in Chicago? Or should they have united with the thousands of white teachers in Chicago schools and the vice president of the Chicago Teachers Union, a white, heterosexual man, to build the movement to save public education in the city?

Probably very few people in history have had as much racist invective directed at them as Barack Obama has—hating him is basically shorthand for racism now. But he has also championed policies that absolved the banks and Wall Street of any responsibility for crashing the economy; as a result, since 2007 ten million people have been displaced from more than four million homes by the foreclosure crisis.[37] Should Black workers put that aside and unite with Obama out of racial solidarity and a shared "lived experience," or should they unite with ordinary whites and Latino/as who have also lost their homes to challenge a political program that regularly defends business interests to the detriment of all working-class and poor people? In the abstract, perhaps these are complicated questions. But in the daily struggles to defend public education, fight for real healthcare reform, or stop predatory foreclosures, these are the concrete questions every movement faces.

The "blind spot" of class within the framework of people like Tim Wise not only leaves them incapable of explaining class division among the oppressed, it also underemphasizes the material foundation for solidarity and unity within the working class. Instead, the concepts of solidarity and unity are reduced to whether or not one chooses to be an "ally." There's nothing wrong with being an ally, but it doesn't quite capture the degree to which Black and white workers are inextricably linked. It's not as if white workers can simply choose not to "ally" with Black workers to no peril of their own. The scale of attack on the living standards of the working class is overwhelming. There is a systematic, bipartisan effort to dismantle the already anemic welfare state. When, in 2013, $5 billion cut was cut from food stamps, it had a direct and deleterious impact on the lives of tens of millions of white working-class people.

In this context, solidarity is not just an option; it is crucial to workers' ability to resist the constant degradation of their living standards. Solidarity is only possible through relentless struggle to win white workers to antiracism, to expose the lie that Black workers are worse off because they somehow choose to be, and to win the white working class to the understanding that, unless they struggle, they too will continue to live lives of poverty and frustration, even if those lives are somewhat better than the lives led by Black workers. Success or failure are contingent on whether or not working people see themselves as brothers and sisters whose liberation is inextricably bound together.

Solidarity is standing in unity with people even when you have not personally experienced their particular oppression. The reality is that as long as capitalism exists, material and ideological pressures push white workers to be racist and all workers to hold each other in general suspicion. But there are moments of struggle when the mutual interests of workers are laid bare, and when the suspicion is finally turned in the other direction—at the plutocrats who live well while the rest of us suffer. The key question is whether or not in those moments of struggle a coherent political analysis of society, oppression, and exploitation can be articulated that makes sense of the world we live in, but that also champions the vision of a different kind of society—and a way to get there.

No serious socialist current in the last hundred years has ever demanded that Black or Latino/a workers put their struggles on the back burner while some other class struggle is waged first. This assumption rests on the mistaken idea that the working class is white and male, and therefore incapable of taking up issues of race, class, and gender. In fact, the American working class is female, immigrant, Black, white, Latino/a, and more. Immigrant issues, gender issues, and antiracism *are* working-class issues.

Conclusion

Racism in the United States has never been just about abusing Black and Brown people just for the sake of doing so. It has always been a means by which the most powerful white men in the country have justified their rule, made their money, and kept the rest of us at bay. To that end, racism, capitalism, and class rule have always been tangled together in such a way that it is impossible to imagine one without the other. Can there be Black liberation in the United States as the country is currently constituted? No. Capitalism is contingent on the absence of freedom and liberation for Black people and anyone else who does not directly benefit from its economic disorder. That, of course, does not mean there is nothing to do and no struggle worth waging. Building the struggles against racism, police violence, poverty, hunger, and all of the ways in which oppression and exploitation express themselves is critical to people's basic survival in this society. But it is also within those struggles for the basic rights of existence that people learn how to struggle, how to strategize, and build movements and organizations. It is also how our confidence develops to counter the insistence that this society, as it is currently constructed, is the best that we can hope to achieve. People engaged in struggle learn to fight for more by fighting for and winning something. But the day-to-day struggles in which many people are engaged today must be connected to a much larger vision of what a different world could look like. Political scientist and radical Michael Dawson argues for "pragmatic utopianism" that "starts where we are but imagines where we want to be . . . based on the utopian imaginings of a much different America—one we are repeatedly told was impossible to obtain—combined with the hardheaded political realism that generated the strategies and tactics necessary to achieve their goals."[38]

Is this neoliberal, gentrified, overpriced, under-resourced society the best our species can create? The *Black Women's Manifesto* provided a very succinct idea of what the "new world" would look like:

> The new world that we are struggling to create must destroy oppression of any type. The value of this new system will be determined by the status of those persons who are presently most oppressed—the low man on the totem pole. Unless women in any enslaved nation are completely liberated, the change cannot really be called a revolution. . . . A people's revolution that engages the participation of every member of the community, including men, and women, brings about a certain transformation in the participants as a result of this participation. Once you have caught a glimpse of freedom or tasted a bit of self-determination, you can't go back to old routines that were established under a racist, capitalist regime.[39]

It is the struggle itself that can compel people to push for more.

In the summer of 2014, the Black working class of Ferguson "caught a glimpse of freedom and tasted a bit of self-determination" when they stood down the police and National Guard and stayed in the streets for Mike Brown. Their local struggle inspired Black people around the country to take to the streets and stand down the police. What began as a narrowly conceived demand for justice for Mike Brown has erupted into a movement largely identified by the slogan "Black Lives Matter." It reflects the political maturation of this stage of the movement. The next stage will involve progressing from protests aimed at raising awareness or drawing attention to the crisis of police violence to engaging with the social forces that have the capacity to shut down sectors of work and production until our demands to stop police terrorism are met. The movement has shown that violent policing does not exist in a vacuum: it is a product of the inequality in our society. The police exert their authority in a fundamentally disordered society. The clearer we can see these threads connecting police mayhem to the disorder in our society, the clearer we can express our need for a different kind of world. This is not simply wishful, utopian thinking. The quotes from Black radicals and revolutionaries throughout this chapter show that this is a familiar conclusion at which those intimately involved in social movements arrive.

At the beginning of this book, I asked why this movement has appeared in this moment, even though police violence and terrorism have been such a common feature of Black life throughout American history. In doing so, I have examined the ideological and political forces that often dramatically slow the fight for Black rights in particular. Historically, the insistence that Black deprivation is rooted in Black culture and in Black people has deflected attention away from the systemic roots of racism, compelling African Americans to look inward instead of making demands on the state and others. But this is a fluid and contradictory process, especially when looking inward reveals that most Black people are working harder than everyone else and still not getting ahead. The space within that contradiction is explosive. We saw it explode in the 1960s, and we can still smell the smoke today. I also explain "colorblindness" not as an aspiration but as a political tool intended to deny the responsibility of the state and free-market capitalism for the disparities that perpetuate racial and economic inequality for African Americans. When we cannot see the historical and contemporary uses of racism, it can be used to further dismantle the public institutions that often stand as the last buffer between poor and working-class people and the street. The hopes initially vested in Obama, who has instead acted to silence and quell Black rebellion, have brought the question to the fore: Can we get free in America?

No one knows what stage the current movement is in or where it is headed. We are very early in the most current rendering of the Black awakening. But we do know that there will be relentless efforts to subvert, redirect, and unravel the movement for Black lives, because when the Black movement goes into motion, it throws the entire mythology of the United States—freedom, democracy, and endless opportunity—into chaos. For the same reasons, the state ruthlessly crushed the last major movement of the Black freedom struggle. The stakes are even higher today because what seemed then like an alternative—greater Black inclusion in the political and economic establishment—has already come and failed. In this sense, the election of Obama completed that political project and has brought us back to this point.

Today, American life is much bleaker for the vast majority of people. The challenge before us is to connect the current struggle to end police terror in our communities with an even larger movement to transform this country in such a way that the police are no longer needed to respond to the consequences of that inequality. As the Black revolutionary C. L. R. James wrote on the historic and transformative power of the Black movement:

> Let us not forget that in the Negro people, there sleep and are now awakening passions of a violence exceeding, perhaps, as far as these things can be compared, anything among the tremendous forces that capitalism has created. Anyone who knows them, who knows their history, is able to talk to them intimately, watches them at their own theatres, watches them at their dances, watches them in their churches, reads their press with a discerning eye, must recognize that although their social force may not be able to compare with the social force of a corresponding number of organized workers, the hatred of bourgeois society and the readiness to destroy it when the opportunity should present itself, rests among them to a degree greater than in any other section of the population in the United States.[40]

CHAPTER 8

Where Is the Black Lives Matter Movement Headed?

The autopsy report confirmed what her neighbors said happened in an apartment complex outside of Houston, Texas. Pamela Turner, a forty-four-year-old grandmother of three, was on the ground, screaming that she was pregnant, trying to connect with the humanity of the police officer who stood over her.

Officer Juan Delacruz ignored her pleas, stepped back, unholstered his gun, and shot five times. Three of his bullets ripped through Turner's body, ending her life. One entered her left cheek, shattering her face. Another tore through her left chest, and the last, her abdomen. The medical examiner ruled it a homicide.

What happened next had been rehearsed many times before. The police put Delacruz on a mandatory three-day administrative (paid) leave; the family secured the services of civil rights attorney Benjamin Crump; the Reverend Al Sharpton delivered the eulogy; and a well-organized and well-attended demonstration forced the police to extend their comments beyond the typical talking points.

In the five years since Mike Brown Jr. was murdered and the streets of Ferguson, Missouri, erupted, police across the United States have killed more than four thousand people, a quarter of them African

American. Five years later, do Black lives matter? Confronted by an array of internal and external obstacles, "the movement" has stalled even as a white supremacist ruled from the White House.

Mike Brown's murder and the uprising it inspired cracked open a period of organizing and protest that boldly aimed to end the reign of police terror in Black poor and working-class communities around the country. For those who think that kind of language is hyperbole, consider the conclusions reached by a 2016 Chicago police commission convened by former mayor Rahm Emanuel after the vicious murder of Black teenager Laquan McDonald by Chicago police officer Jason Van Dyke:

> That outrage [about the killing of Laquan McDonald] exposed deep and longstanding fault lines between black and Latino communities on the one hand and the police on the other arising from police shootings to be sure, but also about daily, pervasive transgressions that prevent people of all ages, races, ethnicities and gender across Chicago from having basic freedom of movement in their own neighborhoods. Stopped without justification, verbally and physically abused, and in some instances arrested, and then detained without counsel . . . *CPD's own data gives validity to the widely held belief the police have no regard for the sanctity of life when it comes to people of color.*[1]

The report itself was evidence of the tremendous pressure generated by movement activists with a Democratic president in office, on the eve of a historic election. Black voters had made Obama president, and the party needed to at least project the appearance of progress.

The Emergence of a Movement

By Obama's second term, what began as a local movement in Ferguson had erupted into a much broader national force. A grand jury's failure to indict the officer who killed Mike Brown Jr. in Ferguson was followed by the failure of a grand jury to indict a New York cop, Daniel Pantaleo, despite video of him choking Eric Garner to death on the streets of Staten Island. In a stupor of rage and disbelief, with hopes shattered like broken glass, young Black people around the country were united by the experiences of police abuse and intimidation.

The watersheds of Ferguson, Cleveland, Los Angeles, Staten

Island, and countless other cities and towns fed the stream that became Black Lives Matter in the late fall and early winter of 2014 and 2015. In December 2014, tens of thousands of people across the country participated in acts of nonviolent civil disobedience. On December 13, 2014, fifty thousand people marched through the streets of New York with chants that connected Ferguson, Missouri, to New York City and then to the nation: "Hands up, don't shoot," "I can't breathe," "Black Lives Matter." There were protests across the nation, in cities large and small. These scattered demonstrations cohered through the chant, demand, and declaration of "Black Lives Matter," in ways similar to the cry of "freedom now" during the Civil Rights Movement.

Even as the professional punditry declared the movement dead after the predictable backlash of police unions and political conservatives, the Baltimore spring spilled into the streets, carried forward by Black children exhausted from the institutional neglect and raw racism that lie beneath lead poisoning, poverty, and charter schools. Measured by the number of formal organizations it sprouted, the movement was barely ever alive, but it thrived in the hearts and minds of young Black people who ached to be heard and seen.

But no movement continues simply because its cause is righteous. Its rise or fall is ultimately determined by a tricky calculus involving strategy, tactics, politics, moves, and countermoves. The Black Lives Matter movement always faced two external challenges, not including the internal struggles that every movement wrestles with. Externally, the movement had to endure the way that its mere existence became a rallying point around which various strands of the white-supremacist right could consolidate. For the most visible activists, that meant dealing with credible death threats along with the more typical deluge of harassment.

Early on as a candidate, Trump made BLM his enemy, describing activists as terrorists and pledging his unwavering support to police.[2] And the FBI, true to its history, began surveilling Black activists and inventing new political categories along the way to communicate the new hazard: "black identity extremists."[3] It wasn't surprising, but it was exhausting, and it could be scary. When Trump decided to make BLM the foil of his white-supremacist candidacy by making naked "law-and-order" appeals and aligning his campaign to the "blue lives matter" hysteria, it put activists and organizations in the crosshairs.

But it was even trickier to navigate the maneuvers of the Democratic Party establishment in its efforts to divide the movement between the pragmatists and those who were rapidly radicalizing in the face of intransigent police power. The Obama administration had a virtual "open door" policy when it came to activists. Their strategy was to make busyness and constant engagement look like progress. This meant having regular contact with activists, empaneling a national policing commission, and empowering the Department of Justice to initiate investigations and compile reports on egregious police departments. Yet, throughout this flurry of activity, it was hard to grasp what was changing. Where was the impact?

The Democratic Party sought, with some urgency, to resolve these issues so that progressives could then turn their full attention to the 2016 election. This meant that the liberal establishment constantly questioned the motives, structure, and demands of the movement in hopes of moving things along. "Who are your leaders?" "What are your demands?" "Give us a solution!" were some of the questions—or rather accusations—directed at the most visible leaders of the movement.

Dinner with the President

This style reflected the influence of nongovernmental organizations, which measure the effectiveness of activism or organizing through a lens of efficiency and tangible results. There was pressure to come up with solutions or policy initiatives as a more "real" and measurable way to confront the issues with policing. When some activists chafed at this particular framing, they were attacked as purists.

For example, when a Black activist from Chicago named Aislinn Pulley refused to go to a closed-door meeting at the White House in February of 2016 because she doubted the sincerity of the Obama administration, president Barack Obama personally called her out.

Obama said, "You can't just keep on yelling at them and you can't refuse to meet because that might compromise the purity of your position. . . . The value of social movements and activism is to get you at the table, get you in the room and then start trying to figure out how is this problem going to be solved. You then have a responsibility to prepare an agenda that is achievable—that can institutionalize the changes you seek—and to engage the other side."4

The president's comments did have a hearing in some parts of the movement. The Black Lives Matter movement was not uniform in its thinking, strategies, or tactics. And those divergent ideas about political objectives and the process through which the movement should arrive at its decisions were deeply contested within the movement. Some activists welcomed White House access and believed it meant they were getting a hearing at the highest level. Brittany Packnett, who was active in St. Louis and Ferguson in 2014, explained why she and others participated in the meeting with Obama:

> To gain the liberation we seek, there remain many critical moments for action and we are wise not to limit the legitimate ones. Our fights will never be won at the policy table alone. Protestors assume risk, build organic democratic accountability in the streets and force organized tactics to take hold. Organizers mobilize the people with strategic and direct action to push systemic change in institutions and policies. Policymakers and institutional leaders are influenced by all manner of people continuing to mount pressure in every space possible to see lasting change. . . I believe this movement's collective, varied work can and has moved mountains but it will take every one of us and every tactic at our disposal to win the freedom we seek.

For others, there were misgivings. Aislinn Pulley, the Chicago activist that Obama chastised for refusing to meet, had a vastly different vision of change compared to the one offered by the president. She wrote an open letter in response to his criticism of her:

> I could not, with any integrity, participate in such a sham that would only serve to legitimize the false narrative that the government is working to end police brutality and the institutional racism that fuels it. For the increasing number of families fighting for justice and dignity for their kin slain by police, I refuse to give its perpetrators and enablers political cover by making an appearance among them. . . . We assert that true revolutionary and systemic change will ultimately only be brought forth by ordinary working people, students and youth— organizing, marching and taking power from the corrupt elites.5

These kinds of tensions and debates in political movements were, of course, not new, especially in Black movements. In 1964, movement strategist Bayard Rustin argued that the Civil Rights Movement and new forms of Black militancy must be prepared to shift "from protest to politics." He argued that "it is clear that Negro needs cannot be satisfied unless we go beyond what has so far been placed on the agenda. How are these radical objectives to be achieved? The answer is simple, deceptively so: *through political power.* . . . We are challenged now to broaden our social vision, to develop functional programs with concrete objectives."

Rustin was suggesting that the shift into formal politics marked a sign of political maturity and could deliver much more substantive change to Black communities than protest alone. He had in mind an expansive social-democratic program pursued by a fresh wave of politicians. (There were barely a hundred Black elected officials in 1964.) We got the politicians (ten years after Rustin's call, there were several hundred Black elected officials)—culminating in the 2008 election of Barack Obama—but not the welfare state.

Obama's public scolding was not precisely over the question of "electoral politics," but you can hear echoes of (a narrowed version of) Rustin's message. Obama was declaring that, in 2016, it was time to stop "yelling" and offer pragmatic solutions that could be acted upon. His response revealed his own impatience with the continuation of Black Lives Matter, now threatening to cause a distraction from the coming general election in 2016. But, more important, his personal intervention was also intended to divide the movement between the "doers" and the "dreamers."

For many activists, the maddening web of police violence and the wider criminal justice system—the fine-and-fee structure, expensive bail, and the arbitrariness of sentencing—required more than roundtables and reports. Many were reaching for structural rather than superficial changes to federal, state, and local criminal justice systems. Some were embracing the politics of abolition and the belief that society would be better off without the entire carceral paradigm. Instead of spending $80 billion a year to put human beings in cages, maybe those resources could be redistributed in such a way as to make people's lives better instead of being used to punish.

In this way, Obama's scold and Pulley's response revealed more than strategic loggerheads on the objective of social movements. Of the many problems in US society Black Lives Matter has exposed, the sharp division within Black politics stands out. The political rancor partly reflected a generational divide, but it also showed a schism between the class anger of Black workers and the class optimism of a tiny Black elite.

Some activists chafed at the paternalism of Obama, who was quick to remind the (mostly white) US public that he was not "Black America's president" while simultaneously code-switching into Ebonics to chastise African Americans to get "Uncle Pookie" off the couch to go and vote.

But it wasn't just Obama. His race antics were a bitter reminder of the ways that Black elected officials often fattened themselves up munching at the trough of Black votes, only to deliver little other than themselves alone as tokens of alleged racial progress.[6] But the reality was that in many cities, Black mayors, Black city council people, Black police chiefs, and police officers oversaw the inequality and oppression that fueled Black Lives Matter.

The naked racism of Donald Trump's description, in July 2019, of Baltimore as a "rodent infested" den where "no human being wants to live" captured the nation's attention, but a broader truth received less—local and national Black elected officials have betrayed their constituents by way of institutional neglect and then have relied on brutal policing to manage the ensuing crisis.

It was this betrayal of promises of "hope" and "change" that rallied the young rebels of Ferguson and then Baltimore, whom Obama and Baltimore mayor Stephanie Rawlings-Blake described as thugs, to act on behalf of millions.

This was the thorny context to Aislinn Pulley's frustration and her rejection of the invitation to chat with the president of the United States. The point here is not whether Packnett's decision to meet with Obama or Pulley's declining was more correct. The reality is that all social movements are expressions of the deep desire for change or reform of the current situation.

For Black Lives Matter, that could be expressed as the hope cops would "stop killing us," but ultimately it was a movement to reform the status quo of policing. But what often happens is that through the course of events, the movement participants come to radically different conclusions about what the objective should be. For many BLM activists, their conclusion began to be that the police could not actually be reformed. This then put them into conflict with the reform nature of the movement itself.

The Tyranny of Structurelessness in the Age of Social Media

However, the bigger problem was the movement's inability to create the space to debate and work out the tension between reform and revolution, or more crudely between body cameras and prison abolition. All movements are confronted with existential debates concerning their viability and longevity. There are always crucial decisions to be made concerning their direction and the best route to get there. But without the opportunity to collectively assess, discuss, or ponder what the movement is or should be, those political disagreements can sometimes devolve into bitter personal attacks.

Among movement activists, acrimonious personal disputes were expressed throughout the social media landscape, creating an archival trove of material for state agents. This also fueled animosity and discord between people who had every interest in collaboration and solidarity. Callout culture summoned attention to every transgression, along with the assumption that the act was committed with the worst of intentions. The goodwill that many imagined and wanted to rest at the heart of the movement could only be built upon trust and genuine relationships. These were difficult to build without formal structures, clear responsibilities, and mechanisms for leadership and accountability.

Indeed, the "organic democratic accountability" that Packnett insisted on was absent. The lack of clear entry points into movement organizing, and the absence of any democratically accountable organization or structure within the movement, left very few spaces to evaluate the state of the movement, delaying its ability to pivot and postponing the generalization of strategic lessons and tactics from one locality to the next or from one action to the next. Instead, the emphasis on autonomy, even at the cost of disconnection from the broader movement, left each locality to its own devices to learn and conjure its own strategy.

The BLM movement claimed to have no leaders, embracing the "horizontalism" of its Occupy predecessor. But all movements have leaders; someone or some group of individuals are deciding that this or that thing will or will not happen; someone decides how this or that resource is used or is not used; someone decides whether this or that meeting will or will not happen. The issue is not whether there are leaders, it is whether those leaders are accountable to those they represent.[7] It also matters how those leaders are determined as leaders. In the case of the meeting with Obama, it appears that the attendees were selected by the Obama administration as individuals or organizations they determined were the leadership of the movement. Perhaps this was unavoidable, but the lack of accountability to the ordinary people who made up the mass of the movement could cause confusion or hard feelings.

But the insistence that there was no leadership even as people were regarded as leaders by the political establishment obscured how decisions were being made and who was to account for them. These problems deepened when it began to feel as if the movement was going in the wrong direction or was stagnant, as it became difficult to determine who to look to for guidance.

This does not mean that "if only" there had been this meeting or that gathering, or even if there had been more democracy in decision making, that the Black Lives Matter movement would have triumphed over police brutality. But it raises the crucial question of how organizers emerge from a lost battle or even a lost war with more clarity about their experience, the lessons learned, and salvaged relationships that may allow them to fight another day with a better sense of what to do the next time around.

Between Hillary Clinton and the "Progressive Foundations"

These tensions within the BLM movement were magnified by the high-profile harassment of activists initiated by Trump's minions and the ongoing manipulation carried out by Democratic Party operatives. The pressure to propel the movement forward while also remaining engaged with officials for whom engagement was intended to create the appearance of progress generated enormous strain on activists. This tension was exacerbated when the Democratic Party nominated Hillary Clinton.

Clinton's campaign slogan, "America Is Already Great," was a rejoinder to Trump's "Make American Great Again." But it also betrayed a level of political detachment that shocked young Black people engaged in a life-and-death struggle, fueling the debate over the best way to advance the struggle. At the same time, activists were sure that if Clinton won, she would be indebted to young Black voters, lending credibility to a strategy that focused on policy initiatives that could have been realized within a Clinton administration.

The momentum of the movement began to wane for a variety of reasons; but the outcome was to make the inside political game seem like a more viable way forward. As the persistence of police abuse and killings made the problem seem intractable, the absence of democratic debate and strategy-making led to the de-emphasis of mass marches and mass actions. Instead, the actions got smaller, more secretive, led by small groups of people who were then vulnerable to arrest.

This cycle of smaller, arrestable actions became a self-fulfilling prophecy as many of those activists decried others' lack of willingness to "sacrifice." The smallness and marginality of the protests became moral cudgels with which to beat people who were not willing to risk arrest. In this context, engaging the political establishment seemed a more realistic route to get something done, at least to some—certainly not all.

This was increasingly the case as supposed progressive foundations tied much of their funding to activists' ability to "get results." Foundation funding flooded into movement organizations almost immediately after the Ferguson uprising. The money was needed and readily accepted as organizers tried to sustain the momentum generated by the Ferguson uprising and the ensuing demonstrations proliferating across the country as police continued to kill African Americans. But the donations, from entities ranging from Google to the Ford Foundation and dozens of others in between, came with more than money or funding in mind. These corporations were most obviously trying to connect the inherent progressive character of social movements to their "brand."

In some cases, such as the Ford Foundation, the money has historically come with an effort to then manipulate the objectives and direction of the movement.[8] Ford was notorious in the 1960s for using its vast resources to nudge Black radicals toward "community development" and Black capitalism, and away from their insurgent potential. Karen Ferguson has written incisively on the ways that Ford leveraged its financial intervention into the 1960s Black freedom movement to promote "responsible" leaders, those it felt could promulgate a political direction with which they agreed.[9]

But this is not just about the Ford Foundation. Megan Ming Francis describes a process of "movement capture" when recounting how foundation donors in the 1920s and 1930s used the lure of funding to help transform the NAACP's political focus on white terrorism and lynching to education, constituting less of a threat to the political status quo.[10]

The influence of foundations remains one of moderation and compromise. The logic is rooted in the reality of these multibillion-dollar organizations that ultimately see themselves as rescuing the system from its excesses. Consider an article recently published by the president of the Ford Foundation, Darren Walker. In the article, Walker counsels the wisdom in "nuance" as a rejection of "extreme" political positions. As he artfully suggests,

> Extreme opposition seems to have entered the playbook of leaders in every category. In this worldview, it's all or nothing, good or evil, the best or worst. . . . Nuance and complexity, meanwhile, are nowhere to be found. And our *extreme* challenges remain *extremely* unsolved.[11]

Walker describes activists in New York City who have been struggling to close the horrible jail Rikers Island as political extremists. Walker was part of a commission that agreed to close Rikers, only to build several smaller jails to replace it. He says it's a compromise—an example of the kind of nuance to which prison and jail abolitionists appear to be impervious. Walker argues that to reject compromise is to "let the perfect be the enemy of progress. If we skip steps, we risk creating a new kind of gap—a gap of missed opportunities and lost alliances."

But all of this is subterfuge for his actual intervention:

> We can see how our capitalist systems have broken down, *while also* appreciating that markets have helped reduce the number of people around the globe who live in poverty. . . .We can be critical of ill-gotten fortunes, *while also* appreciating the current need for

private capital to fund certain valuable public goods, and encouraging wealthy individuals to understand their own privilege and support institutional reforms.[12]

Rarely in this world do you get something for nothing. The tens of millions of dollars the Ford Foundation disseminates to organizations and activists of all stripes come with the intent to redirect or reshape insurgency and disruptions toward more reasonable means. It's never that obvious, because if it were, it would not be effective. Walker here isn't just speaking for Ford—one might consider this to be the objective of most corporations that have the foresight to develop a philanthropic wing as a way to influence the debate over social questions. One of the ways that functions today is with the emphasis placed on policy initiatives and solutions as the practical way to advance a movement or social agenda.

Consider how the Movement for Black Lives policy platform was heralded in ways that made it seem as important as the marches and mobilizations themselves.[13] To be sure, many of the reforms that the policy platform called for were far-reaching and, if implemented, could be transformative. But without a social movement on the ground to create the muscle necessary to coerce the political establishment to shift from its intransigence, how would any of it become achievable?

The ascendance of the policy platform and its projection as a crowning achievement of the movement revealed more about the state of the movement than was intended. In ways similar to the wish-list approach to presidential campaigning, it is easy to call for the moon and stars—and sometimes it is necessary to imagine what freedom might look like—but after demands have been delivered and promises have been made, someone has got to fight to make them a reality. The platform could not answer the central question of how to harness the physical power of a social movement to do just that.

The scrum for foundation dollars could have other unintended consequences. The ability to secure funding undermined the potential of developing more democratic practices within the movement by giving those with the access to funding an outsize voice. With more resources came more authority because of the ways it elevated the profile, presence, and voices of some. This dynamic eventually cut into the kind of unity in purpose necessary to confront the challenge of stopping police abuse and murder. Instead, activists were compelled to compete with one another for funding based on their "unique" contribution to the movement.

These observations aren't intended as some holy screed about how foundation money dirties our movements—though it undoubtedly does. We should stop and ask why corporations that have made billions under US capitalism are so eager to "donate" money to activists, many of whom embrace some version of anticapitalist politics. As I referenced above, foundations' financial influence has *always*, at least through most of the twentieth century and today, been a factor. We can all conceive of homey and quaint ways of raising money for ourselves, but it is difficult to imagine the large scale of activism needed to confront the problems of our society based on bake sales and social events.

But the availability of that money requires even more democracy within our movements. It means decision-making must extend beyond the staffers or the executive board or whoever is drawing a paycheck to those who make up the ranks of the movement. It means that much of our organizing and activism will be messy, slow, and wrongheaded sometimes, but it might also make it easier for everyone to claim ownership of the movement.

The wider participation of everyone with a stake in a Black Lives Matter movement may have resulted in more contact between the different layers of the movement. With the creation of political spaces where these different layers could more closely engage with and influence one another, there may have been a greater urgency placed on the mass movement and mobilizations. Some have concluded that mass mobilizations are no longer necessary; that people just show up and then go home. Of course, that can be one effect, but we should not underestimate the transformative power in the assembly and collective action required to demonstrate together. It is not only about its influence in policy making or in governing institutions but also the ways that power manifests itself among those who make up the ranks of the march.

The radical artist and critic John Berger wrote of mass demonstrations:

> Theoretically demonstrations are meant to reveal the strength of popular opinion or feeling: theoretically they are an appeal to the democratic conscience of the State.[14]

In this sense, Berger wrote, the numbers present at a protest are significant because of their impact on not the state but on those who participate:

> The importance of the numbers involved is to be found in the direct experience of those taking part in or sympathetically witnessing the demonstration. For them the numbers cease to be numbers and become the evidence of their senses, the conclusions of their imagination. The larger the demonstration, the more powerful and immediate (visible, audible, tangible) a metaphor it becomes for their total collective strength.[15]

The point is that movements or mobilizations do not only create the possibility of changing our material condition by exerting the force of many upon the intransigence of the few. Social movements also create arenas where we, ourselves, can be transformed. Mass action breaks us from the isolation of everyday life and turns us into political actors.

In a society that wrongly attributes our successes to our personal ingenuity and blames our failures on personal weakness, the mass movement, that arena of struggle, brings us together to share in our difficulties and show how the solution to so many of our problems is collective. It pierces the prevailing common sense about our society.

The Black radical feminist and organizer Ella Baker understood the need to pierce this bubble of "common sense."

> In order for us as poor and oppressed people to become a part of a society that is meaningful, the system under which we now exist has to be radically changed. This means that we are going to have to learn to think in radical terms. I use the term radical in its original meaning—getting down to and understanding the root cause. It means facing a system that does not lend itself to your needs and devising means by which you change that system.[16]

The collective exhilaration of confrontation and the potential for change opens up the possibility for posing these kinds of questions. Without it, it is hard to break free from the reasonableness and pragmatism as counseled by Obama when he lectured a Chicago activist on the narrow objectives of social movements—to change a law or initiate a policy.

As 2015 and 2016 wore on, no one believed that Trump would win;

instead, activists began to focus on ways they could shift a new Clinton administration on police reform. Of course, Trump was elected, and all the plans to move to Washington, DC, to begin the "inside" phase of the movement never materialized. Today, there are few signs of the grassroots Black Lives Matter movement that in its first years captured the imagination and hopes of young Black people and beyond.

This certainly does not mean that the movement "failed." There continue to be many BLM activists organized and engaged in other forms. It is impossible to imagine that the public appetite for criminal justice reform, including bail reform and the slow but steady decriminalization of marijuana, could be happening without the influence of the Black Lives Matter movement. We are all indebted to the movement for bringing to light the full extent to which Black women, including Black trans women, are also victims of state-sanctioned violence and racist abuse. Many of the organizers who were central to the movement see these new arenas of struggle as a continued expression of the Black Lives Matter movement.

But the mass movement that captured the attention of the world and upended the banal status quo does not exist in the same way. In some ways, that is expected. Nothing stands still, let alone something as alive and dynamic as a social movement. The questions of strategy, tactics, and democracy that emerged as a consequence of the rise of the Black Lives Matter movement have not gone away; in fact, they remain critical to determining how we transform our current situation.

Still Fighting for a Future Where Black Lives Matter

What does the shattered face of Pamela Turner, exploded by a police officer's bullet, tell us about the efforts of the Black Lives Matter movement? It tells us how absolutely central policing is to maintaining the racist, sexist, unequal status quo.

Police unions and elected officials like to portray policing as dangerous, as some kind of bizarre last line of defense between "us" and a murky menacing criminal element "out there." In reality, most policing involves surveilling and harassing poor and working-class people. When Black and Brown people are overrepresented among the ranks of the poor and working class, those people bear the brunt of encounters with police. Being killed by police is a leading cause of death for young Black men.[17] Sociologist Frank Edwards has said that young Black men have "better odds of being killed by police than . . . winning a lot of scratch off lottery games." Pamela Turner, who suffered from schizophrenia, was in the crosshairs of the local police because of several minor infractions that brought her into contact with them. In April 2019, she was served with an eviction notice that resulted in a "criminal mischief" charge and an encounter with the same cop who eventually killed her weeks later.[18]

Policing is the last public-sector service that our government strongly funds as it defunds and neglects all other aspects of the civic infrastructure. As public services across the country are dismantled, hundreds of millions of dollars are unearthed to pay off police brutality and police murder lawsuits. Chicago alone has spent over $800 million since 2004 to settle lawsuits for police brutality and wrongful deaths.[19]

If any other public institution incurred that kind of expense, its budget and service would be shrunk or it would be shut down. For example, when in 2012 the Chicago Board of Education claimed it was running a billion-dollar deficit, its proposed solution was to close fifty-two public schools. But in the midst of revelations about Rahm Emanuel's attempt to cover up the role of police in the murder of Laquan McDonald, the mayor received the blessing of the Chicago City Council to break ground on a new $95 million police academy.[20]

No matter how corrupt, violent, or racist police are, their budgets will never shrink. Elected officials and the rich and powerful whose interests they often represent know that as public expenditures get cut, and as good jobs with benefits get further out of reach, police abuse brings order to a potentially untenable situation. The pain and suffering of Pamela Turner's grandchildren, or Laquan McDonald's mother, or Mike Brown Jr.'s parents are collateral damage in this war to maintain the status quo. It is literally the price of doing business.

Thus, five years later, much of the institutional discussion about police reform remains focused on bad apples, implicit bias, and better training. As a result, the main policy shift has been the widespread use of body cameras. Since 2014, police forces around the country have spent upward of $192 million on body cameras. In Ferguson, where the movement found its heart and soul, there are now more Black police officers than white.[21] Ferguson finally caught up with the rest of the United States. Meanwhile, Black people are stopped 5 percent more and white people are stopped 11 percent less than they were in 2013. Recognizing the stubborn duration of police abuse and violence is less about pessimism than it is about sobriety. There is no quick fix to police brutality. The police are so difficult to transform because the bipartisan political establishment needs them, especially when it decides it has nothing left to give us. It took five long and deadly years for the officials who manage the New York Police Department to fire an officer who choked the life out of a man who was plainly saying, "I can't breathe." It took five years for the Department of Justice to decide that it would not bring federal civil rights charges against Pantaleo, as if his illegal chokehold that took Garner's life was not the textbook definition of a civil rights violation.

But what is the value of protecting the "rule of law" when the law itself prioritizes what is valued by the elite, while ignoring what is valued by most of us? In other words, neither the law nor law enforcement is on our side, and that ultimately makes the movement to reform either extremely difficult. It is usually the case, then, that we get the kind of change we desire when we pressure and coerce the political class, their establishment, and their laws, to see and hear us. And to do that, it matters how we organize, what we think, what we demand, and what we imagine and hope for.

These are key values for any social movement. Democracy, where we see all of our aspirations, our failures, and our endeavors as connected, means trying to bring in as many as possible and figuring out how to make it work. Black lives *can* matter. But it will demand a struggle to not only change the police but to change the world that relies on the police to manage its unequal distribution of the necessities of life.

Acknowledgments

I have written many articles and essays over the years, but I've never written a book until now. A book is hard to write because it takes a long time and requires the kind of single-minded focus that drives away friends and family. It is a solitary affair. It is also very true that a book is impossible to write alone. It is certainly the case with this book. There are too many people to thank for their contributions to a process that has been under way in my mind for a very long time, but there are some without whom this book never could have come into existence. First and foremost, I would like to thank the incredible crew of people at Haymarket Books who have truly bent over backward to get this book out in what must be record time. In particular, I owe special thanks to Anthony Arnove and Julie Fain, who approached me about writing the book in December 2014. I did not think it was possible to take on such a project, having just moved across the country to start a new job while still pining for Chicago. But Anthony and Julie convinced me that I could get it done, and I thank them for giving me the nudge. I also owe a huge thank-you to Haymarket's impressive and professional production crew, without whom an actual book could not have materialized. Thanks to Sarah Grey, Caroline Luft, and Dao X. Tran for their critical copyedits that allowed my voice to rise above typos and misplaced commas. Eric Kerl and Rachel Cohen worked patiently with me to develop a book cover that is powerfully evocative of the movement itself. I also want to thank Rory Fanning, John McDonald, Jim Plank, and Jason Farbman as the ringleaders of Haymarket's impressive marketing and publicity operation.

This book came together relatively quickly because I have been thinking about what are essentially political questions about the road to Black liberation in the United States for most of my adult life. Many comrades, friends, and family have contributed to my deep and rich political education, and this book is certainly a product of those collaborations and discussions. In November 2014 I spent about eight days in Cuba with my father talking about radical Black politics, the nascent Black Lives Matter movement, and the history of the Black liberation movement. I didn't know at the time that I would soon be working on this book, but those conversations were generative and productive and helped me develop the structure of this book. But the comrades with whom I have engaged in political debates and discussions on a regular basis over the last several years have significantly shaped this manuscript: thanks to Brian Bean, Jack Bloom, Elizabeth Breland-Todd, Jordan Camp, Todd Chretien, Brenda Coughlin, Paul D'Amato, Lichi D'Amelio, Akunna Eneh, Joel Geier, Akua Gyamerah, Jesse Hagopian, Shaun Harkin, Ragina Johnson, Brian Jones, Rebecca Marchiel, Marlene Martin, Joan Parkin, Jasson Perez, Khury Petersen-Smith, Jennifer Roesch, Eric Ruder, Elizabeth Schulte, Lance Selfa, Ashley Smith, Sharon Smith, Todd St. Hill, Lee Sustar, and Lee Wengraf.

I have also benefited greatly from conversations with and have learned so much from the insights of Martha Biondi, Michael Dawson, Megan Francis, Ruth Gilmore, Mariame Kaba, Donna Murch, Tiana Paschel, Barbara Ransby, James Thwinda, Rhonda Williams and Gary Younge.

I have also met new colleagues and friends in the Department of African American Studies at Princeton University over the last year, with whom I have had discussions and debates that have made an important imprint on how I think about issues related to Black politics and Black liberation. I owe a special thanks to Eddie Glaude, who allowed me to read his manuscript concerning many of the same issues that I engage with in this book. Eddie has become a true friend with whom I have had some of the most exciting and refreshing debates and discussions about the movement and politics in general. I am also indebted to Imani Perry and Naomi Murakawa—from both of whom I have learned so much through their important writings on race, the state, crime, and justice, and because they have always made themselves available to talk about the world and how we can change it. Wendy Belcher, Ruha Benjamin, Wallace Best, Josh Guild, Tera Hunter, Kinohi Nishikawa, Chike Okeke-Agulu, and Stacey Sinclair constitute an intellectual community at Princeton that is interested in and actively intervening in radical Black politics.

A very special thanks goes to Ahmed Shawki and Alan Maass, both of whom took time out of extraordinarily busy schedules to read and reread the manuscript while offering comments and observations that were critical to shaping what this book has eventually become. You cannot write if you cannot think, and so I want to especially thank Jayne Kinsman for helping me to turn down the noise in my head, which made it possible to write intensively for days at a time. I owe the greatest thanks to my partner in life and best friend, Lauren Fleer. There are too many things that could be said, so I will only say that without Lauren's endless support, love, solidarity, and camaraderie most things in my life would be impossible, let alone writing a book.

Finally, this book is dedicated to the survivors of the state-sanctioned violence that has given rise to what I consider to be the most important and exciting development in the Black freedom struggle in more than a generation. Those left behind to bury their dead have often been the ones to insist that we not forget and continue the struggle to demand justice. They have provided a way out of the darkness of police terror and violence. Those of us who take up the banner for freedom and justice are forever indebted to the bravery of these survivors.

Notes

Introduction

Martin Luther King Jr. and James Melvin Washington, *A Testament of Hope: The Essential Writings of Martin Luther King, Jr.* (San Francisco: Harper & Row, 1986), 316.

1. Matt Apuzzo, "Justice Dept., Criticizing Philadelphia Police, Finds Shootings by Officers Are Common," *New York Times*, March 23, 2015, http://www.nytimes.com/2015/03/24/us/justice-dept-criticizing-philadelphia-police-finds-shootings-by-officers-are-common.html.
2. Ibid.
3. Damien Cave, "Officer Darren Wilson's Grand Jury Testimony in Ferguson, Mo., Shooting," *New York Times*, November 25, 2014, http://www.nytimes.com/interactive/2014/11/25/us/darren-wilson-testimony-ferguson-shooting.html.
4. Krishnadev Calamur, "Ferguson Documents: Officer Darren Wilson's Testimony," NPR.org, November 25, 2014, http://www.npr.org/blogs/thetwo-way/2014/11/25/366519644/ferguson-docs-officer-darren-wilsons-testimony.
5. Maya Rhodan, "Read the Full Text of Obama's Speech in Selma," *TIME*, March 7, 2015, http://time.com/3736357/barack-obama-selma-speech-transcript/.
6. David G. Savage, "Supreme Court Strikes Down Key Section of Voting Rights Act," *Los Angeles Times*, June 25, 2013, http://articles.latimes.com/2013/jun/25/news/la-pn-supreme-court-voting-rights-ruling-20130625.
7. Barack Obama, speech delivered in Philadelphia, March 18, 2008, transcript in *New York Times*, http://www.nytimes.com/2008/03/18/us/politics/18text-obama.html.

8. Alyssa Davis and Lawrence Mishel, "CEO Pay Continues to Rise as Typical Workers Are Paid Less," *Economic Policy Institute*, June 12, 2014, http://www.epi.org/publication/ceo-pay-continues-to-rise/.

9. Antonio Moore, "The Decadent Veil: Black America's Wealth Illusion," *Huffington Post*, October 5, 2014, http://www.huffingtonpost.com/antonio-moore/the-decadent-veil-black-income-inequality_b_5646472.html.

10. Pew Research Center and National Public Radio, *Optimism about Black Progress Declines* (Washington, DC: Pew Research Center, 2007), http://pewsocialtrends.org/assets/pdf/Race.pdf.

11. Ibid.

12. Stokely Carmichael and Charles V. Hamilton, *Black Power: The Politics of Liberation in America* (New York: Random House, 1967), 5–7.

13. Kerner Commission and Tom Wicker, *Report of the National Advisory Commission on Civil Disorders* (New York: Bantam Books, 1968), 10.

14. Pew Research Center and NPR, *Optimism about Black Progress Declines*.

15. Patricia Cohen, "For Recent Black College Graduates, a Tougher Road to Employment," *New York Times*, December 24, 2014, http://www.nytimes.com/2014/12/25/business/for-recent-black-college-graduates-a-tougher-road-to-employment.html.

16. Henry J. Kaiser Family Foundation, "Poverty Rate by Race/Ethnicity," accessed March 20, 2015, http://kff.org/other/state-indicator/poverty-rate-by-raceethnicity/.

17. Jennifer G. Hickey, "Race Gap: Blacks Fall Further Behind Under Obama," *Newsmax*, January 8, 2014, http://www.newsmax.com/Newsfront/obama-blacks-poverty-education/2014/01/08/id/545866/.

18. Matthew Desmond, "Evictions: A Hidden Scourge for Black Women," *Washington Post*, June 16, 2014, http://www.washingtonpost.com/posteverything/wp/2014/06/16/evictions-hurt-black-women-as-much-as-incarceration-hurts-black-men/.

19. Tami Luhby, "5 Disturbing Stats on Black-White Financial Inequality," *CNNMoney*, August 21, 2014, http://money.cnn.com/2014/08/21/news/economy/black-white-inequality/index.html.

20. Jazelle Hunt, "Black Women Face Challenges in Building Wealth," *Sacramento Observer*, April 8, 2015, http://sacobserver.com/2015/04/black-women-face-challenges-in-building-wealth/.

21. Kimbriell Kelly and John Sullivan, "In Fairwood, Dreams of Black Wealth Foundered Amid the Mortgage Meltdown," *Washington Post*, January 25, 2015, http://www.washingtonpost.com/sf/investigative/2015/01/25/in-fairwood-dreams-of-black-wealth-foundered-amid-the-mortgage-meltdown/.

22. Nathalie Baptiste, "Staggering Loss of Black Wealth Due to Subprime Scandal Continues Unabated," *American Prospect*, October 13, 2014, http://prospect.org/article/staggering-loss-black-wealth-due-subprime-scandal-continues-unabated.

23. Chicago Anti-Eviction Campaign, "#CERD Shadow Report Fact Sheet," August 13, 2014, http://chicagoantieviction.org/2014/08/cerd-shadow-report-fact-sheet.html.

24. Laura Gottesdiener, "The Great Eviction: Black America and the Toll of the Foreclosure Crisis," *Mother Jones*, August 1, 2013, http://www.motherjones. com/politics/2013/08/black-america-foreclosure-crisis.

25. Byron Tau, "Obama: 'I'm Not the President of Black America,'" *Politico*, August 7, 2012, http://www.politico.com/politico44/2012/08/obama-im-not-the-president-of-black-america-131351.html.

26. Nia-Malika Henderson, "Cousin Pookie Is Back! And Yes, He Is Still Sitting on the Couch," *Washington Post*, October 20, 2014, http://www. washingtonpost.com/blogs/the-fix/wp/2014/10/20/cousin-pookie-is-back-and-yes-he-is-still-sitting-on-the-couch/.

27. Sam Frizell, "Obama: Ferguson Exposed 'Gulf of Mistrust' Between Cops and Communities," *TIME*, September 28, 2014, http://time.com/3441544/ obama-ferguson-gulf-of-mistrust/.

28. Holly Yan, "Ezell Ford: Autopsy of Unarmed Black Man Shot by Police Shows Key Details," *CNN*, December 30, 2014, http://www.cnn. com/2014/12/30/justice/ezell-ford-police-shooting-autopsy/index.html.

29. Brandon Blackwell, "Cleveland Woman with Mental Illness Died after Police Used Takedown Move, Brother Says," Cleveland.com, November 14, 2014, http://www.cleveland.com/metro/index.ssf/2014/11/cleveland_ woman_with_mental_il_1.html.

30. Associated Press, "Police Pushed, Cuffed Tamir Rice's Sister after Boy's Shooting, Video Shows," *Los Angeles Times*, January 8, 2015, http://www. latimes.com/nation/nationnow/la-na-nn-tamir-rice-video-20150108-story. html.

31. Radley Balko, "The DOJ's Jaw-Dropping Report about the Cleveland Police Department," *Washington Post*, December 5, 2014, https://www. washingtonpost.com/news/the-watch/wp/2014/12/05/the-dojs-jaw-dropping-report-about-the-cleveland-police-department/.

32. Martha Biondi, "From Hope to Disposability," *In These Times*, August 19, 2013, http://inthesetimes.com/article/15438/from_hope_to_ disposability_50_years_after_march_on_washington.

33. Kevin Johnson, "Holder: Change Laws to Let Ex-Convicts Vote," *USA Today*, February 11, 2014, http://www.usatoday.com/story/news/ nation/2014/02/11/holder-voting-rights-ex-felons/5377119/.

Chapter One

Lyndon B. Johnson, speech delivered at Howard University, June 4, 1965," http://www.lbjlib.utexas.edu/johnson/archives.hom/speeches.hom/650604. asp; Barack Obama, speech delivered at Morehouse College, May 19, 2013, http://www.ajc.com/news/news/local/prepared-text-for-president-obamas-speech-at-moreh/nXwk2/.

1. *Twitchy*, "Goldie Taylor Lectures Nicholas Kristof for Suggesting Protesters Focus Less on Michael Brown," January 23, 2015, http://twitchy.com/2015/01/23/goldie-taylor-lectures-nicholas-kristof-for-suggesting-protesters-focus-less-on-michael-brown/.

2. Thomas Jefferson, *Notes on the State of Virginia*, chapter 14 (Paris: 1785), http://xroads.virginia.edu/~hyper/JEFFERSON/ch14.html.

3. Barbara J. Fields, "Slavery, Race and Ideology in the United States of America," *New Left Review* 181, no. 1 (1990): 95–118.

4. Karen Fields and Barbara J. Fields, *Racecraft: The Soul of Inequality in American Life* (London: Verso, 2012), 134.

5. US Congress, et al., *The ISIS Threat: The Rise of the Islamic State and Their Dangerous Potential* (Providence, RI: Providence Research, 2014).

6. Frank Main, "Treasure Trove of Memos Shows Emanuel's Politics in White House," *Chicago Sun-Times*, June 20, 2014, http://chicago.suntimes.com/chicago-politics/7/71/163978/treasure-trove-of-memos-shows-emanuels-politics-in-white-house.

7. Rahm Emanuel, interviewed by Scott Pelley, "Emanuel: Chicago's Escalating Crime about 'Values,'" CBS News, July 10, 2012, http://www.cbsnews.com/news/emanuel-chicagos-escalating-crime-about-values/.

8. ABC7 Chicago, "Obama Addresses Chicago Violence in Message to Students," August 14, 2012, http://abc7chicago.com/archive/8773637/.

9. Hal Dardick and Kristen Mack, "Emanuel Admits He Erred on Details of Protest Rule Changes," *Chicago Tribune*, October 4, 2012, http://articles.chicagotribune.com/2012-10-4/news/ct-met-emanuel-protesters-20120104_1_mayor-rahm-emanuel-protest-leader-nato.

10. Terry Blounte, "Foote: Lynch Sending Wrong Message to Kids," ESPN.com, February 3, 2015, http://espn.go.com/nfl/story/_/id/12272608/arizona-cardinals-linebacker-larry-foote-says-marshawn-lynch-seattle-seahawks-sending-wrong-message-kids.

11. Jonathan Chait, "Barack Obama vs. the Culture of Poverty," *Daily Intelligencer*, March 28, 2014, http://nymag.com/daily/intelligencer/2014/03/barack-obama-vs-the-culture-of-poverty.html.

12. Institute on Assets and Social Policy, "The Roots of the Widening Racial Wealth Gap," report, quoted in Jamelle Bouie, "The Crisis in Black Homeownership," *Slate*, July 24, 2014, http://www.slate.com/articles/news_and_politics/politics/2014/07/black_homeownership_how_the_recession_turned_owners_into_renters_and_obliterated.html.

13. Cohen, "For Recent Black College Graduates, a Tougher Road to Employment."

14. Ta-Nehisi Coates, "Black Pathology and the Closing of the Progressive Mind," *Atlantic*, March 21, 2014, http://www.theatlantic.com/politics/archive/2014/03/black-pathology-and-the-closing-of-the-progressive-

mind/284523/.
15. Quoted in Ronald Reagan, "We Will Be a City upon a Hill," speech delivered to the first Conservative Political Action Conference, January 25, 1974, http://reagan2020.us/speeches/City_Upon_A_Hill.asp.
16. Quoted in Greg Jaffe, "Obama's New Patriotism," June 3, 2015, *Washington Post*, http://www.washingtonpost.com/sf/national/2015/06/03/obama-and-american-exceptionalism/.
17. Michael Dobbs and John M. Goshko, "Albright's Personal Odyssey Shaped Foreign Policy Beliefs," *Washington Post*, December 6, 1996, http://www.washingtonpost.com/wp-srv/politics/govt/admin/stories/albright120696.htm.
18. Reagan, "We Will Be a City upon a Hill."
19. Ta-Nehisi Coates, "Other People's Pathologies," *Atlantic*, March 30, 2014, http://www.theatlantic.com/politics/archive/2014/03/other-peoples-pathologies/359841/.
20. Quoted in Jim Cullen, *The American Dream: A Short History of an Idea That Shaped a Nation* (Oxford: Oxford University Press, 2004).
21. Hal Draper, "Who's Going to Be the Lesser-Evil in 1968?" *Independent Socialist* (January–February 1967), Marxists Internet Archive, https://www.marxists.org/archive/draper/1967/01/lesser.htm.
22. Franklin D. Roosevelt, speech delivered in Chicago, October 14, 1936, http://www.presidency.ucsb.edu/ws/?pid=15185.
23. David M. P. Freund, *Colored Property: State Policy and White Racial Politics in Suburban America* (Chicago: University of Chicago Press, 2007).
24. David Harvey, *Rebel Cities: From the Right to the City to the Urban Revolution* (London: Verso Books, 2012).
25. Freund, *Colored Property*; Arnold R. Hirsch, *Making the Second Ghetto: Race and Housing in Chicago 1940–1960* (Chicago: University of Chicago Press, 1998); Beryl Satter, *Family Properties: Race, Real Estate, and the Exploitation of Black Urban America* (New York: St. Martin's Press, 2009); Kenneth T. Jackson, *Crabgrass Frontier: The Suburbanization of America* (New York: Oxford University Press, 1985); Kenneth L. Kusmer and Joe William Trotter, *African American Urban History since World War II* (Chicago: University of Chicago Press, 2009); Gregory Squires, ed., *Unequal Partnerships: The Political Economy of Urban Redevelopment in Postwar America* (New Brunswick, NJ: Rutgers University Press, 1989).
26. Arnold R. Hirsch and Raymond A. Mohl, *Urban Policy in Twentieth-Century America* (New Brunswick, NJ: Rutgers University Press, 1993); Squires, *Unequal Partnerships*; Gregory D. Squires, *Capital and Communities in Black and White: The Intersections of Race, Class, and Uneven Development* (Albany: State University of New York Press, 1994).
27. N. D. B. Connolly, *A World More Concrete: Real Estate and the Remaking of Jim Crow South Florida* (Chicago: University of Chicago Press, 2014).
28. Penny M. von Eschen, *Race against Empire: Black Americans and Anticolonialism, 1937–1957* (Ithaca, NY: Cornell University Press, 1997);

Mary L. Dudziak, *Cold War Civil Rights: Race and the Image of American Democracy* (Princeton, NJ: Princeton University Press, 2000).

29. Quoted in Leon F. Litwack, *How Free Is Free? The Long Death of Jim Crow* (Cambridge, MA: Harvard University Press, 2009), 82.

30. Ibid., 83.

31. Hirsch, *Making the Second Ghetto*, 65.

32. Lyndon B. Johnson, remarks to the US Chamber of Commerce, April 27, 1964, http://www.presidency.ucsb.edu/ws/?pid=26193#axzz2h3amO72U.

33. Alexander von Hoffman, "The Lost History of Urban Renewal," *Journal of Urbanism* 1, no. 3 (November 1, 2008): 281–301.

34. Landon R. Y. Storrs, *The Second Red Scare and the Unmaking of the New Deal Left* (Princeton, NJ: Princeton University Press, 2013), 2.

35. Ibid., 3–4.

36. Manning Marable, *Race, Reform, and Rebellion: The Second Reconstruction in Black America, 1945–1990* (Jackson: University Press of Mississippi, 1991), 28.

37. Ibid., 31; Von Eschen, *Race against Empire*; Nikhil Pal Singh, *Black Is a Country: Race and the Unfinished Struggle for Democracy* (Cambridge, MA: Harvard University Press, 2004).

38. Karen Ferguson, *Top Down: The Ford Foundation, Black Power, and the Reinvention of Racial Liberalism* (Philadelphia: University of Pennsylvania Press, 2013).

39. Quoted in Alice O'Connor, *Poverty Knowledge: Social Science, Social Policy, and the Poor in Twentieth-Century U.S. History* (Princeton, NJ: Princeton University Press, 2009), 117.

40. Ibid.

41. Ibid., 117–18.

42. Ibid., 122.

43. Martin Luther King Jr., "I Have a Dream," speech delivered at the March on Washington, DC, August 28, 1963, http://www.ushistory.org/documents/i-have-a-dream.htm.

44. Martha Biondi, *To Stand and Fight: The Struggle for Civil Rights in Postwar New York City* (Cambridge, MA: Harvard University Press, 2003), 1.

45. Malcolm X and Alex Haley, *The Autobiography of Malcolm X* (New York: Grove Press, 1965), online edition, 67, http://www.epubsbook.com/2015/4318_67.html.

46. Malcolm X, speech at the founding rally of the Organization of Afro-American Unity, New York, June 28, 1964, http://www.blackpast.org/1964-malcolm-x-s-speech-founding-rally-organization-afro-american-unity.

47. Jack M. Bloom, *Class, Race, and the Civil Rights Movement* (Bloomington: Indiana University Press, 1987), 204.

48. Gerald Horne, *The Fire This Time: The Watts Uprising and the 1960s* (Boston: Da Capo Press, 1997).

49. Johnson, remarks to Chamber of Commerce.

50. Daniel Patrick Moynihan, *The Negro Family: The Case for National Action*

(Washington, DC: US Department of Labor, Office of Policy Planning and Research, 1965), http://www.blackpast.org/primary/moynihan-report-1965.

51. Kenneth Bancroft Clark, *Dark Ghetto: Dilemmas of Social Power* (New York: Harper & Row, 1965), 15.

52. Felicia Ann Kornbluh, *The Battle for Welfare Rights: Politics and Poverty in Modern America* (Philadelphia: University of Pennsylvania Press, 2007), 17–18.

53. William J. Novak, "The Myth of the 'Weak' American State," *American Historical Review* 113, no. 3 (2008): 752.

54. Kornbluh, *Battle for Welfare Rights*, 41.

55. "President Lyndon B. Johnson's Commencement Address at Howard University: 'To Fulfill These Rights,' June 4, 1965," accessed June 9, 2015, http://www.lbjlib.utexas.edu/johnson/archives.hom/speeches.hom/650604.asp.

56. "Negroes, Whites Agree on Riot Victims," *Boston Globe*, August 15, 1967.

57. Martin Luther King Jr., *The Essential Martin Luther King, Jr.: "I Have a Dream" and Other Great Writings* (Boston: Beacon Press, 2013).

58. Philip Sheldon Foner, ed., *The Black Panthers Speak* (Chicago: Haymarket Books, 2014), 51.

59. Colette Gaiter, "Visualizing a Revolution: Emory Douglas and the Black Panther Newspaper," AIGA website, June 8, 2005, http://www.aiga.org/visualizing-a-revolution-emory-douglas-and-the-black-panther-new/.

60. *New York Times* editorial, "The Race Problem: Why the Riots, What to Do?" August 6, 1967, http://timesmachine.nytimes.com/timesmachine/1967/08/06/issue.html.

61. "Negroes, Whites Agree"; Louis Harris, "Races Agree on Ghetto Abolition and Need for WPA-Type Projects," *Washington Post*, August 14, 1967.

62. Kerner Commission and Tom Wicker, *Report of the National Advisory Commission on Civil Disorders* (New York: Bantam Books, 1968).

63. Stan Karp, "Challenging Corporate Ed Reform," *Rethinking Schools* (Spring 2012), http://www.rethinkingschools.org//cmshandler.asp?archive/26_03/26_03_karp.shtml.

64. Nia-Malika Henderson, "What President Obama Gets Wrong about 'Acting White,'" *Washington Post*, July 24, 2014, http://www.washingtonpost.com/blogs/she-the-people/wp/2014/07/24/what-president-obama-gets-wrong-about-acting-white/.

65. Barack Obama, "Remarks by the President on 'My Brother's Keeper' Initiative," Whitehouse.gov, February 27, 2014, https://www.whitehouse.gov/the-press-office/2014/02/27/remarks-president-my-brothers-keeper-initiative.

66. US Department of Justice, Civil Rights Division, *Investigation of the Ferguson Police Department* (Washington, DC: US Department of Justice, 2015), 77, http://purl.fdlp.gov/GPO/gpo55760.

Chapter Two

Naomi Murakawa, *The First Civil Right: How Liberals Built Prison America* (New York: Oxford University Press, 2014), 7.

1. W. E. B. Du Bois, *Black Reconstruction* (Notre Dame, IN: University of Notre Dame Press, 2006), 27.
2. Josh Levin, "The Real Story of Linda Taylor, America's Original Welfare Queen," *Slate*, December 19, 2013, http://www.slate.com/articles/news_and_politics/history/2013/12/linda_taylor_welfare_queen_ronald_reagan_made_her_a_notorious_american_villain.html.
3. Rick Perlstein, *The Invisible Bridge: The Fall of Nixon and the Rise of Reagan* (New York: Simon and Schuster, 2014), 662.
4. Barack Obama, "Remarks by the President on Economic Mobility," speech delivered December 4, 2013, Washington, DC, Whitehouse.gov, https://www.whitehouse.gov/the-press-office/2013/12/04/remarks-president-economic-mobility.
5. Rick Perlstein, "Exclusive: Lee Atwater's Infamous 1981 Interview on the Southern Strategy," *Nation*, November 13, 2012, http://www.thenation.com/article/170841/exclusive-lee-atwaters-infamous-1981-interview-southern-strategy.
6. Rick Perlstein, *Nixonland: The Rise of a President and the Fracturing of America* (New York: Scribner, 2008), 277.
7. *New York Times*, "Haldeman Diary Shows Nixon Was Wary of Blacks and Jews," May 18, 1994, http://www.nytimes.com/1994/05/18/us/haldeman-diary-shows-nixon-was-wary-of-blacks-and-jews.html.
8. Martin Luther King Jr. and James Melvin Washington, *A Testament of Hope: The Essential Writings of Martin Luther King, Jr.* (New York: Harper & Row, 1986).
9. Quoted in Michael and Paul M. Hirsch, eds., *Markets on Trial: The Economic Sociology of the U.S. Financial Crisis: Part A* (Bingley, UK: Emerald Group Publishing, 2010), 151.
10. *Retrospectz*, "Niggermation at Eldon," March 3, 2011, https://retrospectz.wordpress.com/2011/03/03/niggermation-at-eldon/.
11. Dan Georgakas and Marvin Surkin, *Detroit: I Do Mind Dying* (Cambridge, MA: South End Press, 1998), 88.
12. Michael K. Honey, *Going Down Jericho Road: The Memphis Strike, Martin Luther King's Last Campaign* (New York: W.W. Norton & Co., 2007), 497–512.
13. Christian Parenti, *Lockdown America: Police and Prisons in the Age of Crisis* (London: Verso, 2001), 34.
14. Megan Behrent, "The Source of Union Power," *Socialist Worker*, December 19, 2012, http://socialistworker.org/2012/12/19/source-of-union-power.
15. *TIME*, "Nation: The Enduring Mail Mess," March 30, 1970, http://content.time.com/time/magazine/article/0,9171,942204,00.html.
16. Lee Sustar, "Black Power in the Workplace," *Diversity Now*, February 22,

2013, http://diversitynowbyegloballearning.blogspot.com/2013/02/black-power-in-workplace.html.

17. Ibid.

18. Barbara Ehrenreich, *Fear of Falling: The Inner Life of the Middle Class* (New York: Pantheon Books, 1989), 125.

19. Ibid., 121.

20. George Melloan, "Thoughts on Student Rioting Abroad," *Wall Street Journal*, April 19, 1968.

21. Beth Mintz and Michael Schwartz, *The Power Structure of American Business* (Chicago: University of Chicago Press, 1985).

22. Leonard Solomon Silk and David Vogel, *Ethics and Profits: The Crisis of Confidence in American Business* (New York: Simon and Schuster, 1976), 71.

23. Ibid., 48.

24. Alexander Cockburn and Jeffrey St. Clair, *End Times: The Death of the Fourth Estate* (Oakland, CA: AK Press, 2007).

25. Silk and Vogel, *Ethics and Profits*, 64.

26. Richard M. Nixon, "Statement about Federal Policies Relative to Equal Housing Opportunity," speech delivered June 11, 1971, http://www.presidency.ucsb.edu/ws/?pid=3042.

27. Ibid.

28. United States Commission on Civil Rights, *Home Ownership for Lower Income Families: A Report on the Racial and Ethnic Impact of the Section 235 Program* (Washington, DC: Government Printing Office, 1971).

29. Murakawa, *First Civil Right*.

30. Christian Parenti, "The 'New' Criminal Justice System," *Defending Justice*, 2005, http://www.publiceye.org/defendingjustice/overview/parenti_repression.html.

31. US Department of Justice, *Title I: The Omnibus Crime Control and Safe Streets Act of 1968*, Public Law 90–351, https://transition.fcc.gov/Bureaus/OSEC/library/legislative_histories/1615.pdf.

32. Ibid.

33. Heather Ann Thompson, "Why Mass Incarceration Matters: Rethinking Crisis, Decline, and Transformation in Postwar American History," *Journal of American History* 97, no. 3 (2010): 731.

34. Parenti, *Lockdown America*, 12–13.

35. Ibid., 13.

36. Ibid., 19.

37. Devah Pager, *Marked: Race, Crime, and Finding Work in an Era of Mass Incarceration* (Chicago: University of Chicago Press, 2008), 17.

38. Heather Ann Thompson, "The Lingering Injustice of Attica," *New York Times*, September 8, 2011, http://www.nytimes.com/2011/09/09/opinion/the-lingering-injustice-of-attica.html.

39. Thompson, "Why Mass Incarceration Matters," 708.

40. J. Kohler-Hausmann, "'The Attila the Hun Law': New York's Rockefeller

Drug Laws and the Making of a Punitive State," *Journal of Social History* 44, no. 1 (2010): 71–95.

41. Madison Gray, "A Brief History of New York's Rockefeller Drug Laws," *TIME*, April 2, 2009, http://content.time.com/time/nation/article/0,8599,1888864,00.html.

42. Ibid.

43. United States Bureau of Justice Statistics, *Prisoners, 1925–1981* (Washington, DC: Bureau of Justice Statistics, 1982), 2.

44. Manning Marable, *How Capitalism Underdeveloped Black America: Problems in Race, Political Economy, and Society* (Chicago: Haymarket Books, 2015), 125–26.

45. Richard M. Nixon, Public Papers of the Presidents of the United States: Richard M. Nixon, 1973 (Washington, DC: National Archives, 1975), 164.

46. *Crisis* editorial, "Mr. Nixon's Optimism," *Crisis* 80, no. 5 (1973): 149.

47. Joy Darrow, "Ghetto Housing's Future," *Chicago Daily Defender*, January 23, 1973.

48. Quoted in *Crisis* editorial, "Mr. Nixon's Optimism."

49. Alice O'Connor, "The Privatized City: The Manhattan Institute, the Urban Crisis, and the Conservative Counterrevolution in New York," *Journal of Urban History* 34, no. 2 (2008): 339.

50. Ibid.

51. Ibid.

Chapter Three

Manning Marable, *How Capitalism Underdeveloped Black America: Problems in Race, Political Economy, and Society*, 3rd ed. (Chicago: Haymarket Books, 2015), 186; Amiri Baraka, *Tales of the Out and the Gone* (New York: Akashic Books, 2009), 31.

1. Conor Friedersdorf, "Freddie Gray Is Only the Latest Apparent Victim of Baltimore Police Violence," *Atlantic*, April 22, 2015, http://www.theatlantic.com/politics/archive/2015/04/the-brutality-of-police-culture-in-baltimore/391158/.

2. Sabrina Toppa, "The Baltimore Riots Cost an Estimated $9 Million in Damages," *TIME*, May 14, 2015, http://time.com/3858181/baltimore-riots-damages-businesses-homes-freddie-gray/.

3. Oliver Laughland, "Baltimore Unrest: 49 Children Were Arrested and Detained During Protests," *Guardian*, May 7, 2015, http://www.theguardian.com/us-news/2015/may/07/baltimore-children-arrests-freddie-gray-protests.

4. Sheryl Gay Stolberg and Jess Bidgood, "Mistrial Declared in Case of Officer Charged in Freddie Gray's Death," *New York Times*, December 16, 2015, http://www.nytimes.com/2015/12/17/us/freddie-gray-baltimore-police-trial.html?_r=0.

5. Quoted in David Jackson, "Obama Stands By the Term 'Thugs,' White House Says," *USA Today*, April 29, 2015, http://www.usatoday.com/story/theoval/2015/04/29/obama-white-house-baltimore-stephanie-rawlings-blake/26585143/.

6. Quoted in Yvonne Wenger and Luke Broadwater, "Mayor Calls on Black Men to Do More to Stop Violence," *Baltimore Sun*, March 9, 2015, http://www.baltimoresun.com/news/maryland/politics/bs-md-baltimore-state-of-city-20150309-story.html.

7. CBS Chicago, "Cook County Commissioner Wants Shooters Charged as Domestic Terrorists," May 26, 2015, http://chicago.cbslocal.com/2015/05/26/cook-county-commissioner-wants-shooters-charged-as-domestic-terrorists/.

8. Kevin Rector, "Baltimore Prosecutor Asked Police to Target Area Where Freddie Gray Was Arrested," *Baltimore Sun*, June 9, 2015, http://www.baltimoresun.com/news/maryland/crime/blog/bs-md-ci-mosby-email-20150609-story.html.

9. Ibid.

10. Michael B. Katz, *In the Shadow of the Poorhouse: A Social History of Welfare in America* (New York: Basic Books, 1996), 266.

11. Michael K. Brown, et al., *Whitewashing Race: The Myth of a Color-Blind Society* (Berkeley and Los Angeles: University of California Press, 2003), 74.

12. Thomas J. Sugrue, *Sweet Land of Liberty: The Forgotten Struggle for Civil Rights in the North* (New York: Random House, 2008), 505.

13. William Julius Wilson, *The Declining Significance of Race: Blacks and Changing American Institutions*, 3rd ed. (Chicago: University of Chicago Press, 2012), 103.

14. Manning Marable, *Race, Reform, and Rebellion: The Second Reconstruction in Black America, 1945–1990* (Jackson: University of Mississippi Press, 1991), 148.

15. Marable, *How Capitalism Underdeveloped Black America*, 42.

16. Marable, *Race, Reform, and Rebellion*, 148.

17. Ibid., 149.

18. Carmen DeNavas-Walt, et al., *Income, Poverty, and Health Insurance Coverage in the United States, 2010* (Washington, DC: US Census Bureau, 2011), http://www.census.gov/prod/2011pubs/p60-239.pdf.

19. Eugene Robinson, *Disintegration: The Splintering of Black America* (New York: Anchor, 2011), 91.

20. Simeon Book, "Can Negroes Become Big City Mayors?" *Ebony* (March 1966), 30.

21. *The Black Power Mixtape 1967–1975*. DVD. Directed by Göran Hugo Olsson. MPI Home Video, 2011.

22. B. J. Mason, "A Shift to the Middle," *Ebony* (August 1973), 82.

23. Stokely Carmichael and Charles V. Hamilton, *Black Power: The Politics of Liberation in America* (New York: Random House, 1967).

24. Bayard Rustin, "From Protest to Politics: The Future of the Civil Rights Movement," *Commentary* (1965).

25. Grace Lee Boggs and James Boggs, "The City Is the Black Man's Land," *Monthly Review* (April 1966), http://docslide.us/documents/the-city-is-the-black-mans-land.html.

26. Ibid., 42.

27. Martin Luther King Jr. and James Melvin Washington, *A Testament of Hope: The Essential Writings of Martin Luther King, Jr.* (San Francisco: Harper & Row, 1986), 319.

28. Robert E. Weems, *Business in Black and White: American Presidents and Black Entrepreneurs in the Twentieth Century* (New York: NYU Press, 2009), 115.

29. Richard M. Nixon, "Bridges to Human Dignity," speech delivered on NBC Radio, April 25, 1968, box 5, 1968, Press Releases and Nixon Speeches, RNC records.

30. Booker, "Can Negroes Become Big City Mayors?"

31. Leonard N. Moore, *Carl B. Stokes and the Rise of Black Political Power* (Urbana-Champaign: University of Illinois Press, 2003), 56.

32. Ibid., 55.

33. Ibid.

34. Ibid., 58.

35. Quoted in ibid., 63.

36. Quoted in Lee Sustar, "Carving a Niche in the System," *Socialist Worker,* March 15, 2013, http://socialistworker.org/2013/03/15/a-niche-in-the-system.

37. Peniel E. Joseph, *Waiting 'Til the Midnight Hour: A Narrative History of Black Power in America* (New York: Henry Holt, 2006).

38. Huey P. Newton, "The Black Panthers," *Ebony* (August 1969), 110.

39. King and Washington, *Testament of Hope.*

40. Fairness.com, "Congressional Black Caucus," updated 2011, http://www.fairness.com/resources/relation?relation_id=45475.

41. John Conyers Jr., "Politics and the Black Revolution," *Ebony* (August 1969), 165.

42. Ibid.

43. Alex Poinsett, "The Black Caucus: Five Years Later," *Ebony* (June 1973), 64.

44. Quoted in Congressional Black Caucus, *The Black Leadership Family Plan for the Unity, Survival, and Progress of Black People* (Washington, DC: Congressional Black Caucus, 1982), 1.

45. Lee Sustar, "The National Black Political Convention," *Socialist Worker,* March 22, 2013, http://socialistworker.org/2013/03/22/the-national-black-political-convention.

46. Lance Selfa, *The Democrats: A Critical History,* updated ed. (Chicago: Haymarket Books, 2012), 63–84.

47. Thomas J. Sugrue, *The Origins of the Urban Crisis: Race and Inequality in Postwar Detroit* (Princeton, NJ: Princeton University Press, 2005); Betsy Leondar-Wright, "Black Job Loss Déjà Vu," *Dollars & Sense,* May 4, 2004, http://www.dollarsandsense.org/archives/2004/0504leondar.html.

48. Leondar-Wright, "Black Job Loss."
49. Isaiah J. Poole, "Uncle Sam's Pink Slip," *Black Enterprise,* December 1981, 29.
50. *Economist* editorial, "Not So Colour-Blind," December 3, 2009, http://www. economist.com/node/15019840.
51. Marable, *How Capitalism Underdeveloped Black America,* 172.
52. Fredrick C. Harris, *The Price of the Ticket: Barack Obama and the Rise and Decline of Black Politics* (New York: Oxford University Press, 2012), 144–51.
53. Marable, *How Capitalism Underdeveloped Black America,* 171–72.
54. Ibid., 171.
55. Claude Lewis, "Where Are Civil-Rights Leaders?" *Philadelphia Inquirer,* July 24, 1989, http://articles.philly.com/1989-07-24/news/26133979_1_civil-rights-leaders-civil-rights-black-leaders.
56. Marable, *Race, Reform, and Rebellion,* 170.
57. Ibid., 171.
58. Victor Perlo, "Carter's Economic Prescription: Bitter Medicine for the People," *Public Affairs* 58, no. 1 (1979): 1–9.
59. Marable, *Race, Reform, and Rebellion,* 172.
60. D. L. Chandler, "Little Known Black History Fact: 1980 Miami Riots," *Black America Web,* July 11, 2014, http://blackamericaweb.com/2014/07/11/little-known-black-history-fact-1980-miami-riots/2/.
61. Harris, *Price of the Ticket,* 144.
62. Ibid.
63. Ronald W. Walters, *African American Leadership* (Albany: State University of New York Press, 1999); Congressional Black Caucus, *Black Leadership Family Plan.*
64. Ibid.
65. Congressional Black Caucus, *Black Leadership Family Plan,* iii.
66. Walters, *African American Leadership,* 167.
67. Congressional Black Caucus, *Black Leadership Family Plan,* viii.
68. Adolph Reed Jr., *Stirrings in the Jug; Black Politics in the Post-Segregation Era* (Minneapolis: University of Minnesota Press, 1999), 106–9.
69. Ibid., 55.
70. Nathan Bomey and John Gallagher, "How Detroit Went Broke: The Answers May Surprise You—and Don't Blame Coleman Young," *Detroit Free Press,* September 15, 2013, http://archive.freep.com/interactive/article/20130915/NEWS01/130801004/Detroit-Bankruptcy-history-1950-debt-pension-revenue.
71. Howard Gillette Jr., *Camden after the Fall: Decline and Renewal in a Post-Industrial City* (Philadelphia: University of Pennsylvania Press, 2006), 111.
72. Quoted in Ibid., 112.
73. Mike Davis, *The Year Left 2: An American Socialist Yearbook* (London: Verso, 1987), 4.
74. Juan Gonzalez, Linn Washington, and Mumia Abu-Jamal, *Democracy Now!,* interview, May 13, 2015, http://www.democracynow.org/2015/5/13/move_bombing_at_30_barbaric_1985.

75. On the votes, see "Bill Summary & Status 99th Congress (1985–1986) H.R. 5484," http://thomas.loc.gov/cgi-bin/bdquery/z?d099:HR05484; Teka Lark-Fleming, "The Role Black Politicians Play in Systematically Murdering Black People," *Medium*, September 22, 2014, https://medium.com/@blkgrrrl/the-role-politicians-play-in-systematically-murdering-black-people-7f7340cace43#.vo141dofk. On sentencing, see U.S. Department of Justice, "Federal Cocaine Offenses: An Analysis of Crack and Powder Penalties," 2002, 10–11.

76. William J. Clinton, "The Freedom to Die," speech delivered in Memphis, Tennessee, November 13, 1993, http://www.blackpast.org/1993-william-j-clinton-freedom-die.

77. Quoted in Bob Herbert, "In America; A Sea Change on Crime," *New York Times*, December 12, 1993, http://www.nytimes.com/1993/12/12/opinion/in-america-a-sea-change-on-crime.html.

78. Jill Lawrence, "Growth Splinters Black Lawmakers—Views Clash as Caucus Doubles in a Decade," *Seattle Times*, July 27, 1994, http://community.seattletimes.nwsource.com/archive/?date=19940727&slug=1922486.

79. Karen Hosler, "Black Caucus Yields on Crime Bill," *Baltimore Sun*, August 18, 1994, http://articles.baltimoresun.com/1994-08-18/news/1994230118_1_black-caucus-crime-bill-clinton.

80. Quoted in Dara Lind, "Bill Clinton Apologized for His 1994 Crime Bill, but He Still Doesn't Get Why It Was Bad," *Vox*, July 15, 2015, http://www.vox.com/2015/5/7/8565345/1994-crime-bill.

81. Eric Lipton and Eric Lichtblau, "In Black Caucus, a Fund-Raising Powerhouse," *New York Times*, February 14, 2010, http://www.nytimes.com/2010/02/14/us/politics/14cbc.html.

82. Congressional Black Caucus Foundation, "CBCF Announces $1 Million Grant from Walmart," June 9, 2015, http://www.cbcfinc.org/2015-archive/815-cbcf-announces-1-million-grant-from-walmart.html.

83. Jonathan D. Salant, "Corporations Donate to Groups on Both Sides of Voter-ID," *Bloomberg Business*, April 19, 2012, http://www.bloomberg.com/news/articles/2012-04-19/corporations-donate-to-groups-on-both-sides-of-voter-id.

84. Quoted in Lauren French, "Black Caucus Stumps Where Obama Can't," *Politico*, August 23, 2014, http://www.politico.com/story/2014/08/black-caucus-barack-obama-110285_Page2.html.

85. Andra Gillespie, *The New Black Politician: Cory Booker, Newark, and Post-Racial America* (New York: NYU Press, 2012), 9–45.

86. Cathy J. Cohen, *Democracy Remixed: Black Youth and the Future of American Politics* (New York and Oxford: Oxford University Press, 2012), 202–32.

87. Jelani Cobb, "Cory Booker: The Dilemma of the New Black Politician," *New Yorker*, May 22, 2012, http://www.newyorker.com/news/news-desk/cory-booker-the-dilemma-of-the-new-black-politician.

88. Robinson, *Disintegration*, 140.

89. Ibid., 160.
90. Natalie Moore, "Why Are There Fewer Black Teachers in CPS?" WBEZ, July 15, 2015, http://www.wbez.org/news/why-are-there-fewer-black-teachers-cps-112385.
91. Adeshina Emmanuel, "Chicago's Black Unemployment Rate Higher Than Other Large Metro Areas," *Chicago Reporter*, November 16, 2014, http://chicagoreporter.com/chicagos-black-unemployment-rate-higher-other-large-metro-areas/.
92. Fran Spielman, "Black Caucus Going to Bat for Rahm Emanuel in Wilson Courtship," *Chicago Sun-Times*, March 5, 2015, http://chicago.suntimes.com/chicago-politics/7/71/416630/black-caucus-going-bat-rahm-emanuel-wilson-courtship.
93. Ibid.
94. Matt Sledge, "Chicago's Black Population Dwindles, Census Numbers Show," *Huffington Post*, August 4, 2011, http://www.huffingtonpost.com/2011/08/04/chicago-black-population_n_917848.html.
95. Quoted in Mick Dumke, "Why Aldermen Are Mum about Chicago's Violence: They're Not Sure What to Say," *Chicago Reader*, June 3, 2014, http://www.chicagoreader.com/Bleader/archives/2014/06/03/why-aldermen-are-mum-about-chicagos-violence-theyre-not-sure-what-to-say.
96. Manning Marable, *Black Liberation in Conservative America* (Boston: South End Press, 1997), 151.

Chapter Four

Amy Goodman, "The American Dream: Living to 18," *Truthdig*, May 6, 2015, http://www.truthdig.com/report/print/the_american_dream_living_to_18_20150506.
1. Douglas A. Blackmon, *Slavery by Another Name: The Re-Enslavement of Black People in America from the Civil War to World War II* (New York: Doubleday, 2008).
2. "The Black Code of St. Landry's Parish," US Congress, Senate Executive Document No. 2 (Washington, DC, 1865), 93–94, http://www.history.vt.edu/shifflet/blackcode.htm.
3. Ibid.
4. George Rutherglen, *Civil Rights in the Shadow of Slavery: The Constitution, Common Law, and the Civil Rights Act of 1866* (Oxford: Oxford University Press, 2013).
5. Albert D. Oliphant, *The Evolution of the Penal System of South Carolina from 1866 to 1916* (Columbia, SC: State Co., 1916), 5–9.
6. Ibid.
7. "Convict Lease System," *Digital History*, n.d., ID 3179, accessed May 28, 2015, http://www.digitalhistory.uh.edu/disp_textbook.cfm?smtid=2&psid=3179.

8. Khalil Gibran Muhammad, *The Condemnation of Blackness* (Cambridge, MA: Harvard University Press, 2010), 3.
9. David M. Oshinsky, *Worse Than Slavery* (New York: Simon & Schuster, 1997), 97.
10. Ibid.
11. Evelyn Higginbotham Brooks, "African-American Women's History and the Metalanguage of Race," *Signs* 17, no. 2 (1992): 271.
12. Muhammad, *Condemnation of Blackness*, 4.
13. Dorothy E. Roberts, *Killing the Black Body: Race, Reproduction, and the Meaning of Liberty* (New York: Vintage, 1999).
14. Elaine Lewinnek, *The Working Man's Reward: Chicago's Early Suburbs and the Roots of American Sprawl* (Oxford: Oxford University Press, 2014), 153.
15. William M. Tuttle, *Race Riot: Chicago in the Red Summer of 1919* (Urbana-Champaign: University of Illinois Press, 1970); Charles L. Lumpkins, *American Pogrom: The East St. Louis Race Riot and Black Politics* (Athens: Ohio University Press, 2008).
16. Rose Helper, *Racial Policies and Practices of Real Estate Brokers* (Minneapolis: University of Minnesota Press, 1969).
17. Kevin Boyle, *Arc of Justice: A Saga of Race, Civil Rights, and Murder in the Jazz Age* (New York: Macmillan, 2007), 24.
18. Ibid., 111.
19. Muhammad, *The Condemnation of Blackness*, 258–59.
20. Ibid.
21. Tuttle, *Race Riot*, 4–10.
22. Arnold R. Hirsch, *Making the Second Ghetto: Race and Housing in Chicago 1940–1960* (Chicago: University of Chicago Press, 1998), 65.
23. Leon F. Litwack, *How Free Is Free? The Long Death of Jim Crow* (Cambridge, MA: Harvard University Press, 2009), 84.
24. Ibid., 85.
25. "The Race Problem: Why the Riots? What to Do?" *New York Times* editorial, August 6, 1967.
26. Kerner Commission and Tom Wicker, *Report of the National Advisory Commission on Civil Disorders* (New York: Bantam Books, 1968).
27. James Baldwin, "A Report from Occupied Territory," *Nation*, July 11, 1966, http://www.thenation.com/article/159618/report-occupied-territory.
28. *New York Times*, "81% in a Poll See Law Breakdown: 84% Feel Strong President Would Help, Harris Says," September 10, 1968.
29. President's Commission on Law Enforcement, *The Challenge of Crime in a Free Society* (Washington, DC: US Government Printing Office, 1967), 111.
30. Christian Parenti, *Lockdown America: Police and Prisons in the Age of Crisis* (London: Verso, 2001), 15.
31. Lyndon B. Johnson, "Special Message to the Congress on Law Enforcement and the Administration of Justice," speech delivered to Congress, March 8, 1965, http://www.presidency.ucsb.edu/ws/?pid=26800.

32. Naomi Murakawa, "The Origins of the Carceral Crisis: Racial Order as Law and Order in Postwar American Politics," in *Race and American Political Development*, edited by Joseph E. Lowndes, Julie Novkov, and Dorian Tod Warren (New York: Routledge, 2008), 238.

33. David Alan Sklansky, "Not Your Father's Police Department: Making Sense of the New Demographics of Law Enforcement," *Journal of Criminal Law and Criminology* 96, no. 3 (2006): 1224.

34. Ibid.

35. Yamiche Alcindor and Nick Penzenstadler, "Police Redouble Efforts to Recruit Diverse Officers," *USA TODAY*, January 21, 2015, http://www.usatoday.com/story/news/2015/01/21/police-redoubling-efforts-to-recruit-diverse-officers/21574081.

36. Lisa Bloom, "When Will the U.S. Stop Mass Incarceration?" CNN, July 3, 2012, http://www.cnn.com/2012/07/03/opinion/bloom-prison-spending/index.html.

37. Ed Vulliamy, "Nixon's 'War on Drugs' Began 40 Years Ago, and the Battle Is Still Raging," *Guardian*, July 24, 2011, http://www.theguardian.com/society/2011/jul/24/war-on-drugs-40-years.

38. Ezra Klein and Evan Soltas, "Wonkbook: 11 Facts about America's Prison Population," *Washington Post*, August 13, 2013, http://www.washingtonpost.com/news/wonkblog/wp/2013/08/13/wonkbook-11-facts-about-americas-prison-population.

39. University of Chicago Crime Lab, "Incarceration," n.d., accessed June 3, 2015, https://crimelab.uchicago.edu/page/incarceration.

40. Ibid.

41. Kevin Phillips, *The Politics of Rich and Poor: Wealth and the American Electorate in the Reagan Aftermath* (New York: HarperPerennial, 1991).

42. R. Shankar Nair, "Willie's Got a Lesson for Washington," *Chicago Tribune*, February 16, 1995, http://articles.chicagotribune.com/1995-02-16/news/9502160082_1_reagan-revolution-middle-class-wealth.

43. Kevin Phillips, *Wealth and Democracy: A Political History of the American Rich* (New York: Broadway Books, 2003), xvi.

44. Peter Applebome, "The 1992 Campaign: Death Penalty; Arkansas Execution Raises Questions on Governor's Politics," January 25, 1992, http://www.nytimes.com/1992/01/25/us/1992-campaign-death-penalty-arkansas-execution-raises-questions-governor-s.html.

45. Ed Pilkington, "Bill Clinton: Mass Incarceration on My Watch 'Put Too Many People in Prison,'" *Guardian*, April 28, 2015, http://www.theguardian.com/us-news/2015/apr/28/bill-clinton-calls-for-end-mass-incarceration.

46. Radley Balko, "Have Police Departments Become More Militarized Since 9/11?" *Huffington Post*, September 12, 2011, http://www.huffingtonpost.com/2011/09/12/police-militarization-9-11-september-11_n_955508.html.

47. Ibid.

48. Associated Press, "Little Restraint in Military Giveaways," National

Public Radio, July 31, 2013, http://www.npr.org/templates/story/story.
php?storyId=207340981.

49. Joseph D. McNamara, "50 Shots," *Wall Street Journal*, November 29, 2006.

50. Erica Goode, "Incarceration Rates for Blacks Dropped, Report Shows," *New York Times*, February 28, 2013, http://www.nytimes.com/2013/02/28/us/incarceration-rates-for-blacks-dropped-report-shows.html.

51. Mark Berman, "The Breaking Point for Ferguson," *Washington Post*, August 12, 2014, http://www.washingtonpost.com/news/post-nation/wp/2014/08/12/the-breaking-point-for-ferguson/.

52. Brad Heath, "Racial Gap in U.S. Arrest Rates: 'Staggering Disparity,'" *USA Today*, November 18, 2014, http://www.usatoday.com/story/news/nation/2014/11/18/ferguson-black-arrest-rates/19043207/.

53. *USA Today*, "Compare Arrest Rates," interactive map, n.d., accessed January 11, 2015, http://www.gannett-cdn.com/experiments/usatoday/2014/11/arrests-interactive/.

54. Inimai M. Chettiar, "Locking More People Up Is Counterproductive," *Atlantic*, February 11, 2015, http://www.theatlantic.com/features/archive/2015/02/the-many-causes-of-americas-decline-in-crime/385364/.

55. Ibid.

56. Jeremy Gorner and Hal Dardick, "No Back Pay for OT in First Year of New Chicago Police Contract," *Chicago Tribune*, September 5, 2014, http://www.chicagotribune.com/news/local/politics/chi-no-back-pay-on-cop-overtime-in-new-chicago-police-contract-20140905-story.html.

57. Laura Sullivan, "Mentally Ill Are Often Locked Up in Jails That Can't Help," National Public Radio, January 20, 2014, http://www.npr.org/2014/01/20/263461940/mentally-ill-inmates-often-locked-up-in-jails-that-cant-help.

58. Kelley Bouchard, "Across Nation, Unsettling Acceptance When Mentally Ill in Crisis Are Killed," *Portland Press Herald*, December 9, 2012, http://www.pressherald.com/2012/12/09/shoot-across-nation-a-grim-acceptance-when-mentally-ill-shot-down/.

59. Scott Keyes, "It Is Illegal for Homeless People to Sit on the Sidewalk in More than Half of U.S. Cities," *Think Progress*, July 16, 2014, http://thinkprogress.org/economy/2014/07/16/3460553/homeless-criminalization-report/.

60. United States, Bureau of Justice Assistance, and Police Executive Research Forum, *CompStat: Its Origins, Evolution, and Future in Law Enforcement Agencies*, 2013, https://www.bja.gov/Publications/PERF-Compstat.pdf.

61. Ibid.

62. Ibid., 27.

63. Daniel Bergner, "Is Stop-and-Frisk Worth It?" *Atlantic*, April 2014, http://www.theatlantic.com/features/archive/2014/03/is-stop-and-frisk-worth-it/358644/.

64. Ibid.

65. Marina Carver, "NYPD Officers Say They Had Stop-and-Frisk Quotas," CNN, March 22, 2013, http://www.cnn.com/2013/03/22/justice/new-york-stop-and-frisk-trial/index.html.

66. James Q. Wilson and George L. Kelling, "Broken Windows: The Police and Neighborhood Safety," *Atlantic*, March 1982, https://www.theatlantic.com/past/docs/politics/crime/windows.htm.

67. Joseph Goldstein, "Kelly Intended Frisks to Instill Fear, Senator Testifies," *New York Times*, April 1, 2013, http://www.nytimes.com/2013/04/02/nyregion/kelly-intended-frisks-to-instill-fear-senator-testifies.html.

68. Jason Meisner, "Chicago Sued over Police Department's Alleged Stop-and-Frisk Practices," *Chicago Tribune*, April 21, 2015, http://www.chicagotribune.com/news/local/breaking/ct-stop-and-frisk-lawsuit-met-20150421-story.html.

69. John H. Richardson, "Michael Brown Sr. and the Agony of the Black Father in America," *Esquire*, January 5, 2015, http://www.esquire.com/features/michael-brown-father-interview-0115.

70. Campbell Robertson, Shaila Dewan, and Matt Apuzzo, "Ferguson Became Symbol, but Bias Knows No Border," *New York Times*, March 7, 2015, http://www.nytimes.com/2015/03/08/us/ferguson-became-symbol-but-bias-knows-no-border.html.

71. Radley Balko, "How Municipalities in St. Louis County, Mo., Profit from Poverty," *Washington Post*, September 3, 2014, http://www.washingtonpost.com/news/the-watch/wp/2014/09/03/how-st-louis-county-missouri-profits-from-poverty/.

72. Dewan and Apuzzo, "Ferguson Became Symbol."

73. Alain Sherter, "As Economy Flails, Debtors' Prisons Thrive," CBS News, April 5, 2013, http://www.cbsnews.com/news/as-economy-flails-debtors-prisons-thrive/.

74. Joseph Shapiro, "As Court Fees Rise, the Poor Are Paying the Price," National Public Radio, May 19, 2014, http://www.npr.org/2014/05/19/312158516/increasing-court-fees-punish-the-poor.

75. Ibid.

76. Quoted in ibid.

77. Sherter, "As Economy Flails."

78. Jyoti Thottam, "In Texas, Courts Turn Truancy Cases into Cash," *Al Jazeera America*, May 21, 2015, http://america.aljazeera.com/articles/2015/5/21/in-texas-courts-turn-truancy-cases-into-cash.html.

79. Carla Murphy, "NYPD Officers Do Less; City's Young Black Men Exhale," *Colorlines*, January 9, 2015, http://www.colorlines.com/articles/nypd-officers-do-less-citys-young-black-men-exhale.

80. Radley Balko, "U.S. Cities Pay Out Millions to Settle Police Lawsuits," *Washington Post*, October 1, 2014, http://www.washingtonpost.com/news/the-watch/wp/2014/10/01/u-s-cities-pay-out-millions-to-settle-police-lawsuits/.

81. Jonah Newman, "Chicago Police Misconduct Payouts Topped $50 Million in 2014," *Chicago Reporter*, February 25, 2015, http://chicagoreporter.com/chicago-police-misconduct-payouts-topped-50-million-in-2014/.

82. David Schaper, "Chicago Creates Reparations Fund for Victims of Police Torture," National Public Radio, May 6, 2015, http://www.npr.org/sections/thetwo-way/2015/05/06/404545064/chicago-set-to-create-reparation-fund-for-victims-of-police-torture.

83. Joel Rubin, "Federal Judge Lifts LAPD Consent Decree," *Los Angeles Times*, May 16, 2013, http://articles.latimes.com/2013/may/16/local/la-me-lapd-consent-decree-20130517.

84. Balko, "U.S. Cities Pay Out Millions."

85. Dana DiFilippo and David Gambacorta, "Civil-Rights Lawsuits against Police Spiked in 2013," *Philadelphia Daily News*, May 30, 2014, http://articles.philly.com/2014-05-30/news/50185668_1_settlements-chief-deputy-city-solicitor-police-department.

86. Tom McCarthy, "Police Killed More Than Twice as Many People as Reported by US Government," *Guardian*, March 4, 2015, http://www.theguardian.com/us-news/2015/mar/04/police-killed-people-fbi-data-justifiable-homicides.

87. Ibid.

88. Jamiles Lartey, "By the Numbers: US Police Kill More in Days than Other Countries Do in Years," *Guardian*, June 9, 2015, http://www.theguardian.com/us-news/2015/jun/09/the-counted-police-killings-us-vs-other-countries; Matt Agorist, "Police in the US Kill Citizens at Over 70 Times the Rate of Other First-World Nations," *Freethought Project*, January 8, 2015, http://thefreethoughtproject.com/police-kill-citizens-70-times-rate-first-world-nations/.

89. Rob Barry and Coulter Jones, "Hundreds of Police Killings Are Uncounted in Federal Stats," *Wall Street Journal*, December 3, 2014, http://www.wsj.com/articles/hundreds-of-police-killings-are-uncounted-in-federal-statistics-1417577504.

90. Ryan Gabrielson, Ryann Grochowski Jones, and Eric Sagara, "Deadly Force, in Black and White," *ProPublica*, October 10, 2014, http://www.propublica.org/article/deadly-force-in-black-and-white.

91. Rebecca Leber, "Police Officers Are More Likely to Shoot Black Men, Studies Suggest," *New Republic*, August 12, 2014, http://www.newrepublic.com/article/119060/michael-brown-studies-show-racial-bias-police-shootings.

92. Ryan Gabrielson and Ryann Grochowski Jones, "Answering the Critics of Our Deadly Force Story," *ProPublica*, December 24, 2014, http://www.propublica.org/article/answering-the-critics-of-our-deadly-force-story.

93. David Jackson, "Obama Task Force Urges Independent Probes of Police Killings," *USA Today*, March 2, 2015, http://www.usatoday.com/story/news/nation/2015/03/02/obama-task-force-on-21st-century-policing-ferguson/24258019/.

94. David A. Graham, "Walter Scott Shooting: Statistics on North Charleston Police Stops, Police Homicides, and Officer Convictions," *Atlantic*, April 8, 2015, http://www.theatlantic.com/national/archive/2015/04/the-shockingly-familiar-killing-of-walter-scott/390006/.

95. *Guardian*, "The Counted: People Killed by Police in the United States in 2015," interactive database, June 1, 2015, http://www.theguardian.com/us-news/ng-interactive/2015/jun/01/the-counted-police-killings-us-database.

96. Jeff Brady, "Obama: Camden, N.J., Police a Model for Improving Community Relations," National Public Radio, May 22, 2015, http://www.npr.org/2015/05/22/408824877/obama-camden-n-j-police-a-model-for-improving-community-relations.

97. Kate Zernike, "Camden Turns Around with New Police Force," *New York Times*, August 31, 2014, http://www.nytimes.com/2014/09/01/nyregion/camden-turns-around-with-new-police-force.html.

98. American Civil Liberties Union, "Policing in Camden Has Improved, but Concerns Remain," press release, May 18, 2015, https://www.aclu-nj.org/news/2015/05/18/policing-camden-has-improved-concerns-remain.

99. Ibid.

Chapter Five

Tef Poe, "Dear Mr. President: A Letter from Tef Poe," *Riverfront Times*, December 1, 2014, http://www.riverfronttimes.com/musicblog/2014/12/01/dear-mr-president-a-letter-from-tef-poe.

1. Ibid.

2. Daniel Schorr, "A New, 'Post-Racial' Political Era in America," National Public Radio, January 28, 2008, http://www.npr.org/templates/story/story.php?storyId=18489466.

3. Barack Obama, "New Hampshire Primary Speech," *New York Times*, January 8, 2008, http://www.nytimes.com/2008/01/08/us/politics/08text-obama.html.

4. David Corn, "'Black and More Than Black': Obama's Daring and Unique Speech on Race," *Mother Jones*, March 18, 2008, http://www.motherjones.com/mojo/2008/03/black-and-more-black-obamas-daring-and-unique-speech-race.

5. Barack Obama, speech delivered in Philadelphia, PA, March 18, 2008, transcript in *New York Times*, http://www.nytimes.com/2008/03/18/us/politics/18text-obama.html.

6. Cathy J. Cohen, *Democracy Remixed: Black Youth and the Future of American Politics* (Oxford: Oxford University Press, 2012), 118.

7. Ibid., 110.

8. Danny Glover and Harry Belafonte, "Belafonte and Glover Speak Out on Katrina," *AlterNet*, September 22, 2005, http://www.alternet.org/

story/25862/belafonte_%26_glover_speak_out_on_katrina.

9. Cohen, *Democracy Remixed*, 159.

10. Khari Mosley, "Vote for Hope," *Pittsburgh Post-Gazette*, November 2, 2008, http://www.post-gazette.com/opinion/Op-Ed/2008/11/02/Vote-for-hope/stories/200811020185.

11. Dan Martin, "Impassioned Words from Jay-Z in Support of Obama," *Guardian*, November 5, 2008, http://www.theguardian.com/music/2008/nov/05/jayz-falloutboy.

12. Ibid.

13. US Census Bureau, "Voter Turnout Increases by 5 Million in 2008 Presidential Election," press release, https://www.census.gov/newsroom/releases/archives/voting/cb09-110.html.

14. Ibid.

15. Mary McGuirt, "2008 Was Year of the Young Black Voter," ABC News, July 21, 2009, http://abcnews.go.com/politics/story?id=8140030&page=1; Cohen, *Democracy Remixed*, 172.

16. Allison Samuels, "Black Voters Turn Out in Big Numbers for Obama," *Daily Beast*, November 6, 2012, http://www.thedailybeast.com/articles/2012/11/06/black-voters-turn-out-in-big-numbers-for-obama.html.

17. "Most Blacks Say MLK's Vision Fulfilled, Poll Finds," CNN.com, January 19, 2009, http://www.cnn.com/2009/POLITICS/01/19/king.poll/.

18. Ellis Cose, "Meet the New Optimists," *Newsweek*, May 15, 2011, http://www.newsweek.com/meet-new-optimists-67535.

19. Ibid.

20. James Verini, "Is There an 'Obama Effect' on Crime?" *Slate*, October 5, 2001, http://slate.com/articles/news-and-politics/crime/2011/10/the_obama_effect_a_surprising_new_theory_for_the_continuing_crim.single.html.

21. "Obama Effect? Blacks Optimistic in Spite of Economic Struggles," *McClatchy DC*, February 26, 2009, http://www.mcclatchydc.com/2009/02/26/62912_obama-effect-blacks-optimistic.html?rh=1.

22. "Racism in America Is Over," *Forbes*, December 30, 2008, http://www.forbes.com/2008/12/30/end-of-racism-oped-cx_jm_1230mcwhorter.html.

23. George E. Condon Jr., "Has President Obama Done Enough for Black Americans?" *Atlantic*, April 5, 2013, http://www.theatlantic.com/politics/archive/2013/04/has-president-obama-done-enough-for-black-americans/274699/.

24. Chika Oduah, "Poll: Black Americans More Optimistic, Enthused about 2012," *theGrio*, November 7, 2011, http://thegrio.com/2011/11/07/poll-black-americans-more-optimistic-enthused-about-2012/.

25. Vann R. Newkirk II, "The Dream That Never Was: Black Millennials and the Promise of Obama," *Gawker*, December 1, 2014, http://gawker.com/the-dream-that-never-was-black-millennials-and-the-pro-1663448708.

26. Ibid.

27. Quoted in Sherry Wolf, "Why Did Obama Let Troy Die?" *Socialist Worker*,

September 22, 2011, http://socialistworker.org/2011/09/22/why-did-obama-let-troy-die.

28. Greg Bluestein, "Obama Silent as US Murders Troy Davis," *Common Dreams*, September 21, 2011, http://www.commondreams.org/news/2011/09/21/obama-silent-us-murders-troy-davis.

29. Joy Freeman-Coulbary, "Obama Silent on Troy Davis," *Root DC*, September 26, 2011, http://www.washingtonpost.com/blogs/therootdc/post/obama-silent-on-troy-davis/2011/09/21/gIQAH9tIlK_blog.html.

30. Gene Demby, "The Birth of a New Civil Rights Movement," *Politico*, December 31, 2014, http://www.politico.com/magazine/story/2014/12/ferguson-new-civil-rights-movement-113906.html.

31. Doug Singsen and Will Russell, "A Spotlight on Wall Street Greed," *Socialist Worker*, September 28, 2011, http://socialistworker.org/2011/09/28/spotlight-on-wall-street-greed.

32. Chika Oduah, "Poll: Blacks Back 'Occupy,' Want Obama to Be Tougher on Wall Street," *theGrio*, November 9, 2011, http://thegrio.com/2011/11/09/black-americans-favor-occupy-want-obama-to-get-tough-on-banks/.

33. *Socialist Worker* editorial, "We Have to Win Justice for Trayvon," March 21, 2012, http://socialistworker.org/2012/03/21/we-have-to-win-justice-for-trayvon.

34. Krissah Thompson and Scott Wilson, "Obama on Trayvon Martin: 'If I Had a Son, He'd Look Like Trayvon,'" *Washington Post*, March 23, 2012, http://www.washingtonpost.com/politics/obama-if-i-had-a-son-hed-look-like-trayvon/2012/03/23/gIQApKPpVS_story.html.

35. Eric Ruder, "Trayvon Martin Woke Us Up," *Socialist Worker*, July 19, 2013, http://socialistworker.org/2013/07/19/trayvon-martin-woke-us-up.

36. Keeanga-Yamahtta Taylor, "The Terrorists in Blue," *Socialist Worker*, July 30, 2012, http://socialistworker.org/2012/07/30/terrorists-in-blue

37. Lizette Alvarez, "Zimmerman Case Has Race as a Backdrop, but You Won't Hear It in Court," *New York Times*, July 7, 2013, http://www.nytimes.com/2013/07/08/us/zimmerman-case-has-race-as-a-backdrop-but-you-wont-hear-it-in-court.html.

38. Barack Obama, White House press release, July 14, 2013, https://www.whitehouse.gov/the-press-office/2013/07/14/statement-president.

39. Ruder, "Trayvon Martin Woke Us Up."

40. Jennifer Kay, "Trayvon Martin's Mother Says Zimmerman Got Away with Murder," *Huffington Post*, February 25, 2015, http://www.huffingtonpost.com/2015/02/25/trayvon-martin-sybrina-fulton-george-zimmerman_n_6754298.html.

41. Mychal Denzel Smith, "How Trayvon Martin's Death Launched a New Generation of Black Activism," *Nation*, August 27, 2014, http://www.thenation.com/article/181404/how-trayvon-martins-death-launched-new-generation-black-activism#.

42. Alicia Garza, "A Herstory of the #BlackLivesMatter Movement,"

Feminist Wire, October 7, 2014, http://thefeministwire.com/2014/10/
blacklivesmatter-2/.
43. Ibid.
44. Smith, "How Trayvon Martin's Death."
45. Ibid.
46. Barbara Liston, "Dream Defenders Leader Headed to D.C.," *Huffington
Post*, August 24, 2013, http://www.huffingtonpost.com/2013/08/24/dream-
defenders-florida_n_3805651.html.

Chapter Six

Johnson quoted in Michelle Dean, "'Black Women Unnamed': How Tanisha
Anderson's Bad Day Turned into Her Last," *Guardian*, June 5, 2015, http://
www.theguardian.com/us-news/2015/jun/05/black-women-police-kill-
ing-tanisha-anderson.
1. John H. Richardson, "Michael Brown Sr. and the Agony of the Black Father
in America," *Esquire*, January 5, 2015, http://www.esquire.com/features/
michael-brown-father-interview-0115.
2. Kristin Braswell, "#FergusonFridays: Not All of the Black Freedom Fighters
Are Men: An Interview with Black Women on the Front Line in Ferguson,"
Feminist Wire, October 3, 2014, http://www.thefeministwire.com/2014/10/
fergusonfridays-black-freedom-fighters-men-interview-black-women-front-
line-ferguson/.
3. Charles P. Pierce, "The Body in the Street," *Esquire*, August 22, 2014, http://
www.esquire.com/blogs/politics/The_Body_In_The_Street.
4. Mark Follman, "Michael Brown's Mom Laid Flowers Where He Was
Shot—and Police Crushed Them," *Mother Jones*, August 27, 2014, http://
www.motherjones.com/politics/2014/08/ferguson-st-louis-police-tactics-
dogs-michael-brown.
5. Richardson, "Michael Brown Sr."
6. Amnesty International USA, "On the Streets of America: Human Rights
Abuses in Ferguson," October 24, 2014, http://www.amnestyusa.org/research/
reports/on-the-streets-of-america-human-rights-abuses-in-ferguson.
7. Megan Davies and Dan Burns, "In Riot-Hit Ferguson, Traffic Fines
Boost Tension and Budget," Reuters, August 19, 2014, http://www.
reuters.com/article/2014/08/19/us-usa-missouri-shooting-tickets-insight-
idUSKBN0GJ2CB20140819.
8. Anna Brand and Amanda Sakuma, "11 Alarming Findings in the Report
on Ferguson Police," MSNBC, March 4, 2015, http://www.msnbc.com/
msnbc/11-alarming-findings-ferguson-police-department-report.
9. Jon Schuppe, "U.S. Finds Pattern of Biased Policing in Ferguson," NBC
News, March 3, 2015, http://www.nbcnews.com/storyline/michael-brown-
shooting/u-s-finds-pattern-biased-policing-ferguson-n316586.

10. Nathan Robinson, "The Shocking Finding from the DOJ's Ferguson Report That Nobody Has Noticed," March 13, 2015, http://www. huffingtonpost.com/nathan-robinson/the-shocking-finding-from-the-doj-ferguson_b_6858388.html.

11. Joel Anderson, "Ferguson's Angry Young Men," *BuzzFeed*, August 22, 2014, http://www.buzzfeed.com/joelanderson/who-are-fergusons-young-protesters.

12. Johnetta Elzie, "When I Close My Eyes at Night, I See People Running from Tear Gas," *Ebony* (September 2014), http://www.ebony.com/news-views/ferguson-forward-when-i-close-my-eyes-at-night-i-see-people-running-from-tear-ga.

13. Anderson, "Ferguson's Angry Young Men."

14. Jon Swaine, "Ohio Walmart Video Reveals Moments Before Officer Killed John Crawford," *Guardian*, September 24, 2014, http://www.theguardian.com/world/2014/sep/24/surveillance-video-walmart-shooting-john-crawford-police.

15. Josh Harkinson, "4 Unarmed Black Men Have Been Killed by Police in the Last Month," *Mother Jones*, August 13, 2014, http://www.motherjones.com/politics/2014/08/3-unarmed-black-african-american-men-killed-police.

16. Darnell L. Moore, "Two Years Later, Black Lives Matter Faces Critiques, but It Won't Be Stopped," *Mic*, August 10, 2015, http://mic.com/articles/123666/two-years-later-black-lives-matter-faces-critiques-but-it-won-t-be-stopped.

17. Associated Press, "Five Arrested in Ferguson after Protests Break Out over Burned Memorial," *Guardian*, August 12, 2015, http://www.theguardian.com/world/2014/sep/24/ferguson-protest-michael-brown-memorial-fire-police.

18. Trymaine Lee, "Why Vonderrit Myers Matters," MSNBC, October 18, 2014, http://www.msnbc.com/msnbc/why-vonderrit-myers-matters.

19. *Democracy Now!*, "Ferguson October: Thousands March in St. Louis for Police Reform and Arrest of Officer Darrén Wilson," Pacifica Radio, October 13, 2014, http://www.democracynow.org/2014/10/13/thousands_march_in_ferguson_for_police.

20. Donna Murch, "Historicizing Ferguson," *New Politics* (Summer 2015), http://newpol.org/content/historicizing-ferguson.

21. Lilly Fowler, "Al Sharpton Arrives in St. Louis, Seeking Justice for Michael Brown," *Saint Louis Post-Dispatch*, August 12, 2014, http://www.stltoday.com/lifestyles/faith-and-values/al-sharpton-arrives-in-st-louis-seeking-justice-for-michael/article_17152c80-a923-53a4-9ec9-84363709129b.html.

22. "TomP" (username), "Rev. Sharpton Preaches Truth and Action at Michael Brown, Jr. Funeral (with Video)," *Daily Kos*, August 25, 2014, http://www.dailykos.com/story/2014/08/25/1324510/-Rev-Sharpton-Preaches-Truth-and-Action-At-Michael-Brown-Jr-Funeral.

23. Anderson, "Ferguson's Angry Young Men."

24. Erica Ritz, "Jesse Jackson Cornered by Angry Ferguson Protesters: 'When You Going to Stop Selling Us Out?,'" *Blaze*, August 22, 2014, http://www.

theblaze.com/stories/2014/08/22/jesse-jackson-cornered-by-angry-ferguson-protesters-when-you-going-to-stop-selling-us-out/.

25. Braswell, "#FergusonFridays."

26. Matt Pearce, "'Ferguson October' Rally Highlights Divide among St. Louis Activists," *Los Angeles Times*, October 12, 2014, http://www.latimes.com/nation/la-na-ferguson-october-debate-20141012-story.html.

27. Braswell, "#FergusonFridays."

28. Elzie, "When I Close My Eyes at Night.'"

29. Britni Danielle, "'Say Her Name' Turns Spotlight on Black Women and Girls Killed by Police," *Yahoo News*, May 22, 2015, http://news.yahoo.com/her-name-turns-spotlight-black-women-girls-killed-210304072.html.

30. Ella Baker, "Bigger Than a Hamburger," *Southern Patriot 18*, June 1960, History Is a Weapon, http://www.historyisaweapon.com/defcon1/bakerbigger.

31. Amanda Sakuma, "Women Hold the Front-Lines of Ferguson," MSNBC, October 12, 2014, http://www.msnbc.com/msnbc/women-hold-the-front-lines-ferguson.

32. Braswell, "#FergusonFridays."

33. Stephen Bronars, "Half of Ferguson's Young African-American Men Are Missing," *Forbes*, March 18, 2015, http://www.forbes.com/sites/modeledbehavior/2015/03/18/half-of-fergusons-young-african-american-men-are-missing/.

34. Justin Wolfers, David Leonhardt, and Kevin Quealy, "1.5 Million Missing Black Men," *New York Times*, April 20, 2015, http://www.nytimes.com/interactive/2015/04/20/upshot/missing-black-men.html?abt=0002&abg=1.

35. Braswell, "#FergusonFridays."

36. Katherine Mirani, "Nurturing Black Youth Activism," *Chicago Reporter*, October 6, 2014, http://chicagoreporter.com/nurturing-black-youth-activism/.

37. Alicia Garza, "A Herstory of the #BlackLivesMatter Movement," *Feminist Wire*, October 7, 2014, http://thefeministwire.com/2014/10/blacklivesmatter-2/.

38. Barack Obama, "Remarks on Ferguson Grand Jury Decision," *Washington Post*, November 24, 2014, http://www.washingtonpost.com/politics/transcript-obamas-remarks-on-ferguson-grand-jury-decision/2014/11/24/afc3b38e-744f-11e4-bd1b-03009bd3e984_story.html.

39. M. David and Jackson Marciana, "Tanisha Anderson Was Literally Praying for Help as Cops Held Her Down and Killed Her," *CounterCurrent News*, February 28, 2015, http://countercurrentnews.com/2015/02/tanisha-anderson-was-literally-praying-for-help/.

40. Fredrick Harris, "Will Ferguson Be a Moment or a Movement?" *Washington Post*, August 22, 2014, http://www.washingtonpost.com/opinions/will-ferguson-be-a-moment-or-a-movement/2014/08/22/071d4a94-28a8-11e4-8593-da634b334390_story.html.

41. Ferguson Action, "Breaking: Ferguson Activists Meet with President Obama to Demand an End to Police Brutality Nationwide," press release, December 1, 2014, http://fergusonaction.com/white-house-meeting/.
42. Tanya Somanader, "President Obama Delivers a Statement on the Grand Jury Decision in the Death of Eric Garner," White House press release, December 3, 2014, https://www.whitehouse.gov/blog/2014/12/03/president-obama-delivers-statement-grand-jury-decision-death-eric-garner.
43. Kirsten West Savali, "The Fierce Urgency of Now: Why Young Protesters Bum-Rushed the Mic," Root, December 14, 2014, http://www.theroot.com/articles/culture/2014/12/the_fierce_urgency_of_now_why_young_protesters_bum_rushed_the_mic.html.
44. Darryl Fears, "Thousands Join Al Sharpton in 'Justice for All' March in D.C.," Washington Post, December 13, 2014, http://www.washingtonpost.com/national/health-science/sharpton-to-lead-justice-for-all-march-in-dc/2014/12/13/36ce8a68-824f-11e4-9f38-95a187e4c1f7_story.html.
45. Al Sharpton, "It's Been a Long Time Coming, But Permanent Change Is Within Our Grasp," Huffington Post, December 15, 2014, http://www.huffingtonpost.com/rev-al-sharpton/its-been-a-long-time-comi_b_6328806.html.
46. Azi Paybarah, "Amid Tensions, Sharpton Lashes Out at Younger Activists," January 31, 2015, http://www.capitalnewyork.com/article/city-hall/2015/01/8561365/amid-tensions-sharpton-lashes-out-younger-activists.
47. Marcia Chatelain, "#BlackLivesMatter: An Online Roundtable with Alicia Garza, Dante Barry, and Darsheel Kaur," Dissent, January 19, 2015, http://www.dissentmagazine.org/blog/blacklivesmatter-an-online-roundtable-with-alicia-garza-dante-barry-and-darsheel-kaur.
48. Paybarah, "Sharpton Lashes Out."
49. Ferguson Action, "About This Movement," press release, December 15, 2014, http://fergusonaction.com/movement/.
50. Tim Mak, "Capitol Hill's Black Staffers Walk Out to Do 'Hands Up, Don't Shoot!'" Daily Beast, December 10, 2014, http://www.thedailybeast.com/articles/2014/12/10/black-congressional-staffers-plan-ferguson-garner-walkout.html.
51. Nicole Mulvaney, "Princeton University Students Stage Walkout in Protest of Garner, Ferguson Grand Jury Decisions," NJ.com, December 4, 2014, http://www.nj.com/mercer/index.ssf/2014/12/princeton_university_students_stage_blacklivesmatter_walkout_protest_of_garner_ferguson_decisions.html.
52. WhiteCoats4BlackLives, "About," n.d., accessed June 21, 2015, http://www.whitecoats4blacklives.org/.
53. Malaika Fraley and Gary Peterson, "Bay Area Public Defenders Rally for 'Black Lives Matter,'" San Jose Mercury News, December 18, 2014, http://www.mercurynews.com/ci_27163840/bay-area-public-defenders-stand-up-black-lives.

54. Jill Colvin, "Hillary Clinton Denounces Torture, Says Black Lives Matter," *Huffington Post*, December 16, 2014, http://www.huffingtonpost.com/2014/12/16/hillary-clinton-torture-blacks_n_6338154.html.
55. Nia-Malika Henderson, "'Black Respectability' Politics Are Increasingly Absent from Obama's Rhetoric," *Washington Post*, December 3, 2014, http://www.washingtonpost.com/blogs/the-fix/wp/2014/12/03/black-respectability-politics-are-increasingly-absent-from-obamas-rhetoric/.
56. Chatelain, "#BlackLivesMatter Roundtable."
57. Noah Berlatsky, "Hashtag Activism Isn't a Cop-Out," *Atlantic*, January 7, 2015, http://www.theatlantic.com/politics/archive/2015/01/not-just-hashtag-activism-why-social-media-matters-to-protestors/384215/.
58. Ibid.
59. Barbara Ransby, "Ella Baker's Radical Democratic Vision," *Jacobin*, June 18, 2015, https://www.jacobinmag.com/2015/06/black-lives-matter-police-brutality/.
60. Danny Katch, "#BlackLivesMatter Looks to the Future," *Socialist Worker*, February 4, 2015, http://socialistworker.org/2015/02/04/blacklivesmatter-looks-ahead.
61. Moore, "Two Years Later."
62. Hill-Snowdon Foundation, "How to Fund #BlackLivesMatter," June 9, 2015, http://hillsnowdon.org/how-to-fund-blacklivesmatter/.
63. Ryan Schlegel, "Why Foundations Should Support July's Movement for Black Lives Convening," National Committee for Responsive Philanthropy, June 9, 2015, http://blog.ncrp.org/2015/06/movement-for-black-lives-convening.html.
64. Aldon D. Morris, *The Origins of the Civil Rights Movement* (New York: Simon & Schuster, 1986), 234–35.
65. Ibid., 235.
66. Tanzina Vega, "How to Fund Black Lives Matter," CNN, June 5, 2015, http://www.cnn.com/2015/06/05/politics/funding-civil-rights-movement/index.html.
67. Incite! Women of Color Against Violence, *The Revolution Will Not Be Funded: Beyond the Non-Profit Industrial Complex* (Cambridge, MA: South End Press, 2007).
68. Arundhati Roy, *Capitalism: A Ghost Story* (Chicago: Haymarket Books, 2014), 26.
69. Megan Francis, "Do Foundations Co-Opt Civil Rights Organizations?" *HistPhil*, August 17, 2015, http://histphil.org/2015/08/17/do-foundations-co-opt-civil-rights-organizations/.
70. Cory Shaffer, "Cleveland Group Seeks Arrests of Officers Involved in Tamir Rice Shooting," Cleveland.com, June 9, 2015, http://www.cleveland.com/metro/index.ssf/2015/06/cleveland_group_releases_affid.html.
71. John Kopp, "Hundreds in Philly Rally against Police Violence," *PhillyVoice*, April 30, 2015, http://www.phillyvoice.com/hundreds-rally-against-police-violence/.

Notes **271**

72. Claire Z. Cardona and Jasmine Aguilera, "Marches against Police Brutality, for Immigration Reform Take to Downtown Dallas Streets," *Dallas Morning News*, May 1, 2015, http://www.dallasnews.com/news/local-news/20150501-two-marches-take-to-downtown-dallas-streets.ece.
73. Ferguson Action, "Demands," n.d., accessed June 24, 2015, http://fergusonaction.com/demands/.
74. Hands Up United, "Hands Up," n.d., accessed June 24, 2015, http://www.handsupunited.org/.
75. #BlackLivesMatter, "Demands," n.d., accessed June 24, 2015, http://blacklivesmatter.com/demands/.
76. James Forman, *The Making of Black Revolutionaries: A Personal Account* (New York: Macmillan, 1972), 395–96.
77. Annie-Rose Strasser, "The Majority of Fast Food Workers Are Not Teenagers, Report Finds," *ThinkProgress*, August 8, 2013, http://thinkprogress.org/economy/2013/08/08/2433601/fast-food-workers-young/.
78. BYP 100, "Racial Justice Is Economic Justice," n.d., accessed June 24, 2015, http://byp100.org/ff15signup/.
79. *CopyLine*, "Black Youth Project 100 (BYP100) Declares #BlackWorkMatters at Protests in Chicago, New Orleans & New York City," April 20, 2015, http://www.copylinemagazine.com/2015/04/20/black-youth-project-100-byp100-declares-blackworkmatters-at-protests-in-chicago-new-orleans-new-york-city/.
80. Peter Waldman, "NAACP's FedEx and Wal-Mart Gifts Followed Discrimination Claims," *Bloomberg BusinessWeek*, May 8, 2014, http://www.bloomberg.com/news/articles/2014-05-08/naacp-s-fedex-and-wal-mart-gifts-followed-discrimination-claims.
81. Annie Karni, "Rev. Al Sharpton Gets $1M in Birthday Gifts for His Nonprofit," *New York Daily News*, October 3, 2014, http://www.nydailynews.com/new-york/rev-al-sharpton-1m-birthday-nonprofit-article-1.1961881.
82. Owen Davis, "Punitive Schooling," *Jacobin*, October 17, 2014, https://www.jacobinmag.com/2014/10/punitive-schooling/.
83. Jesse Hagopian, "'Why Are They Doing This to Me?': Students Confront Ferguson and Walkout Against Racism," *Common Dreams*, November 30, 2014, http://www.commondreams.org/views/2014/11/30/why-are-they-doing-me-students-confront-ferguson-and-walkout-against-racism.
84. Valerie Strauss, "Just Whose Rights Do These Civil Rights Groups Think They Are Protecting?" *Washington Post*, May 9, 2015, http://www.washingtonpost.com/blogs/answer-sheet/wp/2015/05/09/just-whose-rights-do-these-civil-rights-groups-think-they-are-protecting/.
85. Alessandro Tinonga, "Black Lives Matter on the Docks," *Socialist Worker*, April 30, 2015, http://socialistworker.org/2015/04/30/black-lives-matter-on-the-docks.
86. Sabah, "Stop Using #MuslimLivesMatter," *Muslim Girl*, February 12, 2015, http://muslimgirl.net/10302/solidarity-mean-appropriation/.

87. Robert D. McFadden, "Whitman Dismisses State Police Chief for Race Remarks," *New York Times*, March 1, 1999, http://www.nytimes.com/1999/03/01/nyregion/whitman-dismisses-state-police-chief-for-race-remarks.html.

88. Frank Newport, "Racial Profiling Is Seen as Widespread, Particularly Among Young Black Men," Gallup, December 9, 1999, http://www.gallup.com/poll/3421/Racial-Profiling-Seen-Widespread-Particularly-Among-Young-Black-Men.aspx.

89. Dan Zeidman, "One Step Closer to Ending Racial Profiling," American Civil Liberties Union, October 7, 2011, https://www.aclu.org/blog/one-step-closer-ending-racial-profiling.

90. Sasha Polakow-Suransky, "When the Profiled Become Profilers," *African America*, November 24, 2002, http://www.africanamerica.org/topic/when-the-profiled-become-profilers.

91. Ariel Edwards-Levy, "Americans Say Now Is the Right Time to Discuss Racism, Gun Control," *Huffington Post*, June 22, 2015, http://www.huffingtonpost.com/2015/06/22/charleston-poll_n_7640026.html.

92. Terrell Jermaine Starr, "New Study: More White People See Systemic Problems in Policing after Freddie Gray, but Racial Gulf Remains," *AlterNet*, May 5, 2015, http://www.alternet.org/civil-liberties/new-study-more-white-people-see-systemic-problems-policing-after-freddie-gray-racial.

93. *Guardian*, "The Counted: People Killed by Police in the United States in 2015," interactive database, June 1, 2015, http://www.theguardian.com/us-news/ng-interactive/2015/jun/01/the-counted-police-killings-us-database.

Chapter Seven

1. US Congress, Civil Rights Act of 1866, April 9, 1866, http://teachingamericanhistory.org/library/document/the-civil-rights-act-of-1866/.

2. W. E. B. Du Bois and David Levering Lewis, *Black Reconstruction in America 1860–1880* (New York: Simon & Schuster, 1935), 111.

3. Harry Belafonte, "Harry Belafonte Reflects on Working Toward Peace," Markkula Center for Applied Ethics, n.d., accessed June 28, 2015, http://www.scu.edu/ethics/architects-of-peace/Belafonte/essay.html.

4. Stokely Carmichael and Charles V. Hamilton, *Black Power: The Politics of Liberation in America* (New York: Random House, 1967), 6.

5. Ibid., 197.

6. *Socialist Organizer*, "Malcolm X on Capitalism and Socialism," December 9, 2008, http://socialistorganizer.org/malcolm-x-on-capitalism-and-socialism/.

7. Malcolm X, "Speech at the Founding Rally of the Organization of Afro-American Unity," BlackPast.org, delivered June 28, 1964, New York City, http://www.blackpast.org/1964-malcolm-x-s-speech-founding-rally-organization-afro-american-unity.

8. Socialist Organizer, "Malcolm X."

9. Quoted in Jack M. Bloom, *Class, Race, and the Civil Rights Movement* (Bloomington: Indiana University Press, 1987), 212.

10. Third World Women's Alliance, "Black Women's Manifesto," Duke Digital Collections, 19, 1970–75, http://library.duke.edu/digitalcollections/wlmpc_wlmms01009/.

11. Combahee River Collective, "The Combahee River Collective Statement," April 1977, http://circuitous.org/scraps/combahee.html.

12. Kathleen Cleaver and George Katsiaficas, *Liberation, Imagination and the Black Panther Party: A New Look at the Black Panthers and Their Legacy* (New York: Routledge, 2014), 121.

13. Black Panther Party, "Black Panthers Ten-Point Program," October 15, 1966, https://www.marxists.org/history/usa/workers/black-panthers/1966/10/15.htm.

14. Quoted in Dan Georgakas and Marvin Surkin, *Detroit: I Do Mind Dying* (Cambridge, MA: South End Press, 1998), 17.

15. Roger Guenveur Smith, "Hoover and the F.B.I.," companion website to the documentary film *A Huey P. Newton Story* (Philadelphia: PBS and Luna Ray Films, 2002), accessed June 28, 2015, http://www.pbs.org/hueypnewton/people/people_hoover.html.

16. Tim Wise, "With Friends Like These, Who Needs Glenn Beck? Racism and White Privilege on the Liberal-Left," August 17, 2010, http://www.timwise.org/2010/08/with-friends-like-these-who-needs-glenn-beck-racism-and-white-privilege-on-the-liberal-left/.

17. Robin D. G. Kelley, *Freedom Dreams: The Black Radical Imagination* (Boston: Beacon Press, 2003), 45.

18. Wayne F. Cooper, *Claude McKay: Rebel Sojourner in the Harlem Renaissance: A Biography* (Baton Rouge: Louisiana State University Press, 1996), 179.

19. Philip Sheldon Foner and James S. Allen, *American Communism and Black Americans: A Documentary History, 1919–1929* (Philadelphia: Temple University Press, 1987), 9.

20. Vladimir Ilich Lenin and Doug Lorimer, *Marxism and Nationalism* (New York: Resistance Books, 2002), 137.

21. C. L. R. James, "The Revolutionary Answer to the Negro Problem in the US," Marxists Internet Archive, July 1948, https://www.marxists.org/archive/james-clr/works/1948/07/meyer.htm.

22. Martin Luther King Jr. and James Melvin Washington, *A Testament of Hope: The Essential Writings of Martin Luther King, Jr.* (New York: Harper & Row, 1986), 316.

23. Karl Marx, *Capital*, vol. 1 (London: 1867), chapter 31, Marxists Internet Archive, https://www.marxists.org/archive/marx/works/1867-c1/ch31.htm.

24. Karl Marx, "The Poverty of Philosophy-Chapter 2.1," Marxists Internet Archive, accessed July 21, 2015, https://www.marxists.org/archive/marx/works/1847/poverty-philosophy/ch02.htm.

25. Quoted in Abigail B. Bakan and Enakshi Dua, *Theorizing Anti-Racism:*

Linkages in Marxism and Critical Race Theories (Toronto: University of Toronto Press, 2014), 113.

26. Edmund S. Morgan, *American Slavery, American Freedom: The Ordeal of Colonial Virginia* (New York: Norton, 1975), 381.

27. Bloom, *Class, Race, and the Civil Rights Movement*, 20.

28. Ibid., 18.

29. Hope Yen, "80 Percent of U.S. Adults Face Near-Poverty, Unemployment: Survey," *Huffington Post*, July 28, 2013, http://www.huffingtonpost.com/2013/07/28/poverty-unemployment-rates_n_3666594.html.

30. Associated Press, "4 in 5 Americans Live in Danger of Falling into Poverty, Joblessness," NBC News, July 28, 2013, http://www.nbcnews.com/news/other/ap-4-5-americans-live-danger-falling-poverty-joblessness-v19738595.

31. Associated Press, "Economic Optimism of Whites in U.S. Lags Blacks by Wide Margin, Analysis Shows," CBS News, August 1, 2013, http://www.cbsnews.com/news/economic-optimism-of-whites-in-us-lags-blacks-by-wide-margin-analysis-shows/.

32. Infoplease, "Distribution of Household Income by Race," n.d., accessed June 29, 2015, http://www.infoplease.com/ipa/A0104552.html.

33. Danny Katch, "Confronting the Incarceration Nation," *Socialist Worker*, June 11, 2015, http://socialistworker.org/2015/06/11/confronting-the-incarceration-nation.

34. Infoplease, "Distribution of Household Income by Race."

35. Antonio Gramsci, "Notes for an Introduction and an Approach to the Study of Philosophy and the History of Culture," in *An Antonio Gramsci Reader*, 1932, accessed June 29, 2015, http://www.naturalthinker.net/trl/texts/Gramsci,Antonio/q11-12.htm.

36. Duncan Hallas, "Towards a Revolutionary Socialist Party," 1971, Marxists Internet Archive, https://www.marxists.org/archive/hallas/works/1971/xx/party.htm.

37. Laura Gottesdiener, "10 Million Americans Have Had Their Homes Taken Away by the Banks—Often at the Point of a Gun | Alternet," *Alternet*, August 1, 2013, http://www.alternet.org/investigations/10-million-americans-foreclosed-neighborhoods-devastated.

38. Michael C. Dawson, *Blacks In and Out of the Left* (Cambridge, MA: Harvard University Press, 2013), 194.

39. Third World Women's Alliance, "Black Women's Manifesto," 31.

40. James, "Revolutionary Answer to the Negro Problem."

Epilogue

1. Police Accountability Task Force, *Recommendations for Reform: Restoring Trust between the Chicago Police and the Communities they Serve*, April 2016, https://chicagopatf.org/wp-content/uploads/2016/04/PATF_Final_Report_4_13_16-1.pdf.

2. Walaa Chahine, "Labeling Black Lives Matter As A Terrorist Organization Is Not Only Unjust, It's Dangerous," *Huffington Post*, July 16, 2017, https:// www.huffpost.com/entry/labeling-blm-as-a-terrori_b_10931812; A. L., "Black Lives Matter is not a terrorist organization," *Economist*, https:// www.economist.com/open-future/2018/08/09/black-lives-matter-is-not-a-terrorist-organisation.

3. Alice Speri, "Fear of a Black Homeland," *Intercept*, March 23, 2019, https:// theintercept.com/2019/03/23/black-identity-extremist-fbi-domestic-terrorism/.

4. Michael D. Shear and Liam Stack, "Obama Says Movements Like Black Lives Matter 'Can't Just Keep on Yelling,'" *New York Times*, April 23, 2016, https://www.nytimes.com/2016/04/24/us/obama-says-movements-like-black-lives-matter-cant-just-keep-on-yelling.html.

5. Aislinn Pulley, "Black Struggle Is Not a Sound Bite: Why I Refused to Meet with President Obama," *Truthout*, February 18, 2016, https://truthout.org/ articles/black-struggle-is-not-a-sound-bite-why-i-refused-to-meet-with-president-obama/.

6. Keeanga-Yamahtta Taylor, "Black Faces in High Places," *Jacobin*, May 4, 2015, https://www.jacobinmag.com/2015/05/baltimore-uprising-protests-freddie-gray-black-politicians/,

7. Jo Freeman, "The Tyranny of Structurelessness," *Jacobin*, September 16, 2019, https://www.jacobinmag.com/2019/09/tyranny-structurelessness-jo-freeman-consciousness-raising-women-liberation-feminism.

8. Karen Ferguson, "The Perils of Liberal Philanthropy," *Jacobin*, November 26, 2018, https://jacobinmag.com/2018/11/black-lives-matter-ford-foundation-black-power-mcgeorge-bundy.

9. Karen Ferguson, *Top Down: The Ford Foundation, Black Power, and the Reinvention of Racial Liberalism* (Philadelphia: University of Pennsylvania Press, 2013).

10. Megan Ming Francis, "The Price of Civil Rights: Black Lives, White Funding, and Movement Capture," *Law and Society Review* 53, no. 1 (March 2019): 275–309; Kelsey Piper, "How 'Movement Capture' Shaped the Fight for Civil Rights," *Vox*, February 28, 2019, https://www.vox.com/future-perfect/2019/2/28/18241490/movement-capture-civil-rights-philanthropy-funding.

11. Darren Walker, "In Defense of Nuance," Ford Foundation, September 19, 2019, https://www.fordfoundation.org/just-matters/just-matters/posts/in-defense-of-nuance/.

12. Walker, "In Defense of Nuance."

13. "Vision for Black Lives," M4LB.org, https://m4bl.org/policy-platforms/.

14. John Berger, "The Nature of Mass Demonstrations," *International Socialism* 1, no. 34 (Autumn 1968): 11–2.

15. Berger, "Nature of Mass Demonstrations."

16. Barbara Ransby, *Ella Baker and the Black Freedom Movement: A Radical*

Democratic Vision (Chapel Hill: University of North Carolina Press, 2003).

17. Amina Khan, "Getting Killed by Police Is a Leading Cause of Death for Young Black Men in America," *Los Angeles Times*, August 16, 2019, https://www.latimes.com/science/story/2019-08-15/police-shootings-are-a-leading-cause-of-death-for-black-men.

18. John L. Mone and Jake Bleiberg, "Lawyer: Cop Who Shot Pamela Turner Knew She Was Mentally Ill," Associated Press, May 16, 2019, https://cbsaustin.com/news/local/lawyer-cop-who-shot-baytown-woman-knew-she-was-mentally-ill.

19. "How Chicago Racked Up a $662 Million Police Misconduct Bill," *Crain's Chicago Business*, March 20, 2016, https://www.chicagobusiness.com/article/20160320/NEWS07/160319758/how-chicago-racked-up-a-662-million-police-misconduct-bill; Jonah Newman, "Chicago Spent More than $113 Million on Police Misconduct Lawsuits in 2018," *Chicago Reporter*, March 7, 2019, https://www.chicagoreporter.com/chicago-spent-more-than-113-million-on-police-misconduct-lawsuits-in-2018/.

20. Micah Uetricht and Rachel T. Johnson, "Sixteen Shots and a Conviction," *Jacobin*, October 5, 2018, https://www.jacobinmag.com/2018/10/jason-van-dyke-conviction-laquan-mcdonald.

21. Julie Bosman and Jack Healy, "Returning to Ferguson, Five Years Later," *New York Times*, August 9, 2019, https://www.nytimes.com/2019/08/09/reader-center/ferguson-five-years-later.html.

Index

Georgia, 111, 144, 145
Germany, 130, 144
Giuliani, Rudolph, 124
Glover, Danny, 139
Goode, Wilson, 99
Google, 230
government workers. *See* public-sector
   workers
Gramsci, Antonio, 213
Grant, Oscar, 141, 146
Gray, Freddie, 2, 75–80, 192
Great Migration. *See* Black migration
Great Society programs, 39–40, 42,
   80, 90
Green, Patrick, 127

Hagopian, Jesse, 184
Hamilton, Charles, 8, 84, 94, 196
Hands Up United, 174, 176, 181
Harlem, 27, 38, 41, 114, 116
Harris, Fred, 96
Harvey, David, 31
Hatcher, Richard, 87, 91
Hayes, James, 169
healthcare, xiv, 15, 88, 215
   Carter and, 95
   Commission on Law Enforcement
      and, 117
   environmental racism and, 98
   housing and, 71, 113
   Johnson and, 40
   mental health and, 123–24
   Obama and, 193
health insurance, 11, 93, 214
Highlander School, 178
Holder, Eric, 13, 159, 160
Holtzclaw, Daniel, 164
homelessness, 99, 124, 214
Hoover, J. Edgar, 44, 200
housing, xiv, 63–64, 68, 77, 88, 114. *See*

also Department of Housing and
   Urban Development; evictions;
   mortgage loans
   Black migration and, 113
   evictions and, 236
   federal policy on, 64, 69–71, 93, 103
   public opinion on, 45
   SCLC campaign on, 86
   substandard conditions for Black
      residents, 46–47, 53, 83, 85,
      113, 115
Howard University, 21, 42
hunger, 11, 192, 216
Hurricane Katrina, 10, 139

immigrants, 30, 113, 137, 167, 180, 186
incarceration. *See* prisons and imprisonment
income
   in Baltimore, 78
   Black, 11, 44, 81, 94, 114, 212
   in Camden, 133
   municipal, 119, 124, 183
   taxation of, 120, 127
   welfare and, 52
inequality, 70, 72, 112, 115, 139, 143,
   151, 200
   beneficiaries of, 212
   capitalism and, 205, 206, 218
   debates about racial inequality, 8–10,
      17–18, 23–26, 34, 41–45, 49,
      112, 147
   economic, 5–7, 136, 145–47, 192,
      194, 202
   police and, 162, 167, 217, 219
Institute for Contemporary Studies, 94
institutional racism, xiii–xv, 8, 17, 45,
   48, 50–51, 63, 181
International Longshore and Warehouse Union, 185

Iraq, 10, 130, 136, 188
Islamophobia, 186–88, 212
Israel, xiv

Jackson, Jesse, Sr., 95, 101, 159, 161,
    168, 171–72
Jackson, Thomas, 22
James, C. L. R., 204, 219
Jefferson, Thomas, 23
Jemmott, Zakiya, 154, 166
Jena, Louisiana, 139
jobs programs. *See* federal jobs
    programs
Johnson, Cassandra, 153
Johnson, Lyndon, 21, 34, 39–40, 42–43,
    53, 58, 182
  Cleveland intervention and, 85
  Kerner Commission and, 46–47, 116
  on law enforcement, 65, 117–18
  on urban crisis, 69, 115
Joseph, Peniel, 88
Justice Department. *See* US Depart-
    ment of Justice

Katwiwa, Mwende, 183
Kelley, Robin D. G., 202
Kelling, George L., 124–26
Kelly, Ray, 126
Kelly, Sharon Pratt. *See* Dixon, Sharon
    Pratt
Kennedy, John F., 57, 178
Kennedy, Robert F., 178
Kerner Commission, 9, 18, 46–47, 52,
    70, 116
King, Martin Luther, Jr., 1–2, 178, 193,
    194
  assassination of, 56, 65, 83
  on capitalism, 43
  on electoral power, 84–86, 88
  "evil triplets" concept of, 56, 195,

197, 205
  "I Have a Dream" speech of, 37, 140
  Memphis sanitation strike and, 58,
    101
  "where do we go from here?" by, 198
King, Rodney, 139, 154
Kristof, Nicholas, 23

labor movement, 35, 58–59, 185,
    203–4, 207. *See also* unions
Lane, Lona, 105
Latinos, 5, 68, 173, 183, 186–88,
    214–15
  disposability of, 16
  in Camden, 133
  incarceration rate among, 122
  in Chicago, 104, 214
  killed by police, 131, 211
  in New York, 118, 125, 126
  Obama on, 15
  in Texas, 128
Law Enforcement Assistance Admin-
    istration, 66
Lenin, V. I., 203–4
Lewis, John, 102
Lewis, Oscar, 36
LGBTQ people, 118, 172
  BLM leadership by, xiv–xv, 165–66
  Garza on, 167
  gay liberation movement and, 56
  Moore on, 157
  police violence against, 13, 235
Lincoln, Abraham, 191–92, 207
Lochner, Ralph, 86–87
loitering, 124
Los Angeles, 94, 104, 222
  police murder in, 14, 156
  Rebellion in 1992, 10, 120
  Watts Rebellion in, 39, 114, 116–17
Los Angeles Police Department, 14,

Surkin, Marvin, 57
surveillance, 66, 83, 99, 107–8, 111,
    115, 119, 121, 132, 202
Sustar, Lee, 59

Task Force on Twenty-First-Century
    Policing, 131, 170
taxes, 44, 126–27, 130, 178
    cuts, 6, 32, 54, 95, 98, 104
    municipal funding, 18, 88, 92, 105
    under Nixon, 56
    under Reagan, 120
Taylor, Breonna, xiv, xv
Texas, 114, 128, 180, 190, 221
Third International. *See* Communist
    International
Third World Women's Alliance, 198,
    217
Thirteenth Amendment, 110
Thomas, Clarence, 210
Thompson, Heather Ann, 67
Thurmond, Strom, 95
Till, Emmett, 9, 147, 150
Tometi, Opal, 151, 166
traffic stops, 122, 127, 155, 188
truancy, 128
Trump, Donald, 223, 227, 229, 234
Tulsa, Oklahoma, 164
Turner, Pamela, 221, 235–36
Twitter, 151, 162, 174, 175

unemployment, 81, 103
    1960s, 2, 44, 45, 47, 83, 115
    in Baltimore, 78
    Baraka on, 75
    Biondi on, 16
    Black college graduates and, 28
    Black youth and, 27
    in Camden, 133
    under Carter, 95

ex-convict status and, 164
Katwiwa on, 183
Newkirk on, 143
under Nixon, 70, 71, 98
under Obama, 9, 11, 104, 115, 136,
    138, 142, 146, 168
under Reagan, 93, 94, 96
unions, 42, 93, 132, 137, 185, 205
    air traffic controllers, 94
    Dodge Revolutionary Union Move-
        ment, 199
    Memphis sanitation workers, 58, 101
    police, 79, 223, 235
    postal workers, 59
    public-sector workers, 57, 185, 214
    solidarity with Black Lives Matter,
        185, 186
universities and colleges, 15, 158, 173,
    179, 194
Urban League, 86, 185
USA PATRIOT Act, 121
US Congress, 42
    aides protest, 173
    Black members of, 77, 82, 89–92, 97,
        100–2, 106, 158–59
    Bush to, 188
    business executives on, 62
    "colorblindness" and, 52
    on housing, 31
    Johnson and, 58
    under Nixon, 63
    Roberts on, 5
US Department of Defense, 121
US Department of Justice, 2–3, 49,
    128, 150, 155, 159, 161, 224, 237
US Department of State, 179
US foreign policy, 44, 138, 187–88
    Iraq and, 130, 136
    Vietnam and, 2, 9–10, 55–57, 90,
        195, 199

Study and Discussion Guide

Introduction: Black Awakening in Obama's America

1. From reading the introduction, what are your initial thoughts about the ways anti-Black racism has evolved in the United States since the civil rights era? What is the role of what the author calls "colorblindness" in perpetuating racial oppression in the absence of the overtly racist laws of previous eras?

2. Do you agree with the author that the working class as a whole, "Black, brown and white," has "an interest in exposing the racist nature of US society"? How do you account for the presence of racist ideas among the white working class?

3. What effect has the rise of a Black middle and upper class, as well as the fact that many high-ranking political offices are now held by African Americans, had on Black liberation movements? Does a "Black community" that has a unified set of interests exist?

4. How would you explain the emergence of the Black Lives Matter movement in Obama's America, at a time when Black political and economic power had never been greater? More generally, what are the continuities and differences we can see between the movements for Black liberation that were active in the 1960s and the Black Lives Matter movement?

5. What does the concept of "institutional racism" add to our understanding of racism? If racism is not only, or even primarily, about

individual acts or expression of obvious hate, what does this imply about how racism is generated and maintained and the strategies needed to confront and overcome it? Is working through formal legal and political channels enough to achieve radical change? Can focusing too much energy on those channels actually make it more difficult to achieve such change?

6.   The author asks: "Can the conditions created by institutional racism be transformed within the existing capitalist order?" Do you think there is any specific relationship between capitalism and racism? How might oppression on the basis of "race" relate to class?

7.   The author criticizes the readiness of many Black elected officials to use cultural arguments to blame other Black people for their condition within society. What does this tell us about the way people's interests and understandings of racism change as they are absorbed into mainstream politics? Why might Black elected officials, and the Black middle class more broadly, internalize racist discourses?

Chapter 1: Culture of Racism

1.   The chapter opens with quotes from presidents Johnson and Obama. The former is also later quoted as saying that "freedom is not enough." How do the two presidents' statements exemplify changes in the ways in which racism is understood? What do they tell us about how the idea of the role of government has shifted over the last few decades? What do you think accounts for this shift?

2.   In quoting Barbara Fields, the author advances a "materialist" understanding of racism as an "ideology" that stands for certain "social relations"; she further relates this to the need of capitalism to exploit labor. What does this imply for explanations of racism as simply an unfortunate symptom of tribalistic, ahistorical "human nature"?

3.   This explanation of racism as an ideology developed to legitimize certain social relations implies that its origin is in the ruling class rather than (as arguments attributing racism to "ignorance" often suggest) in the working class. However, the author also states that "ideologies do not work when they are only imposed from above. The key is widespread acceptance, even among the oppressed themselves." How do

ideologies like racism become embedded throughout society and, in particular, how can we account for the internalization of some aspects of racist ideology even by those who directly suffer its effects?

4. While the "culture of poverty" explanation has now become part of racist ideology, the author argues that it originally had a radical potential as a response to a "scientific" racism rooted in eugenics. In order for that radical potential to be realized, is it necessary to develop a "materialist" analysis of culture? If so, what would that look like in this case?

5. The author quotes President Johnson's speech at the chamber of commerce, in which he made the case for a "peaceful revolution" to eliminate ills such as poverty and predicted a "violent change" if this was not done. What does this tell us about the role of the state in managing society and capitalism, and the type of movements needed to gain meaningful concessions?

6. At several points, the author notes convergences between liberal and conservative approaches to race and racism. What explains these convergences? Does liberalism have inherent limits as an antiracist political ideology? Is it able to deal with racism as an institutional and systemic phenomenon structurally related to political economy?

7. Do you think that the conclusions of the Kerner Commission, that "white institutions created it [Black poverty], white institutions maintain it, and white society condones it," still hold today?

8. Are institutional racism and other similar oppressions simply useful and in some sense external to capitalism, or are they necessarily required and generated by capitalism's need to exploit labor and divide the working class? If the latter, then does any effective antiracist politics have to include a strong element of anticapitalist class politics and vice versa?

Chapter 2: From Civil Rights to Coloblind

1. What do the quotes from President Nixon and his chief of staff, H. R. Haldeman, tell us about the degree to which ruling classes perceive working-class, multiracial solidarity as a threat? Do Black people and other racialized groups have a special potential to lead

this kind of solidarity and radicalize a class movement through their leadership? To what degree can we understand racism as an elite project in response to this?

2. What is the relationship between struggles in different areas—for example, in electoral politics, through street movements, housing, and in the workplace? To what extent is achieving radical change dependent on connecting these struggles by, for instance, unions striking against institutional racism, whether or not this occurs directly in their sector?

3. Capitalism and democracy are often presented as being inherently connected, or at least as being uniquely compatible. What do the quotations from Silk and Vogel's survey, in which business leaders questioned the principle of "one man, one vote" and hoped for a more severe recession, suggest about the actual nature of this relationship? Is democracy under capitalism necessarily limited and vulnerable to being rolled back?

4. What was the role of the emerging "colorblind logic" in isolating the Black movement and reversing the achievements of the welfare state? Does it enable a "liberal racism" that does not engage in (and can even denounce) openly racist language but nonetheless relies upon assumptions and supports institutions and policies that perpetuate racism as a structured, social relationship?

5. Do you share Nixon's definition of what a "free and open society" would look like? Can you think of other definitions of "freedom" and "openness" that would require a fundamentally different social foundation?

Chapter 3: Black Faces in High Places

1. The chapter discusses several localities in which police killings made international news. What does the case of Baltimore in particular, with its largely African American political establishment and police, tell us about how racism operates through institutions rather than being a primarily individual failing or due to prejudice?

2. What is the relation of Black elites to the struggle for Black liberation as described in this chapter? Why do you think Black elites often reproduce and reinforce racist narratives about the majority

of the Black population? What can we learn from the differences between the Ferguson and Baltimore contexts?

3. Given the increasing stratification between Black elites and the rest of the Black population, does it still make sense to talk about "the Black community" as a more or less unified group with similar interests?

4. The author writes that "the pursuit of Black electoral power became one of the principal strategies that emerged from the Black Power era. Clearly it has been successful for some. But the continuing crises for Black people, from under-resourced schools to police murder, expose the extreme limitations of that strategy. The ascendance of Black electoral politics also dramatizes how class differences can lead to different political strategies in the fight for Black liberation." If a strategy based on electoral politics has "extreme limitations," does this imply that liberal democracy itself has certain limitations? What is the role of grassroots struggle/social movements in driving change? Why would the interests and strategies of working-class African Americans be different from those of the Black middle classes and elites?

5. How significant is it that the Black breakthrough into electoral politics was achieved at the same time as welfare spending came under attack? In such an environment, is it possible to implement the kind of state policies necessary to improve the lives of the majority of Black people? What is the role of the Democratic Party in relation to radical politics?

6. The difficulty of achieving fundamental change through electoral politics has led many people to dismiss this area of political activity entirely. Do you think it is possible for radical movements to pursue positions of power within the state without succumbing to its conservatizing logic, as described in this chapter, and instead operate "within and against" the state? Can radical change be achieved through existing state institutions, or is it necessary to build separate, alternative structures of power within society? What might these look like?

7. Has this chapter changed your opinion of what "sensible," "mature," or "pragmatic" politics are? Is it in fact unrealistic, even utopian, to believe that fundamental change can be achieved by working entirely within mainstream politics and the existing structures of power?

Chapter 4: The Double Standard of Justice

1. The author writes: "if the task of the police is to maintain law and order, then that role takes on a specific meaning in a fundamentally unequal society." To what extent is it possible to reform the police without a wider and more radical movement that challenges racism within society and opposes state policies that generate inequality?

2. In light of the above, how should we consider suggestions that movements such as Black Lives Matter limit their activism to "specific demands" about police reform?

3. Would you describe the Black Codes instituted after the Civil War as being primarily motivated by a) racism, or b) the need to address the labor shortage caused by the end of slavery? What does this reveal about the general relationship between race and class, and about how racism divides sections of the working class against both one another and their long-term interests?

4. Considering the Black Codes, convict leasing, and other measures discussed in this chapter, do you think "race" has any meaning outside of or prior to social relations, or is it a social construct formed precisely through such relations? If the latter, then are antiracist politics at least as much about changing material social relations as they are about changing social attitudes?

5. Do you think anything fundamental has changed about the way police relate to Black communities since James Baldwin wrote that "they are present to keep the Negro in his place and to protect white business interests, and they have no other function"? Why has the "professionalization" and diversification of police forces failed to address the issue of institutional racism? Could we imagine, for example, a 100 percent Black-staffed and -controlled city police force that remained institutionally racist toward African Americans?

6. What is the significance of the cross-party consensus on the need for "law and order" occurring at the same time as an economic downturn? Can we understand the police and prison system as primarily a way of disciplining the working class and controlling its "surplus" population during times of low economic growth? What is the importance of racism in extending this apparatus?

7. The author writes that "the overwhelmingly racist nature of American policing obscures the range of its reach, but it is in the interests of anti–police brutality activists to point out the specific [racial] *and* the generalized [class] nature of police terror." Do you think that the specific focus of Black Lives Matter helps to advance the general cause of all who suffer at the hands of the police system? Do you think that the slogan "All Lives Matter," often raised in opposition to Black Lives Matter, is intended to link these aspects or to silence Black voices?

Chapter 5: Barack Obama: The End of an Illusion

1. To what extent has the "de-racialization" of Black politics been the condition of the admission of African Americans into electoral politics? Did Obama act, for example, as a "Black president," or simply a president who happened to be Black? How did he contribute to the continuation of "colorblindness" and the upholding of the myth of "the American Dream"?

2. "The American Dream" is just one example of a national myth, and "the American people" is the myth of a national community. Is a politics that seeks to gain acceptance for certain excluded groups within these national imaginaries necessarily a limited one? To what degree would a more radical liberation struggle require an opposition to all forms of nationalist politics and, by extension, the state?

3. Can you draw parallels between Obama's relation to Black liberation and, for example, the relation of Hillary Clinton's presidential campaign to women's liberation? To what extent is the identity of a public individual an indicator of their ability and willingness to represent and improve the conditions of any particular group of people?

4. The author mentions debates held by the Occupy Movement over whether the police should be included in the "99%." How would you analyze the class position of the police and other similar state representatives?

5. How would you summarize the author's argument as to why the radicalization of Black struggle had occurred under a Black pres-

ident and, more generally, at a time when Black political and economic power had never been greater?

6. How did the Occupy Movement help to develop understandings of the relationship between economic and racial inequalities? What was its role in relegitimizing street politics?

Chapter 6: Black Lives Matter: A Movement, Not a Moment

1. How did the aftermath of the killing of Michael Brown in Ferguson illustrate the differences in objectives and strategies of the emerging street movement in relation to established civil rights activists like Al Sharpton? At heart, is this divide a generational one, implying an opposition based on levels of "political maturity," or a political one, implying conflicting aims and interests?

2. How would you explain the prominence of women and queer activists in the broader Black Lives Matter movement? Does this have any implications for how we understand the relationship between oppressions based on gender, sexuality, and race with class?

3. What is "state violence" and why is this concept important? Can it help us understand the intersections of different oppressions? Why does the state target particular groups of people with violence?

4. The author criticizes the "narrowly crafted agendas of the liberal establishment organizations, like Sharpton's National Action Network," which came into conflict with the emerging left street movements. To what extent is liberalism able to advance an adequate systemic or structural critique of the conditions which drive racial oppression, and what might the reasons be for its limitations?

5. While praising the new street movements and contrasting their democratic structures to the ossified establishment organizations, the author also writes that "the larger the movement grows, the more need there will be for coordination." In recent years, movements based on "horizontalism," often explicitly contrasted to "hierarchical" left organizations of previous eras, have become increasingly widespread. How important do you think the form of movements and organizations is in terms of their ability to bring about change? How can a movement retain an internal democratic

culture but also achieve organizational efficacy and efficiency?

6. What role do you think corporate philanthropy has had in de-radicalizing the civil rights–era Black organizations? Is such funding ever apolitical, and can you relate the observations made in this chapter to the wider "NGO-ization" of social movements?

7. How would you distinguish between a reformist movement and a movement that sees, in the author's words, "the struggle for reforms that are possible today" as part of "the struggle for revolution, which is a long-term project"? What would differentiate reforms that are part of such a project from those that are part of a purely reformist agenda?

8. How and why have links developed between Black Lives Matter and organized labor? What accounts for the unique power of organized labor under capitalism?

9. The author writes that "in the contest to demonstrate how oppressions differ from one group to the next, we miss how we are connected through oppression—and how those connections should form the basis of solidarity, not a celebration of our lives on the margins." Without denying the different ways in which oppression is experienced and manifested, a "connection through oppression" implies some kind of commonality. What is the basis of that commonality? How would we distinguish "solidarity" with people's whose oppression you do not personally experience from "allyship"?

Chapter 7: From #BlackLivesMatter to Black Liberation

1. The author quotes Martin Luther King Jr.'s conclusion that "I've come to believe that we are integrating into a burning house." After reading the book, do you think that Black liberation can be achieved within capitalism's "political economy of racism"? Conversely, would the achievement of a socialist society in and of itself signal the end of racism and other forms of oppression?

2. Socialists, and in particular Marxists, are often accused of ignoring or downplaying oppression on the basis of gender, race, sexuality, or other aspects of identity, to focus more or less exclusively on the white male worker. Does this chapter successfully challenge that view? Based on the author's use of Marx and later Marxist thinkers,

and the way she develops their insights, do you think that Marxism provides a useful framework for understanding such oppressions? What is the significance of the long C. L. R. James quote, as well as the author's assertion that "the Black movement is an independent force that has its own timing, logic, and perspective based on the history of racism and oppression in this country. It is also the case that when the Black movement goes into motion, it destabilized all political life in the United States"? Why does the Black movement have this capacity? How can it be both independent and an integral part of wider struggles?

3. The author writes that "under capitalism, *wage slavery* is the pivot around which all other inequalities and oppressions turn." What is meant by the term "wage slavery," and how can this be applied to for-mally free labor? In describing this as the central "pivot" under capital-ism, is the author assigning priority to class relations as a way of under-standing oppression and exploitation? If so, what kind of priority?

4. Why does the author criticize the notion that Black people in po-sitions of power are "acting white" when they reproduce racism?

5. What is the significance of the concept of "contradictory conscious-ness"? How is the "achievement of consciousness" linked to the Marxist distinction between a class "in itself" and a class "for itself"?

6. Do you agree with the author that "immigrant issues, gender is-sues, and antiracism issues *are* working-class issues"? If you agree that they are (or at least should be), then how does the articula-tion of these issues as integral parts of working-class politics differ from the way that they are articulated by middle-class activists and movements? Has this book changed the way you think about con-cepts such as race, class, capitalism, socialism, and democracy?

Chapter 8: Where Is the Black Lives Matter Movement Headed?

1. The author writes that in the wake of the murders of Eric Garner and Mike Brown Jr., "young Black people around the country were united by the experiences of police abuse and intimidation." How do you think growing up in the time of the BLM movement and in the time of prevalent and easily shared video footage has shaped

the racial and political consciousness of young Black adults and Black children? How much impact do you think modern technology is or will have on the efficacy of social movements?

2. Do you agree with activist Aislinn Pulley or Britany Packnett's reasoning on whether to meet with President Obama? Why or why not? How has the dichotomy of change "from above" or "from below" affected other political movements?

3. The author writes that "Black elected officials often fattened themselves up munching at the trough of Black votes, only to deliver little other than themselves alone as tokens of alleged racial progress." Do you agree? How does the fact that the massive increase of Black elected officials since the civil rights era, including a two-term president, has done little to correct systemic racism relate to the idea of the "reform nature of the [BLM] movement"?

4. The author stresses the importance of transparency and accountability in relation to movement leadership. Does this same logic apply to elected government officials? How possible is it to hold elected officials accountable to the people while they hold office? How can we hold movement leaders accountable?

5. Does Ford Foundation president Darren Walker's warning not "let the perfect be the enemy of progress" and the idea of movement purity versus compromise actually work against progress? What do you think of the author's likening of ultimate movement goals as a "wish-list" and asking "for the moon and stars"?

6. In chapter 4, the author examines the history of the police not as "keepers of the peace" but as enforcers of economic disparity. She ends the book with the declaration that for Black lives to matter, we have to "change the world that relies on the police to manage its unequal distribution of the necessities of life." The author sees modern policing in the US as fundamentally racist as an institution, not just as a matter of this or that individual police officer. Why does she reach that conclusion and what evidence does she offer? Do you agree?

7. What conclusions does the author draw as to what will be required to "change the police"? Does this affect your opinion of the viability of change via electoral politics in general?

About Haymarket Books

Haymarket Books is a nonprofit, progressive book distributor and publisher, a project of the Center for Economic Research and Social Change. We believe that activists need to take ideas, history, and politics into the many struggles for social justice today. Learning the lessons of past victories, as well as defeats, can arm a new generation of fighters for a better world. As Karl Marx said, "The philosophers have merely interpreted the world; the point, however, is to change it."

We take inspiration and courage from our namesakes, the Haymarket Martyrs, who gave their lives fighting for a better world. Their 1886 struggle for the eight-hour day reminds workers around the world that ordinary people can organize and struggle for their own liberation.

For more information and to shop our complete catalog of titles, visit us online at www.haymarketbooks.org.

Also available from Haymarket Books

Freedom Is a Constant Struggle
Ferguson, Palestine, and the Foundations of a Movement
Angela Y. Davis

How Capitalism Underdeveloped Black America
Problems in Race, Political Economy, and Society (Third Edition)
Manning Marable, Foreword by Leith Mullings

African Struggles Today
Social Movements Since Independence
Peter Dwyer and Leo Zeilig

The Black Panthers Speak
Edited by Philip S. Foner, Foreword by Barbara Ransby

The Black Power Mixtape: 1967–1975
Göran Hugo Olssen

Capitalism
A Ghost Story
Arundhati Roy

My People Are Rising
Memoir of a Black Panther Party Captain
Aaron Dixon

Detroit: I Do Mind Dying
A Study in Urban Revolution
Dan Georgakas and Marvin Surkin

Who Do You Serve, Who Do You Protect?
Police Violence and Resistance in the United States
Edited by Maya Schenwar, Joe Macaré, and Alana Yu-lan Price,
Foreword by Alicia Garza